Visible Cities

Budapest

A CITY GUIDE

by

Annabel Barber
& Emma Roper-Evans

3rd Edition

SOMERSET LIMITED

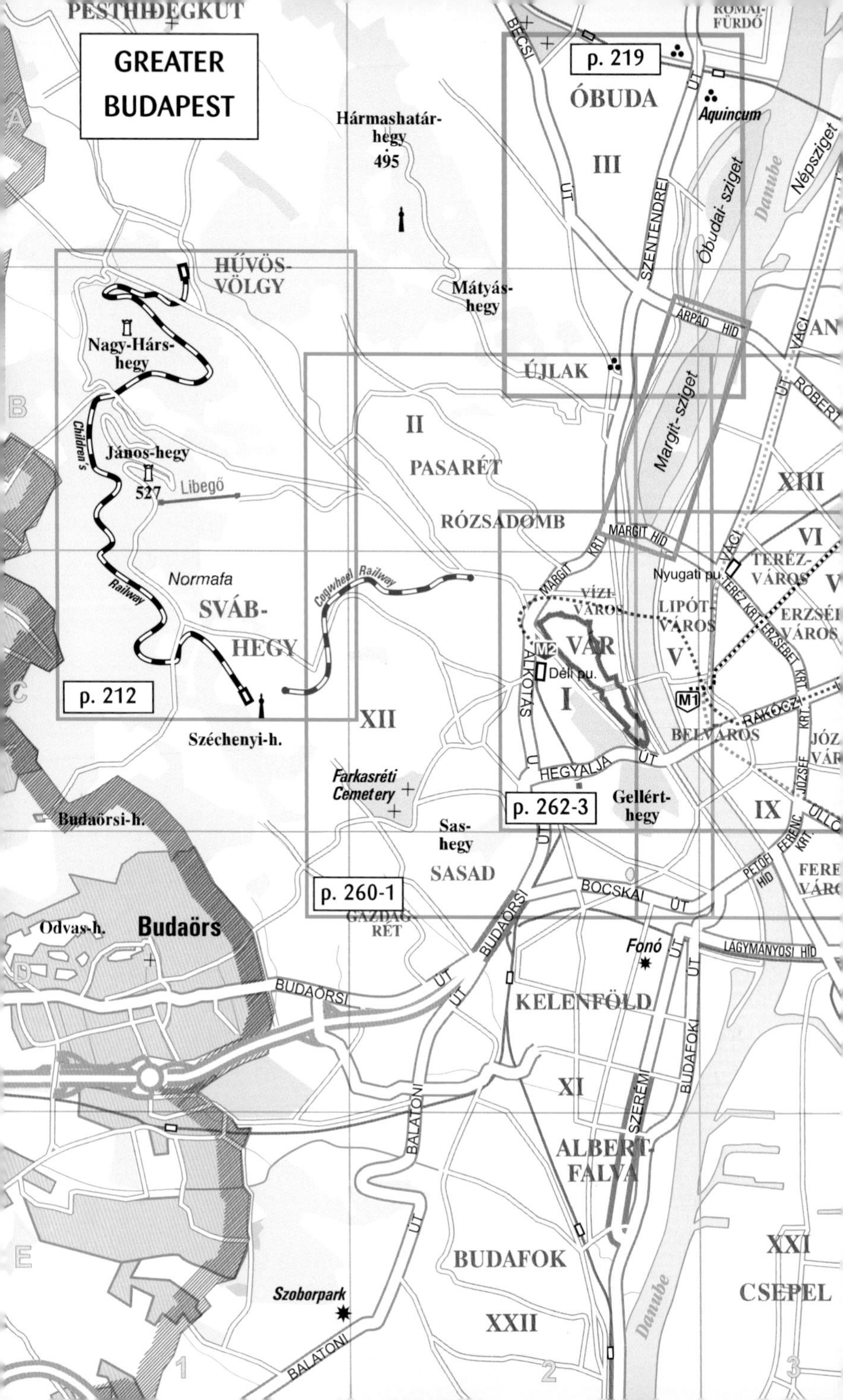
GREATER BUDAPEST
PESTHIDEGKUT
Hármashatár-hegy
495
ÓBUDA
III
Aquincum
Óbudai-sziget
Népsziget
Danube
SZENTENDREI
ÚT
BÉCSI
RÓMAI-FÜRDŐ
p. 219
HŰVÖS-VÖLGY
Mátyás-hegy
Nagy-Hárs-hegy
ÁRPÁD HÍD
ÚJLAK
Margit-sziget
János-hegy
527
Libegő
Children's Railway
II
PASARÉT
RÓZSADOMB
XIII
VI
MARGIT HÍD
MARGIT KRT
Normafa
Cogwheel Railway
SVÁB-HEGY
Nyugati pu.
TERÉZ-VÁROS
VÍZI-VÁROS
LIPÓT-VÁROS
ERZSÉBET-VÁROS
VÁR
V
M2
Déli pu.
I
ALKOTÁS U.
M1
p. 212
XII
Széchenyi-h.
BELVÁROS
RÁKÓCZI
HEGYALJA ÚT
Farkasréti Cemetery
p. 262-3
Gellért-hegy
IX
Budaörsi-h.
Sas-hegy
SASAD
PETŐFI HÍD
FERENC KRT
p. 260-1
BOCSKAI ÚT
GAZDAG-RÉT
Odvas-h.
Budaörs
Fonó
LÁGYMÁNYOSI HÍD
BUDAÖRSI ÚT
KELENFÖLD
XI
BALATONI ÚT
SZERÉMI
BUDAFOKI ÚT
ALBERT-FALVA
XXI
BUDAFOK
CSEPEL
Szoborpark
XXII
Danube
A
B
C
D
E
1
2
3

IV
ÚJPEST
XV
RÁKOS-
PALOTA
ÚJPALOTA
Csömöri-p.
Csömör
FÖLD
PESTÚJHELY
Szilas-p.
RÁKOS-
SZENTMIHÁLY
Rákos-p.
XIV
XVI
SASHALOM
HUNGÁRIA
ZUGLÓ
VERES P. ÚT
KEREPESI ÚT
Keleti pu.
Kerepesi Cemetery
MÁTYÁSFÖLD
JÁSZBERÉNYI ÚT
PESTI ÚT
KŐBÁNYAI ÚT
Jewish Cemetery
KŐBÁNYA
X
p. 258-9
FERENC-
VÁROS
Wekerle-telep
XIX
KISPEST
NAGYKŐRÖSI ÚT
XX
PEST-
ERZSÉBET
HELSINKI ÚT
Ferihegy Airport
XVIII
PEST-
SZENTLŐRINC
A
B
C
D
3
4
5
0
1
2
3 km

office@visiblecities.net
www.visiblecities.net

Layout & design: *Regina Rácz*
Photographs: *Hadley Kincade, Tibor Mester, Attila Kleb, Miklós Gellért, Andrea Felvégi, Jeannette Goehring, Annabel Barber, Thomas Howells, Ágnes Kolozs, Magyar Képek*
Editor: *Maya Mirsky*
Ground plans & colour drawings: *Imre Bába*
Line drawings: *Michael Mansell RIBA*
Maps: *Dimap Bt.*

Acknowledgements:
With thanks to
Mónika Papp, Dr. István Barkóczi, Éva Csenkey, Éva Galambos, Roger Gough

This is the third edition of Visible Cities Budapest: corrections, comments and views will be welcomed.

Other titles in the Visible Cities series:
Visible Cities Barcelona
Visible Cities Dubrovnik
Visible Cities Krakow
Visible Cities Vienna
Further titles are in preparation.

Cover illustration: *Detail of the Schmidl family mausoleum (Béla Lajta, 1903) in the Kozma utca cemetery.*
Previous page: *Hungarian folk motif from the entrance porch of the Applied Arts Museum.*

Annabel Barber has lived in Budapest since 1992. A former editor at Budapest Magazines and food and wine columnist for the *Budapest Business Journal*, she now works as a freelance writer and translator. Emma Roper-Evans has lived in Hungary for twelve years. In 1996 she received the Milán Füst Prize from the Hungarian Academy of Sciences for her literary translations.

ISBN 963 212 986 5

CONTENTS

INTRODUCTION

'Budapest seems a wonderful place... The impression I had was that we were leaving the West and entering the East; the most Western of splendid bridges over the Danube, which is here of noble width and depth, took us among the traditions of Turkish rule...' With those words, Bram Stoker opens one of the most famous stories of all time: *Dracula*. And he was right: Budapest is a wonderful place, bisected by the Danube into leafy and hilly Buda to the west, and Pest to the east, dusty and flat, on a plain that stretches unbroken from the Danube bank to the mountains of Transylvania. Formerly two separate towns, Buda and Pest united in 1873 to form a capital city, administering the affairs of the eastern regions of Austria-Hungary. In its late 19th-century heyday, Budapest was a proud and magnificent city, boasting one of the most booming economies in Europe. Ignominious defeats in two world wars, and fifty years behind the Iron Curtain did much to dim the glitter, but Budapest is resilient. Today it is re-emerging as a city to be reckoned with, reclaiming its place at the heart of the continent, excited about its future, and ever conscious of the exotic aura of difference conferred by its Eastern heritage.

CITY LAYOUT

Eight great bridges span the Danube, the three most central being Margaret Bridge (Margit híd), the Chain Bridge (Lánchíd, *see p. 32*), graceful, white Elisabeth Bridge (Erzsébet híd) and the green, cast iron Szabadság híd (which literally translates as 'Liberty Bridge', though it is always known by its Hungarian name). As long as you orientate to the river, which flows north-south, you will rarely get lost in Budapest. The city is divided into numbered districts, each designated by a Roman numeral, though districts each have names as well: eponymous titles like Józsefváros (Joseph Town), in honour of Habsburg rulers, or more evocative names such as Víziváros (Water Town), for what was once an area of docks, subject to flooding before the Danube was banked up.

Budapest's blue Danube, spanned by the Chain Bridge, with Parliament in the background.

A NOTE ON PLACE NAMES

The Hungarian language is unfamiliar to most non-natives, and to avoid confusion most major sights are given in English (eg: Heroes' Square). Where there is no commonly-used English name (eg: Szabadság tér), the Hungarian is used. A Hungarian-English list of toponyms is given on p. 248.

MAJOR DISTRICTS

Castle Hill (Vár, District I): This limestone crag, rising steeply from the Buda bank of the Danube, was home to the city's royal palace from the middle ages until the Second World War. That palace now houses the Hungarian National Gallery (*see p. 104*). Castle Hill is also home to the Mátyás Church and Fishermen's Bastion (*see pp. 41-3*).

Belváros (District V): This is the heart of Pest, roughly bordered by the Chain Bridge, Szabadság híd, and Deák tér. The area is home to the city's major shopping streets, and also boasts the Dunakorzó, the pedestrian promenade along the Danube (*see p. 34*). Gerbeaud (*see p. 97*), Budapest's most famous coffee house is another landmark in the district.

Lipótváros (District V): Bordered by the Chain Bridge, Margaret Bridge and Bajcsy-Zsilinszky út, this is the 'banking quarter', an area of offices, government ministries and financial institutions centred on the grandiose Parliament building (*see p. 44*) and Szabadság tér (*see p. 48*). An area of wide streets and tall, imposing façades, this part of town is rapidly turning into a lively hub, as cafés and restaurants open up and streets are pedestrianised. St Stephen's Basilica (*see p. 60*) is also here.

Víziváros (District I): A former area of fishermen's cottages and docks between Castle Hill and the Danube, and spilling across Batthyány tér towards Margaret Bridge. Many of the streets still retain their old, higgledy-piggledy quality. The area contains some pretty Baroque churches (*see p. 139*) and the Ottoman-built Király baths (*see p. 90*).

Óbuda (District III): This northerly part of town, beyond Árpád Bridge (Árpád híd) at the far end of Margaret

Panoramic 19th-century view of Buda and Pest.

Island (*see p. 201*), was home to the 2nd-century Roman towns (*see pp. 218 & 222*). Its main sight today is a cobbled square of steep-roofed Baroque houses (*see p. 220*).

Erzsébetváros (District VII): Bordered by Károly körút, Király utca and Rákóczi út, this has traditionally been the Jewish district of Budapest. Dob utca and Kazinczy utca are still the heart of Orthodox Jewish Budapest. An enclosed ghetto was established here during the Second World War. The district's major sights include the grand Dohány utca Synagogue (*see p. 65*).

Józsefváros (District VIII): This district has a distinct identity in people's minds. Traditionally it is known as the Gypsy part of town, and many Roma families live here. The area is not developing as fast as other districts, and still has an old-fashioned feel to it. Though much of it is dilapidated, it has some wonderful buildings, and is fascinating to wander through. Outerlying parts, though, especially at night, can be dangerous. It is home to the Roma Parliament, the Budapest Gypsy Assembly and concert hall (*see p. 130*), as well as to the National Museum (*see p. 114*).

TEN THINGS TO DO IN BUDAPEST

1 Wallow like a pasha in one of the Turkish steam baths (*p. 90*).

2 Treat yourself to a double espresso and a cream cake in one of the city's famed coffee houses (*p. 95*).

3 See the sun-soaked canvases of Károly Ferenczy and the Nagybánya School at the Hungarian National Gallery (*p. 104*).

4 Take a tour of one of the largest parliament buildings in the world, and see the holy crown of St Stephen (*p. 44*).

5 Whoop and weep by turns to the strains of the dulcimer and gypsy fiddle (*p. 128*).

6 Take a box at the Opera, one of the most sumptuous music venues in Europe (*p. 55*).

7 Discover the Antoni Gaudí of Budapest: the architect Ödön Lechner (*p. 78*).

8 See the largest collection of El Grecos outside Spain at the Fine Arts Museum (*p. 112*).

9 Experience one of Communism's best legacies: the Children's Railway in the Buda hills (*p. 211*).

10 See how the wealthy magnates of the 19th-century boomtown lived, at the Postal Museum on Andrássy út (*p. 118*).

Detail of Ödön Lechner's Applied Arts Museum.

LANGUAGE

Hungarian is one of the world's linguistic mysteries. No one knows quite where it came from; it is isolated in a sea of Slavic tongues, though is not Slavic itself, and its closest (yet still distant) relatives are in faraway Finland and Siberia. There is a theory that it is Turkic in origin, and philologists have travelled across the Karim Basin in search of proof, but convincing results have been elusive; it may be that the origins of Hungarian will never be precisely known.

Hungarians are proud of their unique tongue and secretly quite like to believe in their language's reputation as unlearnable. Of course, it isn't: it is dauntingly unfamiliar at first, but has an internal logic that ultimately puts a mongrel language like English to shame.

PRONUNCIATION

Pronunciation, though it seems difficult at first, is always phonetic, and once you know what sounds match what letters, you will be able to pronounce nearly any word without mishap. Sounds that differ from the English alphabet are listed below.

a: similar to the 'o' in 'hot'
á: similar to the 'a' in 'madness'
c: like the 'ts' in 'lots'
cs: like the 'ch' in 'church'
é: like the 'a' in 'baby'
gy: like the 'du' in 'duress'
j: like the 'y' in 'yes'
ö: 'euh', as in 'bird'
ő: much the same as the above, but linger over it
s: 'sh', as in 'shout'
sz: 's' as in 'sound'
ü: like the 'u' in French 'tu'
ű: much the same as the above, but linger over it

HISTORY

A lot of what you see in Budapest is newer than it appears. Classical and Gothic buildings are for the most part Neoclassical and neo-Gothic. Even the much-trumpeted Budapest Baroque was flourishing a good few decades later than the Baroque in many other European countries. This is a direct result of Budapest's turbulent history. Wave upon wave of occupation and subsequent destruction has taken its toll - and when each wave rolled on, it left surprisingly little in its wake.

The Romans were here. The Emperor Trajan established military and civilian townships at Aquincum, a little way north of what is now central Budapest. The Emperor Diocletian built a fortress on the Danube bank in the 3rd century AD, near the present day Elisabeth Bridge. Magyar tribes did not actually enter the Carpathian Basin until the late 9th century, when Árpád led his people down from the Caucasus. The House of Árpád formed a dynasty that ruled Hungary for three centuries.

MEDIAEVAL SPLENDOUR & OTTOMAN CONQUEST

The power of the Árpád dynasty was consolidated by Stephen (István), king and later saint, who converted his people to Christianity and received an apostolic crown from Pope Sylvester II in 1000. Since then, that crown (*see p. 46*) has symbolised the independent Hungarian state and conveyed power and authority on its possessor.

The principal Danube-bank settlement in early mediaeval times was Óbuda (the name means 'old Buda'), to the north of the present city centre. There it remained until the Mongol invasion of 1241 prompted King Béla IV to move his court from the vulnerability of the flat Danube floodplain up to Castle Hill (*see p. 151*). Buda and Pest were two completely separate towns, with Pest more a

'The Baptism of Vajk' by Gyula Benczúr (1875), capturing the moment when the pigtailed chieftain was received into the Christian Church under the name Stephen. He would go on to unite the Magyar tribes and found the Hungarian nation.

Portrait of Sultan Suleiman the Magnificent, conqueror of Buda.

centre of trade and agriculture, and vine-clad Buda the occasional home to the royal court and treasury. During the early mediaeval period, the court was semi-nomadic, moving around Transdanubia (the lands to the west of the Danube), and was not permanently based at Buda. By the 15th century, however, the Renaissance king Mátyás (Matthias Corvinus, 1443-1490) was so wealthy that he held court both at Visegrád, on the Danube Bend north of the city, and in Buda. Mátyás was celebrated as a paragon of cultured humanism, and his palace at Buda is said to have rivalled anything in Europe for opulence and beauty. Visitors gasped at all the cloth of gold, as well as at the dazzling ornamental gardens, fountains and statuary. Besides being home to every pleasure and luxury, the Hungarian court was also a centre of great learning. The famous Bibliotheca Corviniana, which King Mátyás founded, was kept on Castle Hill, and drew scholars to Buda from all over Europe.

As so often happens with a strong monarch, Mátyás's successors found him a hard act to follow. Struggles for the throne ensued, and, inevitably, disaster eventually struck. The boy king Lajos II was drowned in 1526 while retreating from the infamous Battle of Mohács (in southern Hungary), where the Hungarians were crushed by the Ottoman army led by Suleiman the Magnificent. Less than twenty years later the Ottomans had conquered all of Hungary as far as Buda, which they overran in 1541. The country was carved up into three parts, with the Ottomans ruling the south and east to the Danube, Ferdinand Habsburg (brother of the Holy Roman Emperor Charles V) grabbing the north and west, and Transylvania (now part of Romania) becoming a vassal Ottoman state with a certain amount of internal political independence.

The Turks remained in Buda for 140 years. Period woodcuts show a city bristling with minarets - all have now vanished. The Ottomans were finally driven out in 1686 by the armies of Holy Roman Emperor Leopold I, led by Eugene of Savoy and Charles of Lorraine, and only a few relics of their rule survive: a handful of Turkish baths, and a small mausoleum above Margaret Bridge (*see p. 145*).

RECONQUEST, REVOLUTION, REVIVAL

The reconquest of Buda brought devastation, and was followed by a period of extensive rebuilding, when most of the Baroque buildings still extant today went up. The town was no longer a capital city, however. The Habsburg armies had not taken Buda for altruistic reasons; they had conquered it for themselves, and it, together with all of Hungary, fell under Austrian dominion. For much of the 18th century Buda was little more than a provincial backwater. It was not until

The Liberation of Buda in 1686, showing a city ablaze as the united Christian armies under Prince Eugene of Savoy lay siege to it.

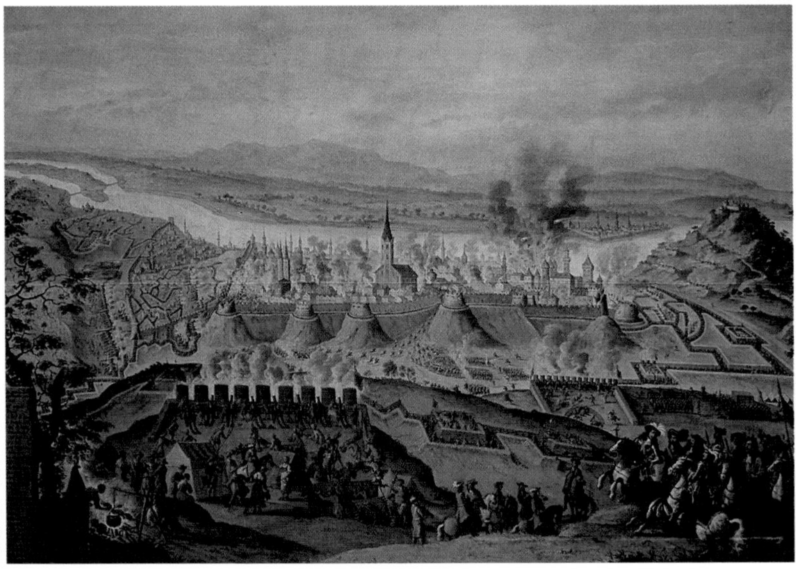

HUNGARIAN NATIONAL MUSEUM

the 'enlightened despotism' of Maria Theresa (1717-1780) and her son Joseph II (1741-90) brought increased freedoms that both Buda and Pest began to flourish again. Maria Theresa, realising the importance that Hungarian symbols of state had for the country, had Buda's Royal Palace rebuilt, returned the right hand of St Stephen, a sacred relic (*see p. 64*), to Hungary, and ennobled many Hungarians. Nevertheless, Vienna was the seat of power and Hungarian affairs were controlled from Pressburg (now Bratislava).

Only in the 19th century did the conception of a united Hungarian capital called Budapest develop. In the first decades of the century, the great reformer Count István Széchenyi undertook to modernise Hungary's feudal, agricultural society. Strongly Anglophile, he visited England repeatedly and came back home full of schemes for steamships and railways to be set up on the English model. He built the first permanent bridge over the Danube and cut the tunnel through the Castle Hill (*see p. 35*).

The feverish spirit of nationalism which coursed through Europe in the mid 19th century did not leave the city untouched. Anti-Habsburg feeling was stirred up on a political level by the fiery oratory of lawyer-turned-revolutionary Lajos Kossuth, and on a popular level by the idealistic young poet Sándor Petőfi. Outright revolution broke out in 1848. Kossuth declared an independent Hungarian capital in the eastern town of Debrecen, while

Sándor Petőfi, romantic poet and freedom fighter, who died in the struggle against Austrian domination in 1849.

PHOTO: BENCE KÉPESSY/ HUNGARIAN NATIONAL MUSEUM

PHOTO: ANDRAS DABASI / HUNGARIAN NATIONAL MUSEUM

Supporters of Lajos Kossuth at an 1848 rally in front of the National Museum.

Petőfi incited the masses to revolt with his inflammatory verses. Things went well for a while, until it became clear that the other ethnic groups within Hungary were unhappy with the new Magyar supremacy. The Croats took Austria's side against the Hungarians, and since Austria was not powerful enough to defeat the recalcitrant Magyars on her own, she called in the Russians to help. Hungary knew that she was beaten, but she still had the spirit to humiliate Austria by surrendering not to the Kaiser but to the Czar. Austria tried to quell that spirit once and for all by ignominiously hanging as many of Hungary's generals as she could get her hands on. The country was desolate: Petőfi had been killed fighting, Kossuth had fled to Turkey, and Count Lajos Batthyány, Prime Minister in Hungary's first independent government, faced the firing squad. It was only in 1867 that the wily old politician Ferenc Deák effected the so-called Compromise between the Habsburgs and the Hungarians. This allowed Hungary its own domestic government, but meant that foreign and military affairs were voted on jointly with Vienna. Under the system known as the Dual Monarchy, Emperor Franz Joseph was to remain Emperor of Austria, while in Hungary he was crowned King. The Compromise Agreement effectively opened up the towns of Buda and

Coronation dinner of Franz Joseph in Budapest in 1867. The Empress Elisabeth, widely rumoured to be in love with the dashing Hungarian Prime Minister Gyula Andrássy, is shown looking coyly at him out of the corner of her eye.

Pest to foreign capital, and also opened the Austrian empire to Hungarian grain from the Great Plain, some of the most fertile arable land in Europe. The resulting explosion of wealth turned what had been two provincial little settlements on the banks of the Danube into a thrusting boomtown.

In 1873 Buda and Pest united to form a single capital city, and a period of furious rebuilding followed. Almost the whole of Pest was torn down, its shabby, squat little houses replaced with glittering palaces and wide, tree-lined boulevards. Once described as the biggest village in Europe, the remodelled city now had to be seen to be believed. People started comparing it with Paris. In 1896 Budapest celebrated its 'Millennium' - 1,000 years since the Magyar tribes first streamed into the Carpathian Basin. The people of Budapest were in confident, buoyant spirits, and they felt in the mood for a massive party. 'Now, at last, our true dawn is breaking,' wrote one ecstatic historian, 'The daystar of Hungary is about to shine in the European firmament.'

CONFLICTING REGIMES

The joy and optimism were not to last. The 20th century was hard on Hungary, and Budapest's buildings still bear the bullet scars of many bloody conflicts. At the Treaty of Trianon that followed the First World War, Hungary lost two-thirds of her territory and Budapest became the capital of a severely truncated country. This loss of territory at Trianon is still seen by the majority of Hungarians as the greatest tragedy

HUNGARIAN NATIONAL MUSEUM

'Join the Red Army!' Propaganda poster from the days of the Republic of Councils.

that has befallen them at any time in their history. The fall of the Habsburg empire was followed by the short-lived 1919 Republic of Councils, or Commune, modelled on the Soviet prototype and led by Béla Kun. It lasted barely a few brutal, triumphant months before Admiral Miklós Horthy and his conservative regime suppressed it and took over. Horthy declared himself Regent (the theory being that he was ruling in place of the Habsburg King Karl IV, exiled in Madeira) and moved into the Royal

Admiral Horthy, Regent of Hungary between the two World Wars.

HUNGARIAN NATIONAL MUSEUM

Palace. Under his leadership a small élite enjoyed a graceful lifestyle, but it was not generally a prosperous time for Budapest. The grand city began to look a little dusty and down-at-heel.

FROM HITLER TO STALIN

The late thirties saw the introduction of restrictive Jewish laws. Though Hungary tried to hold out against outright anti-Semitism, she entered the Second World War on Germany's side, partly because of traditional allegiances, but also encouraged by Germany's promise to salve Hungarian grievances by restoring territory lost at Trianon. In 1944, however, impatient at Horthy's wavering, the German army invaded. Horthy himself was deposed in October, and his government was replaced by the Hungarian Fascists (the Arrow Cross), an ultra-nationalist, anti-Semitic party which allowed Adolf Eichmann to move to Budapest to carry out his 'Final Solution'. A Jewish ghetto was established in the seventh district (*see p. 194*) and deportations began. In April 1945, the Red Army besieged Budapest. The German army retreated across the river, blowing up all the bridges behind them, and holed up on Castle Hill

BTM KISCELLI MÚZEUM FÉNYKÉP GYŰJTEMÉNY

View over the Danube from Castle Hill following the siege of 1945, when the Wehrmacht and the Red Army fought for control of Buda.

in Buda. The Siege of Buda left a smoking ruin of what had been a beautiful Baroque enclave, while Pest also suffered extensive bomb and shell damage.

The immediate post-war period, 1945-48, saw an attempt at democracy with multi-party elections and the re-formation of some of the pre-war parties. However, the cynical 'percentages agreement' concluded between Churchill and Stalin, dividing Europe up into various spheres of interest, saw much of Eastern Europe being sacrificed to the Soviets in return for Greece. Hungary was supposedly divided 50-50 between Russia and the West, but it never happened. Mátyás Rákosi, hardline Communist ideologue and faithful disciple of Stalin, instituted his 'salami tactics', slicing up the Social Democrats and slinging 'Fascist mud' at the right wing. He came to power on the back of rigged elections in 1948, ironically exactly a hundred years since Russia had dealt Hungary her other mortal historical wound. Rákosi instigated one of the worst Stalinist regimes in the region, with the police terror, midnight arrests and show trials so well described by Arthur Koestler in *Darkness at Noon*.

HUNGARIAN NATIONAL MUSEUM

Rákosi as a genial big daddy, presiding over a trio of wholesome youngsters, in a 1950 propaganda poster for the 'Congress of Young Fighters for Peace and Socialism'.

The Hungarian Revolution of 1956

When Stalin died in 1953, the Soviet mirror started to crack. There was rioting in East Berlin the next year, when workers demanded bread. In Poland, the party secretary Gomulka began to call for reform. The Soviet leadership was in disarray: at the 20th Party Congress in Moscow in February 1956, Khrushchev admitted the mistakes of Stalin. This made things a little difficult for Hungary's leader, Rákosi, who not long before had dubbed himself 'Stalin's best pupil'. As a result of the congress, cosmetic changes were made to the Hungarian Communist Party, with Rákosi being replaced for reasons of 'ill health'. But that wasn't enough for the people. Groups of students began meeting, naming themselves after leaders of the 1848 revolution against the Habsburgs (*see pp. 18-19*). Things came to a head on the evening of October 22nd, 1956, with the publication of a manifesto entitled *Sixteen Points by the Hungarian Youth*, a deliberate reference to the 1848 revolutionaries' *People's Twelve Demands*. The document demanded the immediate withdrawal of Soviet troops from Hungarian soil and called for the Communist moderate Imre Nagy to lead the party. Other demands were the reinstatement of the 'class enemy' (the persecuted bourgeoisie, small businessmen, entrepreneurs and yeoman farmers), a free press and trades unions. A protest was planned in Budapest on October 23rd, in support of the strikes in Poland. Delirious with the idea of change, crowds gathered in Heroes' Square to topple the gigantic statue of Stalin. Wire ropes were fastened around him and people came with trucks, bare hands and sheer courage to pull him down. He crashed to the pavement that same night, only his huge boots remaining. The Hungarian army was reluctant to fire on its own people, so the State Security Department (ÁVO) was called in to quell the riot. Their brutality was such that they only made matters worse, and ÁVO operatives were lynched and hanged from lamp posts in retaliation. On October 25th a peaceful demonstration outside the parliament was fired on by security force snipers. The Politburo held an emergency session, and on the 27th a compromise was reached. Imre Nagy formed a government. The Soviet Union and Hungary's own hard-liners at first seemed happy to accept peace at this price, but when it became clear that Nagy intended to abolish the one-party system and withdraw Hungary from the Warsaw Pact, the Stalinists began to panic. 'Soviet assistance' was called for, and Red Army tanks were put on standby to invade. On the 31st a former machinist, János Kádár, was offered leadership of the country if he broke the back of the revolution. Though Kádár had initially supported the uprising, and had even been imprisoned by Rákosi, this chance at power proved greater than his conscience. He formed a new, pro-Moscow government. Imre Nagy, still insisting that Hungary was independent of Moscow, appealed to the West for aid. Britain and France were deep in the Suez crisis, and the United States had a presidential election to deal with. No aid was forthcoming. On November 4th the Soviet tanks rolled into Budapest. The battle raged for twenty-two days. Hungarian army units joined the revolutionaries, guns were handed around, prisons emptied. But the might of the Soviet empire was too great. Hundreds of civilians were killed and thousands wounded. Almost a quarter of a million people (around 2% of the population) fled the country. In June 1958, Imre Nagy, who had been offered clemency by the new regime, was executed after a summary trial.

HUNGARIAN NATIONAL MUSEUM

Face of despair: an unknown refugee of the 1956 revolution, homeless and displaced, probably photographed in a camp in Vienna.

GOULASH COMMUNISM

Kádár spent the next few years arresting and liquidating the revolutionary leaders. Around 2,000 executions were carried out and 25,000 prison sentences delivered. Kádár then declared an understated amnesty with his famous line, 'Anyone who is not against us is for us'. He went on to become the most moderate leader in the Eastern Bloc, the initiator of 'Goulash Communism', a system which allowed a secondary economy to grow, with people working in the state sector by day and for themselves by night. A sort of second Biedermeier age dawned. Governed by a state every bit as absolutist as the empire under the Habsburgs, the people had no say in their own affairs and little chance to influence the course of their own lives. And yet they were prosperous and content to a degree. Limited numbers of Western goods were available in the shops; everyone had their East German, rattletrap car; everyone had central heating; everyone had summer holidays by Lake Balaton or the Black Sea; those who wanted could have a small house and vineyard in the country. Gorbachev, impressed by Kádár's record, once said that his perestroika had been partly inspired by the Hungarian model.

INTO THE FUTURE

When in 1989 the Red Star was finally removed from the tip of the Parliament building, Hungary, as a result of Kádár's measures, was not as paralysed by the emergence of a market economy as might have been expected. Budapest itself has changed with extraordinary speed over the last fifteen years, and is now a bustling, prospering modern capital. Many Hungarians feel that accession to the European Union has at last placed them where they have always wanted to be: at the heart of Europe, better known and better understood, independent and autonomous, but with the support of their neighbours, and - for once! - politically on the right side. Perhaps now, at long last, the predictions of those optimistic, excited late 19th-century voices will come true: 'Budapest will be a world metropolis, and crowds of people will flock from far and wide to see it'.

A Handful of Dates

896 (approx.) The seven Magyar tribes arrive in the Carpathian Basin.

1000 Pope Sylvester II grants a crown to Stephen, first Christian monarch of Hungary.

1241 Invasion by the Mongols, who lay waste most of the country.

1476-90 King Mátyás makes Buda a centre of learning and luxury.

1541 Capture of Buda by the Ottomans.

1686 Expulsion of the Ottomans from Buda by the Habsburgs.

1848-9 Hungary's anti-Habsburg bid for independence is crushed.

1867 Compromise Agreement between Hungary and Austria creates the Dual Monarchy of Austria-Hungary.

1919 Short-lived Soviet-style commune under Béla Kun.

1920 The Treaty of Trianon deprives Hungary of two-thirds of her territory.

1948 Hungary officially becomes a Communist state.

1956 Anti-Soviet uprising brutally crushed.

1989 Fall of Communism.

2004 Accession of Hungary to the European Union.

PART II

GUIDE TO THE CITY

MAJOR SIGHTS

These sights are marked on the map on the following page.

❶ THE CHAIN BRIDGE: The most beautiful of all the bridges across the Danube - *p. 32.*

❷ THE ROYAL PALACE: Former residence of the Habsburg emperors, surrounded by traces of glorious and inglorious history - *p. 35.*

❸ THE MÁTYÁS CHURCH: Buda's oldest and most exotic-looking church - *p. 41.*

❹ PARLIAMENT: Symbol of sublime self-confidence, now home to St Stephen's Crown - *p. 44.*

❺ THE OPERA HOUSE: Possibly the most beautiful in the world - *p. 55.*

❻ HEROES' SQUARE: A parade-ground on a monumental scale, to celebrate a thousand years of nationhood - *p. 57.*

❼ ST STEPHEN'S BASILICA: Sheer magnificence, dedicated to Hungary's founding monarch-saint - *p. 60.*

❽ THE DOHÁNY UTCA SYNAGOGUE: Budapest's grandest temple - *p. 65.*

❾ VÁCI UTCA: Includes a celebrated market and coffee house - *p. 69.*

The Chain Bridge, Budapest's most enduring symbol.

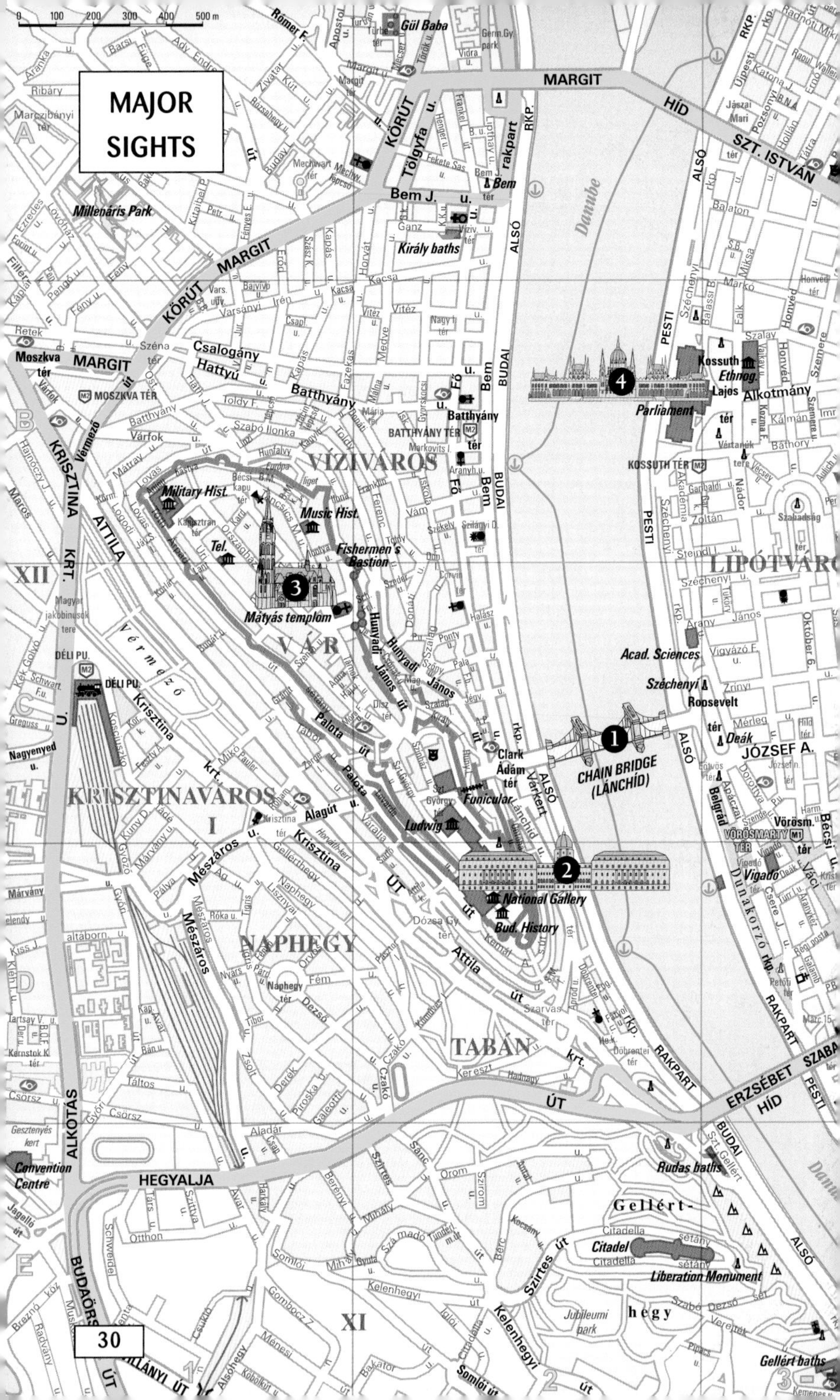
0 100 200 300 400 500 m
MAJOR SIGHTS
Gül Baba
MARGIT HÍD
SZT. ISTVÁN
Millenáris Park
Király baths
Danube
Moszkva tér
MOSZKVA TÉR
BATTHYÁNY TÉR
VÍZIVÁROS
Military Hist.
Music Hist.
Tel.
Fishermen's Bastion
Mátyás templom
VÁR
Parliament
Kossuth
Ethnog.
KOSSUTH TÉR
LIPÓTVÁROS
Acad. Sciences
Széchenyi
Roosevelt tér
Deák
CHAIN BRIDGE (LÁNCHÍD)
Clark Ádám tér
Funicular
Ludwig
National Gallery
Bud. History
VÖRÖSMARTY TÉR
Vigadó
DÉLI PU.
KRISZTINAVÁROS
NAPHEGY
TABÁN
ERZSÉBET HÍD
Rudas baths
Gellért-hegy
Citadel
Liberation Monument
Jubileumi park
Gellért baths
Convention Centre
HEGYALJA
BUDAÖRSI ÚT
XII
I
XI
1
2
3
4

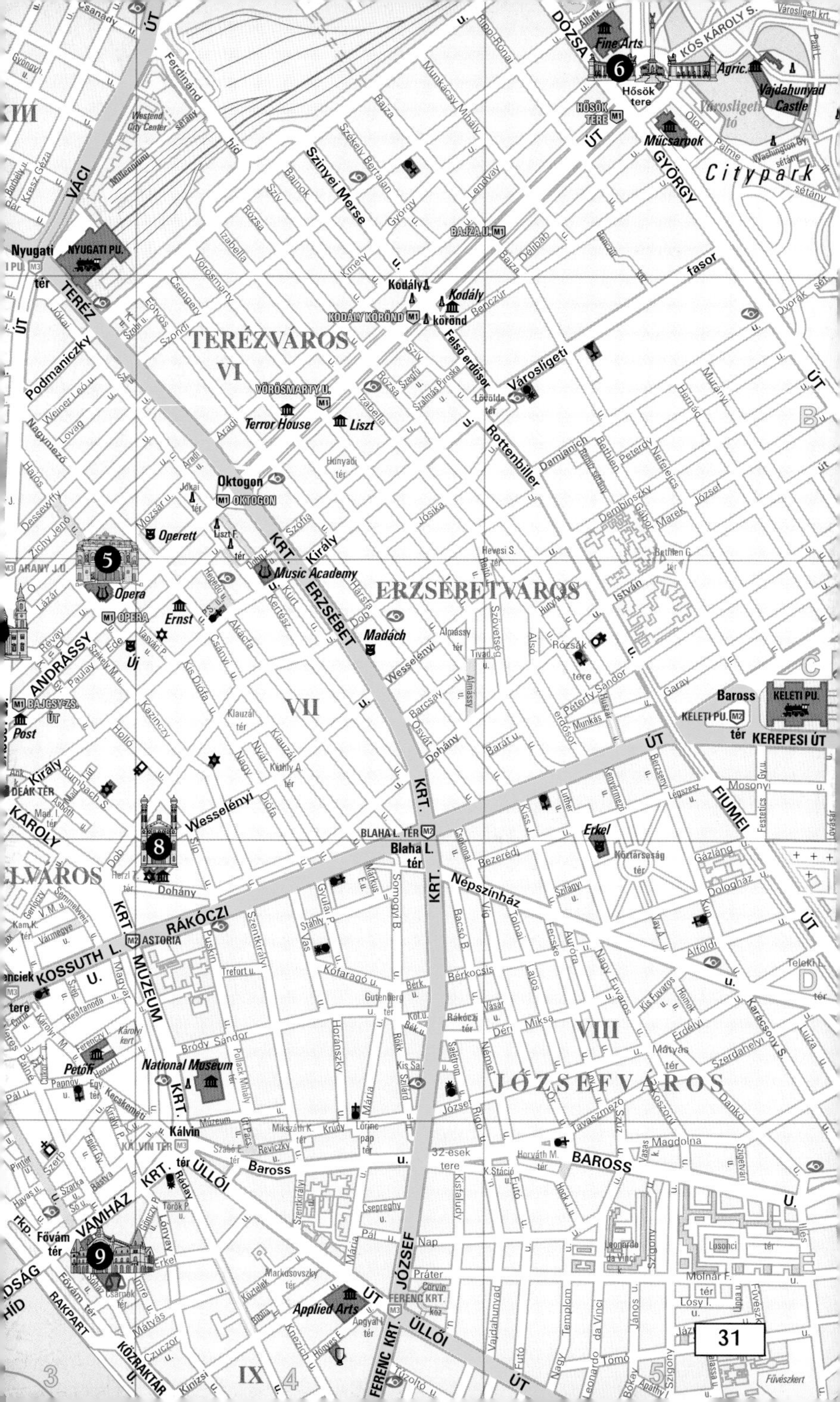

TERÉZVÁROS
VI
ERZSÉBETVÁROS
VII
VIII
JÓZSEFVÁROS
IX
Cityparck
Városliget
Fine Arts
Hősök tere
Agric.
Vajdahunyad Castle
Műcsarnok
Nyugati
NYUGATI PU.
Westend City Center
Kodály körönd
KODÁLY KÖRÖND
Terror House
Liszt
VÖRÖSMARTY U.
Oktogon
OKTOGON
Operett
Music Academy
Opera
OPERA
Ernst
Új
Madách
Post
BAJCSY-ZS. ÚT
DEÁK TÉR
Baross
KELETI PU.
KEREPESI ÚT
BLAHA L. TÉR
Blaha L. tér
Erkel
Köztársaság tér
ASTORIA
National Museum
Petőfi
Kálvin
KÁLVIN TÉR
Fővám tér
Applied Arts
FERENC KRT.
ANDRÁSSY
VÁCI ÚT
TERÉZ KRT.
ERZSÉBET KRT.
RÁKÓCZI ÚT
MÚZEUM KRT.
KOSSUTH L. U.
VÁMHÁZ KRT.
ÜLLŐI ÚT
JÓZSEF KRT.
BAROSS
FIUMEI ÚT
DÓZSA GYÖRGY ÚT
Népszínház
Wesselényi
Dohány
Király
Rottenbiller
Városligeti fasor
Podmaniczky
Nagymező
Hajós
Dessewffy
Zichy Jenő
Rumbach S.
Akácfa
Kazinczy
Klauzál tér
Rózsák tere
Dembinszky
István
Damjanich
Bethlen
Peterdy
Garay
Gutenberg tér
Rákóczi tér
Mátyás tér
Horánszky
Mária
Krúdy
Bródy Sándor
Pollack Mihály
Szentkirályi
Vas
Kőfaragó u.
Somogyi B.
Bacsó B.
Nagy Fuvaros
Karácsony S.
Dankó
Szerdahelyi
Vajdahunyad
Templom
Leonardo da Vinci
Tömő
Tűzoltó
Knézich
Kinizsi
Ráday
Török P.
Lónyay
Erkel
Közraktár
Rakpart
Füvészkert
Losonci tér
Molnár F. tér
Lósy I.
Magdolna
Horváth M. tér
32-esek tere
Práter
Corvin
Nap
Pál u.
Csepreghy
Baross
Szabó E. tér
Reviczky
Múzeum
Mikszáth K. tér
Lőrinc pap tér
Kis Stáció
Futó
Hock J.
Szigony
Bókay
Apáthy
31

THE CHAIN BRIDGE & ROOSEVELT TÉR

As the Eiffel Tower is to Paris and the Statue of Liberty is to New York, so the Chain Bridge is to Budapest: its quintessential symbol, stamped on all Hungarian hearts and reproduced on thousands of souvenir keyrings, snowstorm paperweights and coffee mugs.

In December 1820 a young nobleman and officer, Count István Széchenyi, stationed on the eastern bank of the Danube, received news that his father had died in Vienna. At that time there was nothing but a pontoon bridge across the river, and ice floes that hard winter had put it out of use. Frustrated and immobilised, Széchenyi languished on the Pest riverbank for a week before the bridge could be reopened. The incident led him to make a vow: he would pay for a proper, fixed bridge whatever the cost. It took him nearly thirty years to do it; the Chain Bridge, designed by the Englishman William Tierney Clark and built by Scots engineer Adam Clark (no relation), was officially opened only in November 1849, just as the defiant Hungarian uprising against the Habsburgs was humiliatingly crushed. In a bitter twist of fate, the first man to cross the bridge was Baron Julius Jacob von Haynau, Commander-in-Chief of the Austrian army in Hungary, leading his victorious troops into the Hungarian capital. And Széchenyi, after a severe nervous breakdown, was eventually installed behind the doors of the Döbling Mental Institution in Vienna, where he remained until he took his own life in 1860. Today the Chain Bridge or Széchenyi Lánchíd, the first

PHOTO: BENCE KÉPESSY / HUNGARIAN NATIONAL MUSEUM

Count István Széchenyi (1791-1860), popularly known as the 'greatest Hungarian', who masterminded the building of the Chain Bridge.

permanent bridge in Budapest, is still the most magnificent bridge across the Danube.

The square into which the bridge leads on the Pest side of the river is Roosevelt tér, site of the Hungarian Academy of Sciences, the imposing dark honey-coloured building on the left as you come across the bridge. The academy was founded by Széchenyi in 1825 - he is said to have donated an entire year's revenue to the project, and he took rooms in a hotel on the same square so that he could watch the construction work. Széchenyi caused a sensation when the academy opened by making his inaugural speech in the vernacular Hungarian instead of Latin, which in those days was still the lingua franca of officialdom in the Habsburg empire.

BTM KISCELLI MÚZEUM FENYKÉP GYŰJTEMÉNY

Count Széchenyi's beloved Chain Bridge in 1945, after the Red Army had taken Buda.

Tucked behind the statue of Széchenyi that now graces the centre of the square is an ancient acacia tree, propped up on wooden stilts and reputedly the oldest tree in Budapest. Behind that is the Four Seasons Hotel, housed in the Gresham Palace, an Art Nouveau-style building by Zsigmond Quittner and József Vágó, constructed in 1907 for the London-based Gresham insurance company. Its most famous features are its graceful peacock gateways, its glass-roofed atrium, and the stained glass windows and wrought iron banisters in its stairways. Between the two world wars, the building's café was the haunt of the Gresham Circle of artists, which included Béla Czóbel and István Szőnyi, former members of the Nagybánya School (*see p. 106*). Their artistic philosophy favoured lyricism and humanism, and took a reactionary stand against the radical avant garde of the day.

The statue of István Széchenyi presides over Roosevelt tér, in front of the Hungarian Academy of Sciences, which Széchenyi founded.

One of the Gresham Circle's favourite places to take the air was the Dunakorzó, the Danube promenade between Roosevelt tér and Elisabeth Bridge. It has been a popular sauntering spot for decades, and its pavement cafés offer superb and dramatic views of Buda's Castle Hill on the opposite bank. A row of magnificent hotels once stood here, patronised by the kings and dukes of Europe and the magnates of America. But the Second World War took its toll and the hotels were flattened. New hotels have been built, but they are considerably less magnificent.

Vigadó tér, about halfway along the Dunakorzó, fills up with a craft market in summer and is dominated by the eclectic Vigadó concert hall (1865). The bronze statue sitting on the railings beside the Vigadó tér tram stop is *Little Princess*, a 1990 work by László Márton and a much-exploited photo opportunity.

THE ROYAL PALACE & ENVIRONS: SOUTHERN CASTLE HILL

Clark Ádám tér & the Sikló

The grassy roundabout on the Buda side of the Chain Bridge is named Clark Ádám tér in honour of the Scots engineer who built the bridge. Adam Clark fell in love with Budapest, married a Hungarian, and lived in the city for the rest of his days, in a house at the end of Lánchíd utca. The tunnel that cuts through Castle Hill is also Clark's work. It was built between 1853 and 1856 at the instigation of István Széchenyi, who had the foresight to understand that the Chain Bridge could only be an effective link between Buda and Pest if Buda's hinterland was then made accessible to the traffic that drove over it. The tunnel is parabolic in shape, to better bear the weight of the hill. Hungarian children are told that the Chain Bridge is rolled into it to keep dry when it rains.

To the left of the tunnel as you face it, in a small patch of garden, is the 0-kilometre stone, an elliptical sculpture in the shape of a stylised zero, marking the spot from which all Hungarian milestones take their reference. The best way to approach Castle Hill from here is to take the funicular (*sikló*), which first made the steep ascent in 1870, when it was constructed on the orders of Széchenyi's son Ödön. The stepped carriages were built in the 1980s but are faithful replicas of the 19th-century originals. The *sikló* runs from 7.30am to 10pm every day every except the 1st, 3rd and 5th Monday of every month, when it is closed for maintenance.

The *sikló* brings you out on top of Castle Hill, a limestone outcrop rising steeply from the western bank of the Danube and separating the river from the hilly Buda hinterland. Because of its easily defensible position, it was chosen as the site for the royal palace in the 13th century, during a massive Mongol invasion which swept across the country, bringing devastation in its wake. For three centuries after that, Hungarian monarchs occupied Castle Hill, until Sultan Suleiman took Buda in 1541 without a shot being fired. The city remained in Ottoman hands for a hundred and fifty years, until the Ottoman army was defeated in a bloody and destructive siege in 1686. The victorious Christian armies claimed the palace for the Holy Roman Emperor and Archduke of Austria, Leopold von Habsburg.

THE ROYAL PALACE OF BUDA

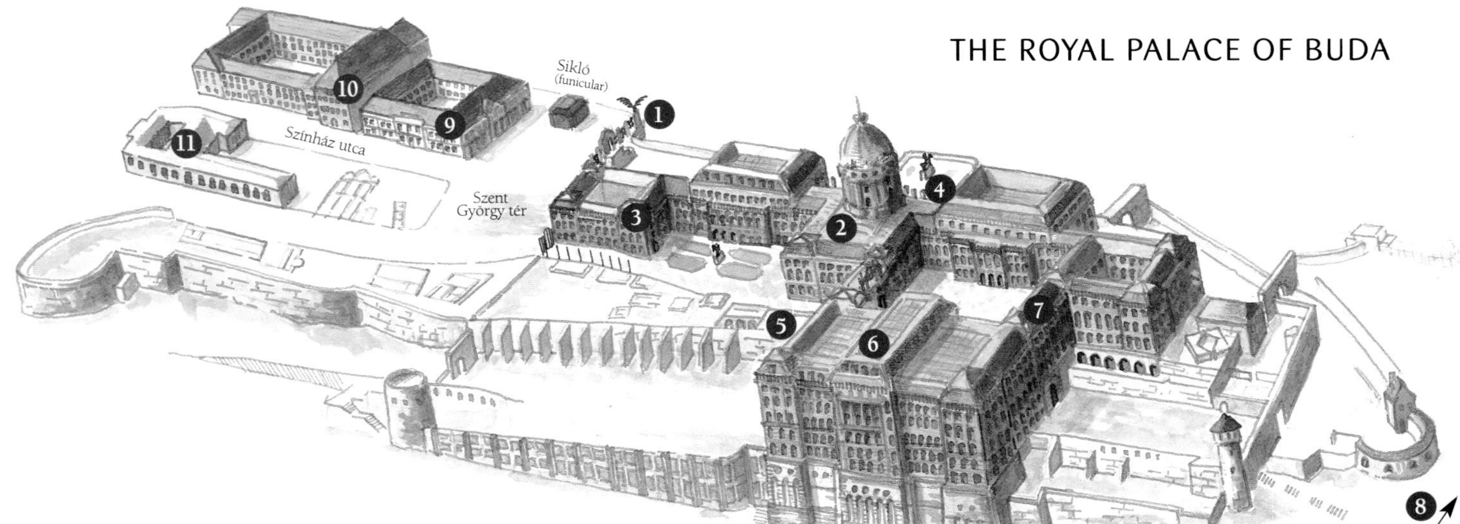

1 Turul
2 National Gallery
3 Ludwig Museum
4 Eugene of Savoy
5 Mátyás Fountain
6 Széchenyi Library
7 Budapest History Museum
8 Ottoman Gravestones
9 Sándor Palota
10 Hungarian Dance Theatre
11 Former Defence Ministry

What to See

1 THE TURUL: Guarding the gateway to the Royal Palace is an immense bronze bird, wings outstretched, with a sword in its talons. This is the turul, mythical bird of the ancient Magyars: Árpád, the warrior chief who led the seven Magyar tribes into the Carpathian Basin, is said to have sprung from its loins.

2 HUNGARIAN NATIONAL GALLERY: Buda's golden age came during the reign of King Mátyás Corvinus (1458-1490). He had the Buda palace completely rebuilt in the Renaissance style, and contemporary accounts marvelled at its splendour, claiming that there was no finer building, even in Italy. In 1663 the Turkish chronicler Evlia Chelebi wrote that as soon as he saw the palace, he dropped to his knees and touched his forehead to the ground, giving thanks to Allah for allowing him to see Buda. Though the Ottomans admired the palace, and carried many of its treasures away to Istanbul, they did not use it as a royal residence, instead quartering janissaries and horses there. In 1686, when the Ottomans were ousted from Buda, the palace was destroyed in the fighting. And although it was rebuilt in the Rococo style by Maria Theresa, she and her successors only used it for imperial visits to the Hungarian capital. It was remodelled again, partly by Opera House architect Miklós Ybl (*see p. 77*), and partly by Alajos Hauszmann (architect of the Ethnographic Museum) during the reign of Franz Joseph. It was used as a royal residence for the last time during the regency of Miklós Horthy between the wars. During the Second World War it was badly bombed and had to be entirely rebuilt.

The Hungarian National Gallery is housed in the former palace's main wing. Its collections are described in detail on pp. 104-110.

3 LUDWIG MUSEUM: A permanent collection of contemporary art plus temporary shows. For more detail see p. 113.

4 STATUE OF EUGENE OF SAVOY: Both soldier and statesman, Prince Eugene of Savoy fought in the Austrian army that beat the Ottomans back from the gates of Vienna in 1683. Three years later he had come into his own as a commander, and led the Christian troops to victory in Buda. The statue, which stands on the castle parapet overlooking the river, was erected in 1900.

BTM KISCELLI MÚZEUM FÉNYKÉP GYŰJTEMÉNY

The Habsburg Steps and entrance portico on the Danube-facing façade of the Royal Palace. Photographed in 1903.

❺ THE MÁTYÁS FOUNTAIN: A 1904 piece by Alajos Stróbl, whose works, chiefly portrait sculptures, are found scattered all over the city. This romanticised scene commemorates a legendary incident from the life of King Mátyás Corvinus. One day while out hunting, he was espied by a beautiful young girl, Szép Ilonka, who fell instantly in love with him, not realising who he was. When she discovered his true identity, mortified at the hopelessness of her love, she died of grief. Mátyás is portrayed at the top, standing proudly over a stricken stag. Ilonka sits shyly on the right, with a frightened fawn by her side. On the left is Mátyás's Italian chronicler, aquiline-featured and aloof, with observant eagle eyes and a falcon on his wrist. Below them, Mátyás's thirsty hounds lap from the fountain.

❻ SZÉCHENYI LIBRARY: The library is housed in the so-called 'Ybl wing' of the palace, so named because it was built to the designs of Miklós Ybl, architect of the Opera House. It faces away from the river and was protected from the brunt of the

BTM KISCELLI MÚZEUM FÉNYKÉP GYŰJTEMÉNY

The palace ballroom after Soviet bomb raids in 1945.

fighting when the Red Army marched in from the east in 1945. The result is a less badly damaged wing, and one which gives more of a flavour of how the palace would have looked when Franz Joseph presided over it. A tall gateway guarded by stern and stalwart lions leads through into an inner courtyard. The lions on the inner side of the gate have their hackles up, growling malevolently at intruders into the royal sanctum. The Széchenyi Library on the right is Hungary's main reference library and keeps copies of all works published in the country. A corridor round the side of it (entrance under the lion gateway) is lined with an exhibit documenting the history of the palace, including archive photographs of its pre-war splendour and subsequent devastation. At the end of the corridor is a lift, which for 10 forints takes you down to the other side of the hill.

7 BUDAPEST HISTORY MUSEUM: The fragmentary (literally) nature of the museum's collection demonstrates just how much was destroyed in all the wars and sieges Buda has lived through - and how little survives. The first-floor display on Budapest from the defeat of the Ottomans up to the Second World War is interesting. The oldest exhibits are underground in the former cellars. '*In the royal palace,*' wrote a Turkish chronicler in 1526, '*there was a temple, stuffed with idols, its walls filled with the images of base giaours. Gilded paintings, portraits of the Hungarian sultans, adorned it in glorious array.*' That temple has long gone, but its brick-vaulted crypt survives. It was restored and re-consecrated as a chapel in 1990. A Gothic vaulted undercroft, the '*gótikus terem*', also survives. Apart from that, you are confronted with a pitiful array of salvaged remains: ceramic stove tiles, glazed floor tiles, and carved marble door and window frames of great beauty and skilled manufacture, often made of characteristic ruddy marble from the Pilis Hills north of Budapest, marble that is still very much a part of the city's stonework. These fragments can only let us conjecture how magnificent the palace must once have been.

The museum also gives you access to the fortifications of Buda's southern ramparts: a tall lookout tower and a round bastion with gun placements. *Museum open 10am-6pm. Closed Tuesdays except in summer.*

8 OTTOMAN GRAVESTONES: Just below the round bastion, in a grassy park with a view of Gellért Hill, is a handful of traditional Ottoman gravestones, characteristically topped

Turbanned gravestones on southern Castle Hill, remains of a Turkish cemetery.

with turbans. Enclosed behind a rail fence, these are the only remnants of a Turkish cemetery that once occupied these slopes.

❾ SÁNDOR PALOTA: A fine Neoclassical building built in 1806 and designed by Mihály Polláck (*see p. 76*), it now houses the offices of the President of the Hungarian Republic, hence the chains, barricades, limousines and uniformed guards. It was here, in 1941, that Hungarian Prime Minister Count Pál Teleki committed suicide after Germany advanced against Yugoslavia. Both countries were Hungarian allies, and Teleki had hoped to reconcile them. Immediately opposite the main entrance to the building is an excavation area and small garden containing the reconstructed ground plan of a royal chapel built here in the middle ages, the burial place of Mátyás Corvinus's first wife. The teenage queen died in childbirth in 1465.

❿ HUNGARIAN DANCE THEATRE: This building has been used as a concert hall since the late 18th century - Beethoven performed here in 1800. Before that it was home to a community of Carmelite nuns; the auditorium is the nunnery's former church. Next door to the theatre is the Rivalda restaurant, which in summer sets out tables in the old nunnery courtyard. Just beyond the entrance to Rivalda is a small area of flowerbeds containing lavender and other aromatic plants, created in commemoration of the nuns' former physic garden.

⓫ FORMER DEFENCE MINISTRY: This bleak, shell-shocked hulk remains as testimony to what most of Castle Hill looked like in 1945, after the Red Army had finally driven the retreating Nazis from Buda. The building is still completely unrestored.

CENTRAL CASTLE HILL: THE MÁTYÁS CHURCH & FISHERMEN'S BASTION

MÁTYÁS CHURCH

(Mátyás templom) Buda I, Szentháromság tér
Open Mon-Sat 9am-5pm; Sun 1pm-5pm.

Large and imposing, the Mátyás Church (Mátyás templom) has had many incarnations in its 750-year history. It was founded in 1255 by King Béla IV, after he moved his court up to Castle Hill from Óbuda. Though officially dedicated to the Blessed Virgin, the church gets its popular name from an escutcheon bearing the coat of arms of King Mátyás Corvinus (who reigned 1458-1490), which you can see about halfway up the outside of the south tower.

The towering, neo-Gothic Mátyás Church.

Mátyás married twice, both times in this church. His first wife was the twelve-year-old daughter of Podjebrad of Bohemia, who died almost immediately because, as one writer darkly expressed it, 'her tender body was not strong enough to withstand the rigours of cohabitation'. His second wife, Beatrice, daughter of the King of Naples, was made of much robuster stuff. She encouraged him to patronise the arts and undertook the task of civilising him and his court, inviting Italian cooks and craftsmen to Hungary, introducing her husband to the concept of 'quality not quantity' when it came to wine, and frowning on his carousing at mealtimes, his belching and farting contests, and his tendency to eat with his hands and come away from table with beard and clothing spattered with sauce. Beatrice, in other words, helped Mátyás turn himself from a mediaeval warrior - lion on the battlefield, hooligan at home - into a cultured Renaissance monarch. But when the Turks captured Buda in 1541, Hungary's Renaissance glory vanished forever. The Mátyás Church was transformed into a mosque named after Suleiman the Magnificent, and a celebration was held here to mark the Ottoman victory. Fortunately the church's treasures had already been moved to Pressburg (now Bratislava) for safekeeping. When Buda was recaptured in 1686, the church came under the auspices of the Jesuits. In 1867 the Compromise Agreement between Hungary and Austria established the Dual Monarchy of Austria-Hungary, and the Emperor Franz Joseph was crowned King of Hungary here, to the strains of Liszt's *Coronation Mass*. In the late 19th century the church was completely remodelled, and any fragment that remained of the original 13th-century stonework was incorporated into the new design. The result, concocted by the architect Frigyes Schulek and completed in 1896, is a neo-Gothic fantasy, based on popular 19th-century ideas of the middle ages as an age of gilded chivalry and rose-tinted piety.

The interior of the church (*NB: entry fee*) is very striking, with columns and vaulting exuberantly painted in geometric designs (supposedly mediaeval in inspiration) and floral patterns (inspired by Hungarian folk motifs). The design was by one of Hungary's finest 19th-century fresco and genre artists, Bertalan Székely. Despite the vaulting and the stained glass windows, the church does not feel like a Gothic cathedral: its atmosphere is too mysterious and Eastern. Kodály's *Budavári Te Deum* received its debut performance here in 1936, as part of the 250th anniversary celebration of the recapture of Buda from the Turks, and the church is still an important concert venue.

Fishermen's Bastion

The Fishermen's Bastion, built by Schulek in 1902, is so named because this stretch of Buda's defensive walls was traditionally guarded and maintained by the

The Fishermen's Bastion draws its guiding inspiration from the Far East.

guild of fishermen. It consists of a meringue-pie arrangement of neo-Romanesque arcades, and towers topped with pinnacled turrets that seem to take their inspiration from the jungle temples of Cambodia. 'Kitsch but beautiful' was the 1930s writer Antal Szerb's verdict. Its greatest advantage is that from the top you get one of the city's best panoramic views. Nestling in the bastion's embrace is a 1906 equestrian statue of King Stephen (*see p. 88*), the work of Alajos Stróbl.

NB: For a walking tour of the Castle Hill, beginning outside the Mátyás Church, see p. 151.

Where to Eat on Castle Hill

In summer there is a café and bar inside the Fishermen's Bastion, offering unaparalleled views out over the Danube. For coffee, cake and cosiness there is the tiny Ruszwurm (*see p. 99*), Budapest's oldest café, at Szentháromság utca 7. For something more substantial, Rivalda (*see p. 236*) offers Hungarian fusion cooking, and Arany Kaviár (*see p. 235*) serves Russian menus fit for a Czar.

PARLIAMENT, ST STEPHEN'S CROWN & SZABADSÁG TÉR

Parliament

(Parlament) Pest V, Kossuth Lajos tér 1-3

Tours in English lasting 45 minutes run at 10am and 2pm every day. The ticket office is at Door X, to the right of the main steps. Ask the guard to let you through.

The Hungarian Parliament, an immense piece of neo-Gothic grandiloquence, was built over a period of two decades (1884-1904) by the architect Imre Steindl. It is the third largest parliament building in Europe, after the Reichstag and the Palace of Westminster. In fact Steindl is thought to have been influenced by Westminster in his choice of the Gothic Revival style. In 1872 he submitted a giant-domed neo-Gothic entry for the competition to design the new Reichstag. He didn't win, but was highly commended, and this spurred him on to design something similar for his native Hungary. The result is a colossal palace standing right on the river, on sedgy land that had to be drained and stabilised before building could begin. By the time it was finally completed, its neo-Gothic style looked hopelessly out of date in a city that was learning to relish the sensuous pleasures of Art Nouveau, and critics scornfully compared it to both a Turkish bath and a wedding cake. Today it seems madly huge for such a small country, but in its day it administered the affairs of a significant stretch of the Habsburg empire, stretching from the Tatra Mountains to the Carpathians in one direction and to the Adriatic in the other. Inside the building, the walls and pillars are decorated in gold - it's real gold leaf above head height, while within arm's reach the gilding is just gold paint, so that no one can profit from peeling it off. Numbered cigar-holders line the window sills outside the debating chamber so that a smoking politician didn't need to waste his good Havana when he went in to vote; he merely set it down in, say, No. 3, and relit it after he had cast his lot. The stained glass in all the windows is by the foremost masters of the time, including Miksa Róth (*see p. 119*). Parliament's most prized exhibit is the crown (*see p. 46*) of the canonised King Stephen (István).

The square on which the parliament building stands, Kossuth Lajos tér, is one of the largest in the city, home to some eye-catching architecture, not least the Metro station, which hits you with the sheer audacity of its ugliness. It is a

1972 work by Béla Pintér, also the architect of the Hilton Hotel up on Castle Hill. Standing with your back to the Parliament, the building in front of you on your right, with the ground-floor colonnade, is the Agriculture Ministry. The busts all along the colonnade commemorate horticulturalists, vets, animal breeders and agricultural revolutionaries who helped develop Hungary's rich farmlands. Two Socialist-Realist statues stand outside it: the stripped-to-the-waist, young-Adonis 'Boy Reaper', and the sturdy-legged, broad-hipped 'Girl Agronomist'. Built in a neo-Renaissance style in 1885, the building was one of the competing designs for the new parliament. It came third, and was erected as a sort of consolation prize. If you inspect the colonnade more closely, you will notice that its walls are dotted with small bronze balls, put there to symbolise the bullets fired on 'Bloody Thursday' in 1956. On October 25th, 1956, thousands of people gathered in front of Parliament to protest against the Stalinist regime. The Politburo panicked and snipers and tanks shot at the peaceful crowd. This only served to steel the will of the people still further, and gun battles took place on the streets until the Soviet tanks finally emerged victorious a few weeks later. Much of the damage you see on the city's façades today does not date from the Second World War but from 1956. In the grassy area in front of Parliament stands a broad basalt column bearing an eternal flame, erected in 1996 on the 40th anniversary of Bloody Thursday.

The debating chamber in Budapest's Parliament.

St Stephen's Crown

The holy crown of St Stephen is not only an exquisite work of art, it is a physical symbol of power and authority. Hungarian subjects traditionally owed allegiance not to the monarch but to the crown he wore: rising up in rebellion against the monarch might be considered justified, but any word or action against the crown was treason. At the beginning of Mátyás Corvinus's reign, the crown was missing, having been traded to Holy Roman Emperor Frederick III for 8,000 gold coins, and thus the king ruled by right of parliament. As soon as Mátyás ransomed the crown back, in 1464, he ruled by right of the crown, and summoned parliament only twice more.

Scholars disagree on whether this is the very same crown that Pope Sylvester II sent to King Stephen in the year 1000. Some say it is; others say that it is in fact two crowns joined together. It clearly consists of two parts: a Byzantine circlet adorned with pearls and cloisonné enamel panels, and a Latin cross-piece, with delicate gold filigree work and semi-precious stones. The Latin section is thought to be the older and more likely to have been used by Stephen. The enamel panels on the circlet show God the Son at the front and the Byzantine emperor Michael Ducas (reigned 1071-1078) at the back (though his image is believed to have been fixed on later, in place of an original icon of

the Virgin and Holy Ghost. The gold cross-piece has an enamel image of God the Father, creator of sun, moon and stars, at the top, and eight of the apostles down the sides. The cross at the top was most likely bent by accident, but theories persist that it was fashioned like that deliberately, mimicking the angle of the earth's axis (23.5°), to symbolise Hungary's temporal sway.

The crown has been in danger more than once. In 1439, wanting to secure the succession of her baby son, the mediaeval Queen Elizabeth, newly widowed by the death of her husband, Holy Roman Emperor and King of Hungary Albert II, smuggled the crown in her baby's cradle to the baby's clandestine coronation: the weight of the royal infant almost squashed it flat. In 1848, rather than allow it to fall into Habsburg hands, some zealous revolutionaries advocated throwing the crown into the Danube. When the Communists first came to power in 1919, there were numerous calls for the crown to be melted down. Béla Kun, leader of the Soviet-style Republic of Councils, planned to auction it off in Germany, but his regime was toppled before this could happen. When the Communists again came to power after the Second World War, the crown was smuggled out of the country and out of their reach. Its journey took it to Fort Knox, where it lay incarcerated until 1978, when President Carter formally returned it to Hungary. A lot of people on both sides of the Atlantic were against its return while the country was still Communist, but Carter insisted. It was accompanied by a distinguished delegation, including the Nobel Prize-winning chemist Albert Szent-Györgyi (*see p 147*). Today it is once again the symbol of the Hungarian state, and a treasured piece of the nation's patrimony, watched over by a platoon of guards in ceremonial uniform.

(*Contd. from p. 45*) On the other side of the road from the flame you will see the stately Ethnographic Museum (*see p. 117*), another contender in the parliament design competition. Along the balustrade on the roof are statues to Rhetoric, Painting, Geometry and the Arts and Sciences - the architect, Alajos Hauszmann, may have hoped that the MPs within would be as cultured. At the far end of the square, again on the grass outside Parliament, is a gigantic statue of Lajos Kossuth, after whom the square is named, striking nationalist fervour into the hearts of ordinary Hungarians. A lawyer by profession and radical thinker by instinct, he provided the brains and the vision behind the 1848 uprising, while the romantic poet Sándor Petőfi (*see p. 88*) provided the fire and the emotion. Kossuth was not captured by the Austrians and, unlike many of his companions, did not die a martyr's death. Instead he fled to Turkey, from where he made his way to London, where he lived for a time just off the Portobello Road. The story goes that once, when he stood up to address a crowd of British radicals, he spoke English with such an impenetrable accent that the crowd remarked how similar Hungarian sounded to their own tongue.

Szabadság tér

On weekdays this whole area is buzzing with office workers, bank clerks and civil servants, swarming in and out of the lofty buildings that flank the wide, geometric streets. The novelist and essayist Sándor Márai wrote that many such areas of Pest went up virtually overnight in the early 20th century, all 'covered with clouds of dust. Building went on at every street corner, the capital city of the great, rich, happy empire was having its image built, feverishly fast, and on a greatly exaggerated scale'. Just where slum dwellings had once stood, lapped by the muddy Danube and packed in next to timber yards and factories, graceful streets and great neo-Renaissance blocks were raised. This particular part of town became the commercial centre and the money has stayed, with Szabadság tér still home to the Hungarian National Bank. The grassy expanse in the square's centre boasts a café where you can sit and enjoy the view. Sights numbered on the plan opposite are described in full on the following pages.

SZABADSÁG TÉR

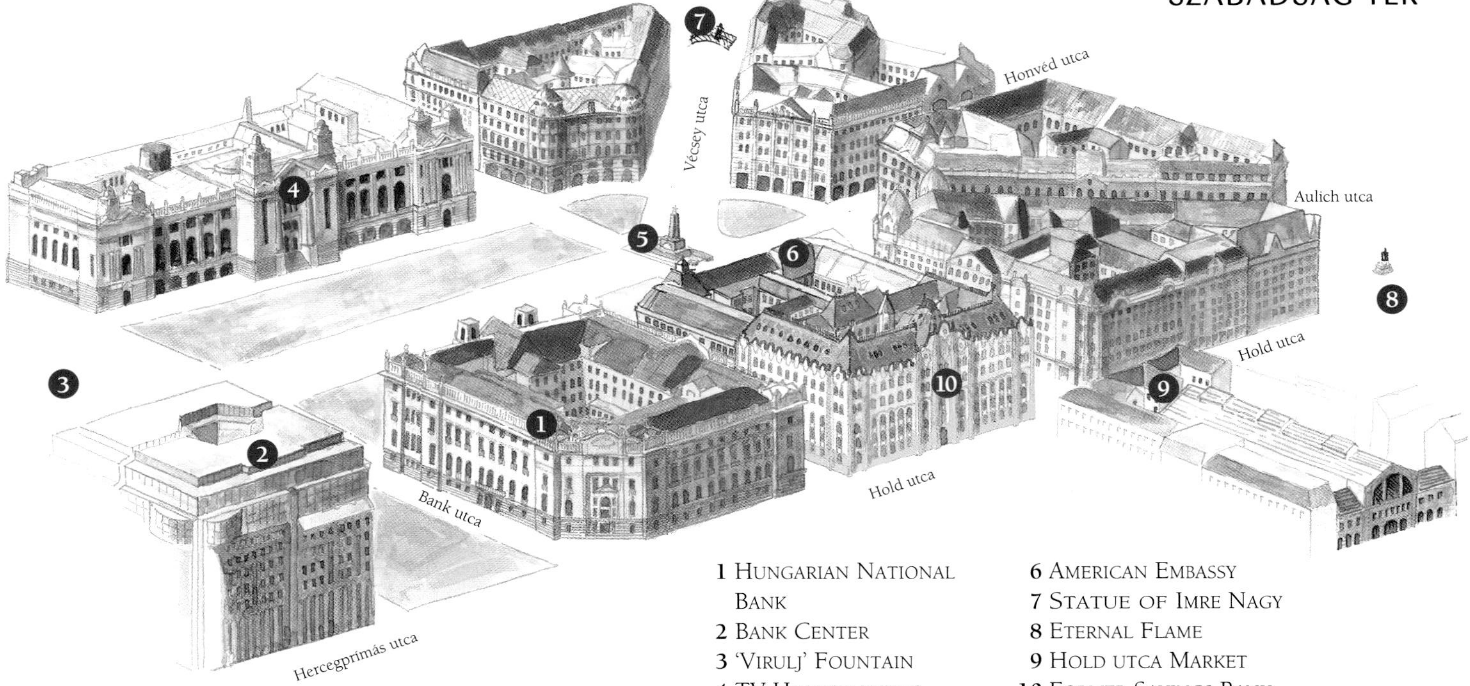

1 Hungarian National Bank
2 Bank Center
3 'Virulj' Fountain
4 TV Headquarters
5 Soviet Memorial
6 American Embassy
7 Statue of Imre Nagy
8 Eternal Flame
9 Hold utca Market
10 Former Savings Bank

❶ THE HUNGARIAN NATIONAL BANK: Built in 1905, this is one of the few buildings in Budapest where the façade is really made of stone and not moulded plaster over brick. Finely carved reliefs run all the way round the building, tracing the history of commerce and finance.

❷ THE BANK CENTER: A gleaming modern banking and office complex built in 1996 by József Finta (b. 1935), who is responsible for most of the Danube-bank hotels, none of which show him in a very flattering light. This is a more successful undertaking with its glassed over atrium, central glass pyramid and four towers all shimmering in chrome, polished marble and glass. It has an air of confidence, in keeping with its function.

❸ THE 'VIRULJ' FOUNTAIN: Szabadság tér was once little more than a marshy wasteland where the citizens of Pest dumped their refuse. Count István Széchenyi (*see p. 88*) drew up plans to fill it with trees, getting his wife to plant the first saplings, which she did with the invocation '*Virulj!* - Flourish!'. The bas-relief on the ornamental drinking fountain commemorates this event.

❹ STATE TV HEADQUARTERS: Built in the same year and by the same architect (Ignác Alpár) as the National Bank, this vast, imposing building originally housed the Hungarian Stock Exchange.

❺ THE SOVIET MEMORIAL: This 1946 memorial is the only Communist-era monument not to have been uprooted and taken to the Statue Park (*see p. 120*). It was erected two years before Hungary officially threw in her lot with the Soviet Bloc,

Minting money: a detail from the façade of the Hungarian National Bank.

and was built over the final resting place of Russian soldiers who fell in the Second World War. Hungary signed an agreement to let it stay, and it remains as almost the only overt reminder of half a century of history behind the Iron Curtain. Its Soviet star now winks across at the American Embassy.

Memorial to the Red Army soldiers who died in the battle for Budapest in 1945.

❻ THE AMERICAN EMBASSY: The Embassy is the place where Cardinal Mindszenty, Catholic primate of Hungary, took refuge after the 1956 revolution was crushed. Mindszenty in fact spent most of his life behind bars. He was first imprisoned in 1919, for speaking out against the Communist government of Béla Kun. During the Second World War he was incarcerated again, for denouncing the deportation of Jews. He was jailed for a third time after a show trial in 1949, for refusing to support the Stalinist system. In 1956 he was released by rebel forces, and took refuge in the American Embassy when the Soviet tanks took Budapest. The Hungarian police had the building watched at all times lest he try to escape. Masked Hallowe'en party guests were even stopped and made to disrobe in case one of them was the Cardinal. Fifteen years went by before an agreement between the government and the Vatican (in 1971) allowed him to leave. The extent of his fame and courage can be seen in Peter Glenville's award-winning 1955 film *The Prisoner*, with British actor Sir Alec Guinness in the title role. Shot before the '56 revolution, it refers to Mindszenty's imprisonment by the Communist regime, and features the famous 'Bishop's move' as the Cardinal glides across a chequered floor. Mindszenty died in Vienna in 1975.

❼ THE STATUE OF IMRE NAGY: Vértanuk tere, a tiny, leafy square, takes its name from the country's *vértanuk* or martyrs, thirteen rebel generals executed by the Habsburgs in 1849, following the defeat of the Hungarian bid for independence from Austrian rule. The square now contains the statue of another doomed would-be reformer, Imre Nagy (1896-1958), who as Prime Minster led a bid for independence from Soviet-style Communism, putting an end to forced collectivisation and turning away from the dubious glamour of heavy industry. Disgruntled by this turn of events, the Soviet Union backed a coup to oust him. In the autumn of 1956 Budapest took to the streets in protest (*see p. 24*). When the Soviet tanks moved in to crush the revolution, Nagy was offered sanctuary in the Yugoslav Embassy, only to be later sacrificed by Tito, who realised there was room for only one black sheep in the Soviet flock, and wasn't prepared to jeopardise his own position to save Nagy. The KGB arrested him, and although they promised clemency, he was executed only two years later, in 1958.

Retracing your steps into Szabadság tér, take a quick detour up Honvéd utca to see No. 3. This Art Nouveau jewel was built by Emil Vidor in 1903. Commissioned by the art collector Béla Bedő, it draws on the international strands of Art Nouveau, using Jugendstil, Belgian and French elements fused with Hungarian motifs. Ceramic sunflowers adorn the balconies, with two bearded Babylonian figures above them. If someone is entering or leaving the building, snatch your chance to go inside to admire the

Statue of Imre Nagy, the Communist moderate Prime Minister condemned to death after the 1956 revolution.

Roofscape of Ödön Lechner's former Savings Bank, a building which horrified many a stalwart citizen when it was unveiled in 1901 (see following page).

floor tiles, pillared stairway, and surviving stained glass.

8 THE ETERNAL FLAME: The approach to this is up Aulich utca, on which stands (at No. 3) a 1901 example of classic Art Nouveau. At the very top is a lovely glazed mosaic of a woman plucking an apple, a veritable Secession Eve. Below that squirrels scamper under the eaves. Women struggle with writhing serpents above the second floor windows, and under the first floor balcony another woman, a vision of narcotic bliss, is surrounded by the heads of opium poppies. Frog corbels support the balcony itself, on either side of the front door. At the end of the street is the eternal flame, which burns for Count Lajos Batthyány, first Prime Minister of an independent Hungary. He held office in the anti-Habsburg revolutionary government formed in 1848. The following year the Habsburgs called on the Russian army to defeat the Magyars, and Batthyány faced a firing squad in the barracks that at that time covered most of Szabadság tér.

❾ HOLD UTCA MARKET: This is one of a number of handsome 19th-century market halls erected around the city. For market lovers it is always worth browsing the stalls and admiring the hangar's ornate latticed girders and airy spaces. You can buy coffee and cakes or a pancake inside.

❿ FORMER SAVINGS BANK: This is Secession architect Ödön Lechner's masterpiece (*see p. 80*), built as a Post Office Savings Bank in 1901 and now part of the Hungarian National Bank. Its experimentalism caused horror and consternation when it was unveiled. On workdays you can go into the foyer to admire some of the interior detail.

An Art Nouveau ceramic adorns an early 20th-century façade (Aulich utca 3, described on previous page).

WHERE TO EAT AROUND SZABADSÁG TÉR

For a full meal, there is Biarritz at Kossuth tér 18 (corner of Balassi Bálint utca, *see p. 232*), serving light, Mediterranean-inspired dishes. Pizza, pasta and salads are the province of Pizza Marzano (the Hungary franchise of Pizza Express) at Vécsey utca 5. If all you need is a quick cup of coffee, you can get the real thing at Java, which faces the eternal flame on the corner of Hold utca. Alternatively there is the Szalai cukrászda at Balassi Bálint utca 7 (*see p. 100*), an old survival from pre-capitalist days, with home-baked cakes and fresh lemonade. Café Picard at Falk Miksa utca 10 (*see p. 232*) merges good coffee with Italian-style snacks and light lunches.

THE OPERA HOUSE

Pest VI, Andrássy út 22. www.opera.hu
Tours in English tours given daily at 3pm & 4pm.
Tickets for tours are sold in the Opera House shop.
For additional information about the Opera House, see p. 124.

Even if you don't see an opera, the Budapest Opera House is a major sight in itself. It was conceived, at least in part, by member of parliament and city planner Baron Frigyes Podmaniczky. As head of the Budapest Opera Committee, he had ambitious plans for a grand new building on Budapest's grand new radial avenue. An inn of ill repute stood on the chosen site, full of highwaymen and robbers planning fresh assaults on the good citizens of the town. One night Podmaniczky, enraged that this den of iniquity should stand in the way of his grandiose plans, stormed into the place armed with a cudgel, furiously knocking over tables and scattering the shifty clientele. Not long afterwards the place was closed down and work began on one of Budapest's most spectacular buildings. Designed by Hungary's greatest Historicist architect, Miklós Ybl, it was

Sumptuous gilt and plush in the Opera House interior.

constructed between 1875 and 1884, and ever since has been a symbol of civic and cosmopolitan pride. It is undoubtedly Ybl's finest achievement, marking the high watermark of Historicist eclecticism in Budapest, using Baroque elements in a mainly neo-Renaissance construct. Built at a time when opera houses were going up all over Europe, Ybl's building vies with them all for sheer refinement. The foremost fresco artists of the day were brought in to cover the interior from top to toe in Grecian allegory and belle époque fantasy. The main entrance is flanked by two seated statues by Alajos Stróbl, one of Franz Liszt and the other of Ferenc Erkel, composer of the Hungarian national anthem, the *Himnusz*. Above these stand the muses Erato, Thalia, Melpomene and Terpsichore, their names picked out in gilded Greek lettering. The Opera is said to have cost a million forints in gold to build, money which was entirely put up by the Emperor Franz Joseph, keen to demonstrate that he wasn't a Habsburg ogre - though he received little recognition for his generosity. To be fair, though, he in turn gave little recognition to the architect. 'It is very beautiful. I like it very much,' was all the effusion he could muster, and this, for what is arguably the loveliest opera house in Europe, is not saying much. The architect of the Vienna Opera, when faced with a similar lack of imperial enthusiasm, had despairingly committed suicide.

One of a pair of impassive stone sphinxes, guarding the Opera House entrance.

HEROES' SQUARE

(Hősök tere)

This wide and extravagant parade ground was laid out by the architect Albert Schickedanz for the Hungarian millennium celebrations of 1896, when the country celebrated 1,000 years since Árpád and his men galloped into the Carpathian Basin to occupy the area for the Magyars. The history books put Árpád's arrival at a year or two before 896, but the story goes that the millennium monuments were not ready in time, so Hungary pragmatically pushed offical history forward a bit. In the centre of the square is a tall Corinthian column topped with a statue of the Archangel Gabriel holding aloft St Stephen's crown. Gabriel is said to have appeared to Pope Sylvester II in a dream, telling him to send an apostolic crown to the king of Hungary, to legitimise his position as one of the defenders of Christendom. Today that crown is displayed in the Hungarian Parliament (*see p. 46*). At the base of Gabriel's column is Árpád himself and the chieftains of the seven Magyar tribes who followed him into

Monumental Heroes' Square, with its central column topped by the Archangel Gabriel, and the Magyar pantheon of fame in a semi-circular arc behind.

Hungarian heroes in the shadow of the apostolic cross.

the Carpathian Basin. Behind the column, in stately semi-circular file, are kings and heroes from Hungarian history, with allegorical charioteers of War and Peace above the colonnade's inner corners. Originally the kings and heroes were mainly members of the Habsburg dynasty. Deemed unacceptable and removed during the brief Republic of Councils that followed the First World War, they were restored under Admiral Horthy, only to be consigned to utter oblivion after 1945. Since that time their places have been taken by figures from the dim and distant mediaeval past, resurrected to serve as uncontroversial role models (a similar reason lies behind their recent prominence on Hungarian banknotes).

Heroes' Square is flanked by two Hellenistic buildings, also the work of Schickedanz. On the left is the Fine Arts Museum (Szépművészeti Múzeum, *see p. 111*), and on the right the Műcsarnok (Palace of Art), an important venue for contemporary art shows. Behind Heroes' Square stretches City Park (Városliget), home to the Széchenyi baths (*see p. 93*) and the city zoo. One of the park's main monuments can be seen from Heroes' Square: the turreted Vajdahunyad Castle (Vajdahunyadvár). It began life as an architectural folly, constructed as a temporary gimmick for the millennial festivities of 1896. In the end it proved so popular that it was rebuilt to last, and has been here ever since. The architect

(Ignác Alpár) was given the brief to include sections representing every architectural style to be found in Hungary and the territories she controlled. The part facing the ornamental lake (an ice rink in winter) is a copy of the Vajdahunyad Castle in what is now Hunedoara, Romania. It is home to the Agriculture Museum, which is full of marvellous steam-powered leviathans for threshing and winnowing, and Stalinist-era posters of beaming peasants and muscular farm hands. The castle's most famous pastiche is its chapel, a copy of the 13th-century abbey church from Ják in western Hungary.

Where to Eat Around Heroes' Square

Robinson in City Park (*map p. 263, A5*) will give you a more than decent lunch at a reasonable price. Sit out on the deck over City Park Lake in summer and watch the ducks dabbling. (*Reservations recommended. Tel: 422-0222.*) Other options are Gundel and the next-door Bagolyvár (*for both see p. 235*). Reservations are recommended at both. For coffee and cake, head down to the Lukács at Andrássy út 70 (*see p. 98*).

Vajdahunyad Castle in City Park.

ST STEPHEN'S BASILICA

Pest V, Szent István tér

Entry to the basilica itself is free. There is a small entry charge for the treasury and roof panorama.

This church had a long gestation period: construction took fifty-five years, between 1851 and 1906, and its slowness became such a local joke that the expression 'when the Basilica is finished' became a Hungarian equivalent of 'pigs might fly'. It was the work of three architects. József Hild started the project, drawing up plans for a large Neoclassical basilica along the lines of Hungary's great basilica at Esztergom. The side façades are mainly Hild's work. After Hild's death, Miklós Ybl (*see p. 77*) took over, and reworked the plans in a more flamboyant, neo-Renaissance style. The main entrance and the façade flanking Bajcsy-Zsilinszky út are his. But he too died before the Basilica was finished, and a third architect was brought in to complete it. Nothing went smoothly for this church. In the 1860s, the first dome collapsed and had to be completely remodelled, so that when the inaugural mass at last took place, in 1906, Emperor Franz Joseph was seen to look nervously up at the ceiling to make sure it wasn't caving in.

In the summer you can climb to the top of the (now stable) dome and enjoy superb views. Coming back down to earth again, it is odd to realise that the grand tympanum announcing 'the way, the truth and the life' contains a public toilet.

Winter view of the Basilica's Italianate west façade.

Detail of the Basilica's main west door.

Inside the Basilica

The interior of the Basilica was decorated by notable artists of the day, who contributed frescoes, mosaics and statues on the theme of Hungary's Christian and Catholic identity in a region where the Muslim and the Orthodox were strong - and often hostile - presences. St Stephen (c. 975-1038), to whom the Basilica is dedicated, was a descendant of the tribal leader Árpád. He was born the son of a pagan chieftain and given the name Vajk, but for political reasons his father, Géza, chose to give him a Christian education; he learned to speak Latin, the language of the Holy Roman Empire, was converted to Christianity and baptised Stephen. When he succeeded his father, he set about using the new religion ruthlessly, uniting the warring tribes that fought for control, expunging Hungarian nomadic traditions of how power was divided and inherited and suppressing the practice of the old religion among his people. He succeeded, more or less, and in 1000 was officially crowned king, the first Christian monarch of a united Hungary.

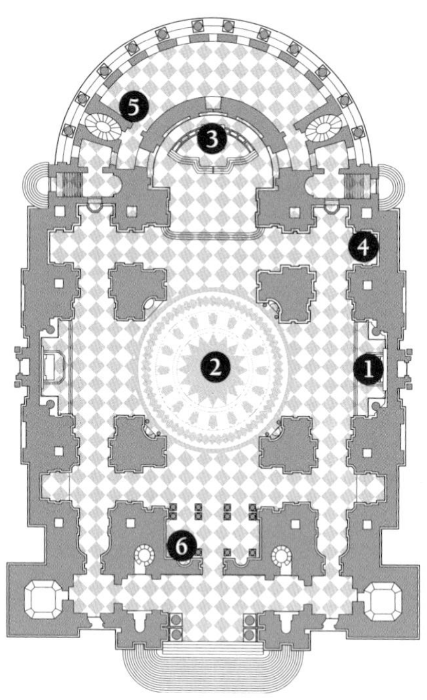

1 The Patrona Hungariae Altar
2 The Dome
3 The High Altar
4 The Szent Imre Chapel
5 The Szent Jobb
6 Saint Rita

1 The Patrona Hungariae Altar

The altarpiece is by Gyula Benczúr, a 19th-century artist who painted many mythical and semi-mythical moments from Hungary's history. This one shows the Blessed Virgin being invited to extend her patronage over Hungary, symbolised by St Stephen's crown. To the left of the altar is a statue of King Stephen's son Imre, canonised together with his father in 1083. Imre showed great promise as a young man. He was educated by the Venetian cleric Gellért (*see p. 209*), and grew up bold and virtuous. Alas, he never succeeded to the throne, as he was gored to death by a wild boar at the age of 24. The statue on the right is St Margaret (Margit). Born a princess of the Árpád dynasty, she eschewed marriage and royal privilege, and lived a life of austere self-denial as a nun on Margaret Island (*see p. 201*).

2 The Dome

The dome, 96 metres high, rests on four thick pillars, three of which are adorned with statues of Hungarian saints: the canonised King Ladislas (László), to whom a variety of miracles were attributed; St Elizabeth of Hungary, who took the veil after her husband died on crusade to Jerusalem in 1227, and who was tormented to death by her confessor, the cruel and sadistic Conrad; and Bishop Gellért, portrayed with the young Prince Imre. Above these, in the pendentives, are mosaics of the four Evangelists. In the centre of the cupola is a fresco of God the Father.

3 The High Altar

A life-size Carrara marble statue of St Stephen, to whom the basilica is dedicated, presides over a tableau reminiscent of Heroes' Square (*see p. 57*), with the archangel Gabriel holding the holy crown above the saint-king's head.

4 The Szent Imre Chapel

Below the altarpiece, in a small reliquary monstrance, is a finger bone belonging to Queen Gizella, mother of Imre and wife of King Stephen. Gizella was a Bavarian princess, sister of the Holy Roman Emperor Henry II, and was chosen as Stephen's wife in order to keep the peace between Hungary and the Holy Roman Empire. In 996, at the age of about eleven, she travelled down the Danube with her retinue, into the land of the barbarian Magyars, to marry the illiterate warrior prince Stephen, only recently baptised. When Stephen died without an heir (his son predeceased him), Gizella was kept a political prisoner by the warring factions battling for the throne. According to nomadic tradition, the eldest tribal chieftain

St Elizabeth of Hungary.

had seniority, and would have claimed her as his bride and thus seized power, but she eventually escaped back to Germany, where she retired to a nunnery near Passau, becoming its abbess in due course. She was beatified in 1911.

5 The Szent Jobb

The Szent Jobb ('holy right hand') is the right fist of King Stephen. It was found intact, though retracted into a clenched position through desiccation, when the king's body was reinterred in 1060. It is Hungary's holiest relic and is displayed in an ornate reliquary casket. Insert a 100-forint coin and the casket lights up. On St Stephen's Day (August 20th) the hand is ceremonially paraded around the city. *Chapel open Mon-Sat 9am-4.30pm (May-Sep); 10am-4pm (Oct-Apr); Sun 1pm-4.30pm.*

6 Saint Rita

This wonderfully expressive statue of the melancholy mystic and saint shows her holding a crown of thorns to symbolise her meditation on Christ's passion, meditation said to have been so intense that she caused a psychosomatic wound to appear in her forehead. Rita (1377-1447) married against her own wishes and was beaten and maltreated by her husband. When he died she retired to a nunnery, until tuberculosis carried her off. She is the patron saint of unhappily married women and the desperate. Notice how the prie-dieu in front of her effigy has been worn by decades of supplicants' knees.

What to See & Where to Eat in Szent István tér

Szent István tér, the broad square in front of the basilica, contains two fountains, one dedicated to St Stephen and the other to his mother, the Blessed Gizella. The house at No. 15, a 1907 work by Béla Lajta (*see p. 82*), is interesting for its Secession-style copper and pyrogranite frontage. Once a wholesaler's warehouse, it is now the Hungarian Foreign Trade Bank. In front of the basilica on the right is the bar-restaurant Negro (*see p. 234*). On the left is Leroy, decorated like a Bollywood film set, but serving respectable food. Other places to eat include the ever-popular Café Kör, at Sas utca 17 (*see p. 232*). Its menu is traditional Hungarian with a contemporary twist. At Zrínyi utca 18 you will find the cosy Café Montmartre.

THE DOHÁNY UTCA SYNAGOGUE

(Dohány utcai zsinagóga)
Pest VII, Dohány utca 2
Open Mon-Thur 10am-5pm; Fri 10am-3pm; Sun 10am-2pm.

The Dohány utca Synagogue is situated at an angle to Károly körút, between Deák tér and Astoria. If you duck into some of the courtyards on the opposite side of the road, you will see traces of the old Pest city walls. It is no coincidence that the synagogue sits just outside the old city limits - Jews were forbidden to live in the city in the 18th century, leading to the establishment of a Jewish quarter just outside the walls, with their main synagogue built to stare defiantly back at the Roman Catholic town. This arresting building, completed in 1862, was built by the Viennese architect Ludwig Förster, assisted by Frigyes Feszl. It is the second largest synagogue in the world, with seating capacity for almost 3,000.

The exterior, with its onion domes and structural polychromy, seems a romantic fusion of pseudo-Moorish and pseudo-Byzantine, although the Budapest Jewish community was almost strictly Ashkenazi. In fact, though the twin towers are reminiscent of the belltowers on a Christian church, they are actually intended to evoke the two columns that fronted the Temple of Solomon, as described in the book of Kings: '*And he set up the pillars in the porch of the temple: and he set up the right pillar, and called the name thereof Jachim: and he set up the left pillar,*

Orientalist exterior of the Synagogue.

Resplendent polychromy inside the Dohány utca Synagogue.

and called the name thereof Boaz'. The Christian feel of these twin towers may be deceptive, but it is interesting that Förster himself was a gentile, and the interior of the Synagogue is certainly unusual. Its plan, with a central nave and open seating galleries at the sides, is much like that of a Lutheran church. While in an Orthodox synagogue the *bimah* (raised platform from which the Torah is read) is placed in the centre, Förster has located it at the east end, near the ark, where the Torah scrolls are kept. There may be another reason for this, however, as the synagogue was not built for an Orthodox congregation, but for the Neologic community, whose reformed liturgy called for a less central location of the *bimah*. Organ music was also important to the services. Though the Dohány utca Synagogue now only fills with worshippers on High Holidays, its organ is famous, and has turned the temple into an important concert venue.

To the left of the main Synagogue entrance is the Jewish museum (*open Mon-Thurs 10am-3pm; Fri & Sun 10am-2pm*). It houses ancient Jewish ritual objects and has a harrowing exhibition on the Holocaust in Hungary, which cost the life of over half a million people. A plaque outside the museum, on the Synagogue's main façade, commemorates Theodore Herzl, father of Zionism (*see p. 193*), who was born in 1860 in a house on this site.

In 1944 the area behind the Synagogue was turned into an enclosed Jewish ghetto. Its gates were next to the Synagogue, in Wesselényi utca. A small plaque now commemorates this fact. In the courtyard behind the main building is the domed Heroes' Temple, also a functioning place of worship, originally built to commemorate Jews who died in the First World War. Beyond this is the cobbled Raoul Wallenberg Park, named in honour of the Swedish diplomat who did so much to save Jewish lives in the Second World War (*see overleaf*). In its centre is a moving memorial by the sculptor Imre Varga. It takes the form of a metal weeping willow tree, planted on the site of the mass graves of victims of the Holocaust. Each leaf bears the name of one of the dead. At present only the lower branches are leaved, but gradually the tree is filling up as more and more families add a leaf in remembrance.

For a walking tour around the former Jewish district of Pest, see p. 193.
Other Budapest synagogues are described in the Religious Monuments section on p. 143.

Where to Eat near the Synagogue

The family-run kosher café Fröhlich at Dob utca 22 serves the best *flódni* (an apple, poppy seed and walnut slice) in town (*NB: closed Friday afternoons and weekends*). For a slap-up Italian meal in elegant surroundings, head for Fausto's at Dohány utca 5 (*see p. 233*). For a simpler, traditional Budapest lunch, there is the ever-popular Kádár Étkezde, a short walk away at Klauzál tér 9 (*map p. 263, C4*). An *étkezde* (literally 'eatery') is a cross between a canteen and the dining room in a humble pension. If trade is brisk, expect to share a table. If kosher food is what you are after, and you prefer to sink into a chair right away, there is the Kék Nefelejcs (Blue Forget-me-not) at Dohány utca 10, only a few yards from the Synagogue entrance.

Raoul Wallenberg (1912 - ?)

Born into a prominent Swedish family, Wallenberg was originally destined for a business career. He studied architecture and Russian, and in the 1930s worked in the building trade in South Africa and Palestine. He came to Budapest in 1944 to work for the Swedish legation. As a neutral country, Sweden could offer diplomatic immunity to Jews, and thus save them from deportation. The 'official' passes issued by Wallenberg (examples can be seen in the National Museum) absolved Jews from wearing the yellow star, and gave them free passage out of the country. When the Horthy government was overthrown in October 1944, the Hungarian Fascist party (the Arrow Cross) seized command, and things became more complicated for Wallenberg. It was then that he began to create 'safe houses'. By hanging the Swedish flag outside the door, he turned buildings into neutral Swedish territory, allowing Jews to take refuge inside. Stories of Wallenberg's courage abound. He would stand beside columns of Jews being marched out of Hungary and hand out food, medicine and Swedish passes. He clambered onto the roofs of the deportation waggons and stuffed protective passes in through the slats. Then he would jump onto the tracks and announce that all those with passes were to leave the train. He is estimated to have saved about 100,000 Jewish lives. When the Russians entered Budapest in January 1945, Wallenberg attempted to collaborate with them. Suspicious of his claims, and believing him to be a western spy, the NKVD (later the KGB) arrested him. He was never seen again. According to Soviet statements, he died in Moscow's Lubyanka prison in 1947. Other claims suggest that he was murdered in Hungary, and that he never reached the Soviet Union. There are even suggestions that he survived. The fate of Raoul Wallenberg, the brave and compassionate 'righteous gentile', is a mystery that has never been solved.

VÁCI UTCA

This is Budapest's most famous shopping street - not lined with wonderful emporia, perhaps, but then Budapest is not a city for shoppers. Nevertheless, Váci utca has been home to the city's best retailers for well over a century. At its southernmost end is the Vásárcsarnok, the city's central market hall. First opened in 1897, it was originally served by a network of under-floor channels allowing barges to unload produce direct to the individual stallholders. An international competition was organised for its design, and the judges awarded first prize to a team of French architects. But nothing had ever been said about actually executing the winning plans, and the building that was commissioned was designed by a Hungarian contestant, Samu Pecz. Inside, the spacious interior offers row upon row of produce and meat stands: humbler, local fare straight from the field and allotment on the left hand side, and fresh, exotic fruits from around the globe on the right, in the *gazdagsor* ('rich row'). Upstairs you will find stalls selling fried fish and spicy sausage, served on paper plates with fresh bread

The exuberant Vásárcsarnok (Central Market Hall), temple of fine fresh produce, which stands at Váci utca's southern end.

Inside the graceful iron-framed hangar of the Vásárcsarnok.

and mustard. It is all meant to be washed down with a glass of beer or a shot of pálinka, Hungary's traditional strong fruit brandy.

From here Váci utca stretches northwards for around a kilometre, bisected by the wide and busy feeder road for Elisabeth Bridge. The section between the market hall and the bridge is broader, more spacious, and pleasanter to wander. The narrower section above the bridge is the more traditional shopping section, still home to a number of quaint and attractive shops. To visit a few of them, turn right up Régi Posta utca after the modern C&A department store at No. 16. Immediately on your right, you can turn into an underpass under the Fontana building to find Anda Emilia, one of Hungary's top designers of women's clothing. A Hungarian folk art store is immediately opposite you as you come back out, and further up on the same side is a clutch of pretty, old-fashioned shops: gloves and hats, hand-bound notebooks and blank journals, and Kaczián, an establishment specialising in ties. Opposite, at No. 19, is a little leather goods shop, and back on the left hand side, at the corner of Petőfi Sándor utca, is the clothing store Sasch, which until very recently was the gorgeous Brammer drapery store. The beautiful 1920s showcase fittings, mahogany-wood shelves and old measuring tables are still in place, as are the lovely stuccoed ceiling and chandeliers, but the bolts of cloth have tragically been evicted. Moving up the street, with Brammer on your left, you soon come to a row of three architectural masterpieces. The Rózsavölgyi music store at No. 5 is one of the oldest - and the best - sources of sheet music and classical CDs in town. It is also housed in a building that is an important example of the transitional style between Art Nouveau and Functionalism (Béla Lajta, 1912). Next door is a building with an Art Nouveau mosaic adorning the top of the façade, the work of Miksa Róth (*see p. 119*). Next door to that is a very early pre-Modernist building, clearly betraying the influence of Viennese architect Otto Wagner in the way it is faced with stone tiles fixed on with large, deliberately visible rivets. Back on Váci utca, the Philanthia

Above: Art Nouveau in Váci utca: the Philanthia florist. Left: Struggling to be free of the clutches of winter: the central statue on Vörösmarty tér.

flower shop at No. 9 is a treat for all lovers of Art Nouveau. The interior is superbly preserved.

Very soon after this, Váci utca reaches Vörösmarty tér, a broad pedestrian square centred by a 1919 statue of the romantic poet Mihály Vörösmarty (1800-1855) (in winter he's wrapped up in a polythene bubble to preserve the Carrara marble from the depredations of snow and ice). A Christmas crafts market fills the square during Advent. At no. 3, on your right as you enter from Váci utca, is the Luxus áruház, built by the same architects who designed the Liszt Music Academy. Deceptively plain on the outside, it has a beautiful Art Nouveau main staircase within. The department store, once the top of the line for Communist Hungary, now seems very old-fashioned, even provincial, but it has a certain charm, and there is often something worth a second glance on the bargain rail on the second floor.

Dominating the far end of the square is the famed Gerbeaud coffee house (*see p. 97*). Directly outside it is the entrance to the Földalatti (literally 'underground'), the yellow metro line, which runs from here to the opera house, Heroes' Square and the Széchenyi baths. This was the second underground railway in the world after London's Metropolitan line, and therefore the first in continental Europe, as locals rarely tire of reminding you. It was completed in 1896, in time for the Hungarian millennium (*see p. 57*), and Emperor Franz Joseph was one of its first passengers.

ARCHITECTURE

Eclectic Budapest is one of the most architecturally beguiling cities in Europe. Besides a few remnants of the Baroque and some crumbling Gothic fragments, the story of its cityscape is a relatively recent one. Almost all of central Pest was built between 1880 and the turn of the 20th century, in Historicist styles drawing on the mediaeval, the Renaissance and the Baroque. Pest is a triumph of town planning, and while the Second World War destroyed much, many of its inner streets remain essentially unchanged. At one point around the turn of the last century, Budapest was developing faster than New York, and whole blocks went up seemingly overnight. The glory of the façades is obvious, but scratch the surface and you will see that huge blocks of what appear to be ashlar and rusticated masonry are in fact no more than cheap brick coated with wire and moulded plaster.

The Institute for the Blind, one of a number of late 19th-century buildings inspired by the Eastern-tinctured architecture of Ödön Lechner (see p. 78).

Gothic dwarf arcade on a house in Buda's Castle District.

The arrival of Secessionist architecture (Hungary's Art Nouveau) in the early 20th century brought with it new concepts, with its sinuous lines and emphasis on decoration. Between the wars, Modernist influences began to make themselves felt, yet even the starkest Hungarian buildings of the 1930s are relieved with playful motifs. After 1948, Socialist Realism laid its ideological hand on architecture - but the hand, although heavy, did produce a lot of interesting buildings, as the giddy rush of idealism took form in powerful (if kitsch) depictions of the power of the people. In the 1970s, as the ideology began to run out of steam, functional tower blocks mushroomed to meet burgeoning housing needs. Meanwhile, the architecture of past ages was allowed to crumble, and buildings that over the decades had stood fast through bomb raids, shelling and looting, began simply to fall down through neglect.

Restoration is beginning, though, and new buildings are increasingly designed to complement, not ignore, their surroundings. Always remember to look upwards: the glaring shopfronts or sooty and graffitied entryways are often no clue to the riot of gorgeous ornamentation above, all the more lovely for being slightly down at heel.

AN OVERVIEW OF STYLES

Gothic

During the Árpád dynasty (972-1301), Buda grew into the prosperous capital of a newly Christianised nation, and as such it became an important bulwark against the pagan and infidel east, offering pilgrims to Jerusalem safe passage at least as far as Constantinople. Monasteries and convents following the rule of St Benedict sprang up, and monarchs endowed churches and chapels. The Mongol invasion of 1241 destroyed much; what was rebuilt was again destroyed or left to fall into ruin during the Ottoman period (1541-1686). Today only vestiges remain, and the best place to see them is on **Castle Hill**. Almost all its Baroque town houses are built on Gothic foundations; some preserve interesting fragments of masonry, for example the house (now a restaurant) at **Országház utca 20** (*illustrated opposite*), which preserves a dwarf arcade on its upper storey. Many Castle Hill entranceways have carved Gothic sedilia: for example the **Fortuna Passage** on Hess András tér (*map p. 262, C1*). A small vaulted chapel and Gothic chamber, remnants from the mediaeval royal palace undercroft, are preserved in the **Budapest History Museum** (*see p. 39*).

Baroque

Buda was not recaptured from the Ottomans until 1686, by which time the Counter-Reformation had triumphed in the Habsburg dominions, the Jesuits were a powerful force, and the humanist Renaissance was well and truly a thing of the past. King Mátyás Corvinus's Buda is said to have been a Renaissance jewel, but we have only the chroniclers' word for it - no convincing traces remain. The Christian reconquest brought Baroque architecture to Hungary: noble palaces, churches and merchants' houses went up in the Viennese style. The best secular Baroque architecture in the city can be found on **Castle Hill**: the colour-wash façades are picked out in white stucco work, much of it in the Zopf style, with bell-pull swags of foliage resembling the pigtail on a periwig (*zopf* in German, hence the name). The best of the few sacred Baroque survivals are the **Church of St Elizabeth** on Fő utca (*see p. 139*), and the **University Church** in central Pest (*see p. 136*).

Neoclassicism

In keeping with much of the rest of Europe, Budapest embraced the Neoclassicist style in the early 19th century. The republican symbolism of the architecture of ancient Greece and Rome was apparent to revolutionaries everywhere, and it became immensely popular in anti-Habsburg, anti-monarchist Budapest. In its clean, dignified and graceful lines, the style also represented a welcome break from the sumptuous ornamentation of the Baroque. Though much of Budapest's Neoclassical architecture was lost to the Second World War, two fine buildings remain: The **Sándor Palota** (1806, *see p. 40*) on Castle Hill, and, by far the most famous, the **National Museum** (1846, *for information about the Museum collection, see p. 114*). Both are the work of **Mihály Pollack** (1773-1855). Though he was born in Vienna, Pollack became a citizen of Pest in 1802. He was a leading member of the Beautification Commission, set up in 1805 to develop the city, and this gave him considerable influence on its layout and design. The National Museum is his masterpiece. Its impressive portico, supported on eight fluted Corinthian columns, is clearly meant to evoke an ancient Greek temple. The main entrance is explicitly modelled on the Erechtheion in Athens, and the sculpted figures in its tympanum are allegories of Pannonia flanked by Science and Art. Sadly for Pollack, construction was delayed a number of times, notably by a catastrophic flood in 1838, when the waters reached chest-height, sweeping away most of the mud-brick buildings of old Pest. When the grand Museum edifice was eventually completed in 1846, there were many critics who found its style old-fashioned and out of keeping with the spirit of the times.

Portrait of Mihály Pollack with his design for the National Museum.

HUNGARIAN NATIONAL MUSEUM

Historicism

Typical Historicist façade in Pest.

This term is used to describe a number of styles that flourished from the mid to the late 19th century. What unites them is the fact that they were all imitations of something that had gone before: neo-Romanesque, neo-Gothic, neo-Renaissance, etc. Many of Budapest's Historicist buildings are an eclectic blend of elements from a number of 'neo' styles. A sort of etiquette existed on what style was appropriate to what kind of building. The neo-Gothic would be used for a church (as in the **Mátyás Church**) or, because the style echoed Hungary's own mediaeval glory, a government building (the **Hungarian Parliament**). The neo-Byzantine or Orientalist style was deemed appropriate for places of entertainment and amusement (the **Vigadó**) or for synagogues. Theatres, because they were venues for show and display, favoured the neo-Baroque. The neo-Renaissance was used for symbols of prosperity and civic pride (the **Opera House** and **mansions on Andrássy út**), and because of its connotations of the age of science and enlightenment, it was also used for academic buildings (the **Hungarian Academy of Sciences**). Budapest Historicism reached its apogee in the late 19th century, when a booming industrial sector made the city rich and the 1867 Compromise Agreement established the dual Austro-Hungarian monarchy, giving Hungary status within the empire. Hungary's foremost Historicist architect was **Miklós Ybl** (1814-1891). When he was buried, his funeral cortège had to stop at numerous buildings en route to the cemetery, to commemorate the man whose stamp was so firmly impressed on the face of the city. The Opera House is his, as is most of **St Stephen's Basilica**, many of the patrician palaces in the 'magnates' quarter' behind the National Museum, and the Széchenyi Library wing of the **Royal Palace**.

The Secession & Ödön Lechner

Art Nouveau - le Style Moderne, as it is called in France - was indeed something truly modern, truly new. It was genuinely different; not a harking back to the past, but an expression of confidence in the present and the future. This spirit found particular resonance in Austria-Hungary: while the Habsburg court and official tastes still clung to Historicism, voices in the crown lands were calling for a new direction. The term 'Secession', which describes Austrian, Bohemian and Hungarian Art Nouveau, encapsulates the impetus of the new trend: a desire to break away or secede from the stolid academicism of the past. In Hungary's case there was another impetus, too, in the desire to find a style that was Hungarian; a national style. The man who created it was **Ödön Lechner** (1845-1914). He is to Budapest what Gaudí was to Barcelona: a creative genius, a man who wanted to leave no surface unadorned (because, as he pointed out, the birds have eyes too), a lover of colour and of texture, a patriot - and an intensely nationalistic one at that. His buildings were divisive: enthusiastically received by

Ceramic representation of Lechner's Geological Institute.

certain sections of the public, they were reviled by traditionalists. Though his creations are not to all tastes, he was a true original, more than just another Art Nouveau purveyor of whiplash curves, swirling foliage, and idealised female forms.

Major Buildings by Ödön Lechner

Applied Arts Museum (*Iparművészeti Múzeum*) - Built between 1893 and 1896, this extraordinary building is a milestone in Hungarian architecture. Previously museums had always been housed in western Historicist-style buildings; it was a sort of unwritten rule. Lechner rejected this. He believed that the East, not the West, was the cradle of Hungarian civilization, and that Hungarian models of beauty, as well as all the patterns and motifs of the Hungarian cultural conscious and unconscious, were informed by the Orient. His Applied Arts Museum is a sort of cross between Moghul palace and Moorish Alhambra, all graceful white, icing-sugar arches within and majolica pinnacles without. The Emperor Franz Joseph, when called upon to inaugurate the museum, was appalled at what he saw, and performed the ceremony through gritted teeth. *Buda IX, Üllői út 33-37. Open Tue-Sun, 10am-6pm (see also p. 115). Map p. 263, E4.*

Ödön Lechner's Eastern-inspired Museum of Applied Arts.

Geological Institute (*Földtani Intézet*) - In this building Lechner continues with his 'Persian carpet' style of architecture. Exposed brickwork creates a reticulated pattern on the

Ödön Lechner in his characteristic fez-style cap, symbol of his cultural allegiance to the Orient.

façade. On the roof four stalwart Atlas-figures, moustachioed and with braided hair like ancient Magyar tribesmen, sit with a cerulean globe on their shoulders. The blue colour scheme is continued inside with the carved doors that line the corridors. There is ornament everywhere, even in the bathrooms. The building was built in 1899 for the Hungarian Geological Institute, and has remained its home ever since. Exhibits of fossils and other secrets of the earth's crust compete for your attention with painted folk motifs - stylised hearts, pomegranates and tulips - from somewhere deep in Hungary's lost Oriental subconscious. *Pest XIV, Stefánia út 14. The building and its collection are open to the public Thur, Sat & Sun 10am-4pm. Map p. 258, C4.*

Former Savings Bank (now part of the Hungarian National Bank) - Built in 1901, this is Lechner's masterpiece (*see illustration on p. 53*). A riot of colourful majolica tiles teamed with exposed brickwork is topped by an undulating roof, making it one of the most spectacular buildings in the city.

The Geological Institute: children come to look at the fossils; adults will also enjoy the architecture.

Detail of Váci utca 11, a façade covered in pyrogranite ornamentation. Pyrogranite - a weather-resistant clay - was developed by the Zsolnay factory (see p. 116), and used by Lechner for almost all his Budapest buildings.

Look for the winged serpents on the side towers and the engaged pillars of unrendered brick, which rise like tree trunks to the sky, complete with ceramic bees making for the hives at the top. When it was unveiled, it met with considerable official resistance, and a decree was passed declaring that public money was no longer to be spent on such radical projects. *Pest V, Hold utca 4. Map p. 262, B3*

Former Sipek-Balázs Villa - This pink blancmange castle was built in 1905 as a private villa overlooking City Park. Today it belongs to the Hungarian Association for the Blind. The exterior is interesting for its asymmetry, with a tapering chimney soaring into the sky. The original wrought-ironwork is preserved, as is the ground floor winter garden with its double layer of glazing, and an undulating, composite stone bench beside the front door. *Pest XIV, Hermina út 47. Map p. 258, B4.*

The Sipek-Balázs Villa, a rare example of a private residence designed by Lechner.

The Transition to Modernism

Art Nouveau could not survive the First World War. Even before war broke out, people were beginning to question it. How justified was all that confidence, after all? God was dead and humanity was in crisis. In the early years of the 20th century, in response to the troubled times, an interesting style arose in Hungary, a fusion of the folk-inspired elements of the Hungarian Secession with international Functionalism. The best exponent of this was **Béla Lajta** (1873-1920), who initially worked under Lechner before branching out in his own direction. In many of his earlier works he draws explicitly on folk themes. The elongated beehive shape he used in his famous mausoleum in the **Jewish cemetery in Kozma utca** (*pictured on p. 144*) is drawn from the *suba*, the sheepskin cloak worn by shepherds to protect themselves from the bitter blizzards of the Great Plain. The shape of the *suba* and its architectural corollary, the catenary or parabolic arch, was much beloved by architects of the Hungarian folk revival school. Lajta's **Újszínház theatre** (1910, *map p. 263, C3*) adopts a

Sacerdotal temple of pleasure: the former Parisiana nightclub (now the Újszínház theatre), by Béla Lajta (1910).

Modern housing to meet modern needs: Napraforgó utca.

cleaner, more modern approach, and the influence of Semitic architecture is strong. Its semi-blind façade, topped with crenellations, is built of marble but is reminiscent of the traditional adobe architecture of Mesopotamia. Lajta went on to articulate his later works by a conspicuous use of horizontals (**Szervita tér 5**, *map p. 262, D3*) and verticals (**Széchenyi School**, Vas utca 11, *map p. 263, D4*). Both buildings are dated 1912. In the case of the Széchenyi School, the vertical emphasis is broken only by abstract motifs. When it was unveiled, one critic asked who were the more fortunate, the teachers or the pupils, to attend such a model and well-designed school.

The Folk Revival & Károly Kós

Like many of his contemporaries, Kós (1883-1977) was intent on creating a Hungarian style, but he looked to the Middle Ages for his inspiration. A devotee of John Ruskin and the Arts and Crafts Movement, he delved into the mediaeval folk past to create a new style. He was inspired by the village architecture of his native Transylvania, and employed its sloping roofs, steep gables, carved weather-boarding and tiled turrets in much of his work. His most famous piece in Budapest is the **bird house** (*madárház*) **in the zoo** (Pest XIV, Állatkerti körút 6-12, *map p. 258, B3*), built in 1911. He also planned the centre of the **Wekerle telep**, a model housing estate in the suburb of Kispest (*map p. 5, D4*), which has a consciously rural atmosphere. When Hungary lost Transylvania after the First World War, Kós returned there for good. He died in Cluj.

Functionalism

Decrying the use of ornament for ornament's sake, the Functionalists were less interested in craftsmanship than in the innovations made possible by technology. Influenced by Walter Gropius and the Bauhaus in Germany, and by Adolf Loos in Vienna, the Hungarian exponents of the style (notably **László Vágó** and **Farkas Molnár**) were followers rather than pioneers, but still created some outstanding buildings. Like architects all over Europe in the 1920s, they were commissioned not only to create cubic villas for avant-garde patrons, but were also called upon to address metropolitan housing problems. Enter the era of reinforced concrete. The **Napraforgó utca housing estate** in Buda (*map p. 260, A1*) is a good example of Hungarian Functionalists at work. The challenge was to create comfortable, affordable housing on a small site on the banks of a deep

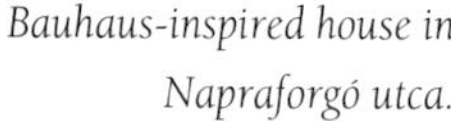

Bauhaus-inspired house in Napraforgó utca.

ditch. Constructed in 1931, it was modelled on the German Werkbund's Weissenhofsiedlung in Stuttgart (1927), to which Mies van der Rohe had been an important contributor. The Napraforgó estate consists of twenty detached and semi-detached houses with small gardens and roof terraces (the roof terrace was one of the elements of Le Corbusier's five-point programme). Twenty-two architects were involved in the project, including Molnár (No. 15), Vágó (Nos. 1 and 11) and the Olympic swimming champion and architect Alfréd Hajós (No. 17). He was also the architect of the **Andrássy Hotel** (*see p. 242*), formerly a Jewish boarding house, at Andrássy út 111, and the **Nemzeti Sport public swimming pool** on Margaret Island (*see p. 207*). To get to Napraforgó utca, take the No. 5 bus from Március 15. tér or Moszkva tér to the end stop at Pasaréti út, from where it is a short walk.

Farkas Molnár created a number of other apartment blocks and individual villas, mainly in the Buda Hills. Particularly interesting is his geometric cube-and-cylinder composition at **Lejtő utca 2/a**, overlooking Apor Vilmos tér (*map p. 261, D3*), which won a prize in the 1933 Milan Triennale.

Socialist Realism

Drawing on the architectural tenets of history's most famous republics, ancient Athens and Rome, the first decade and a half of Communist control of Hungary was architecturally fruitful. Though the goalposts were routinely moved by party mandate, and architects who had once won plaudits found themselves having to fall ritually on their swords, much of what went up in the 1950s, when both ideology and idealism were riding high, was aesthetically successful. The late 1940s saw architects still clinging to the forms of international Modernism. The **'White House'**, formerly the Ministry of the Interior and now parliamentary offices, on the Pest bank beside Margaret Bridge (Széchenyi rakpart 19, *map p. 262, A3*), and the **MÉMOSZ building**, headquarters of the architects' trades union (Dózsa György út 84/a, *map p. 263, A5*) are good examples. Both are the work - at least in part - of Lajos Gádoros. István Nyíri's 1949 **Erzsébet tér bus station** (*map p. 262, C3*), now a listed building, is another.

Later these buildings were criticised as pandering to the models of bourgeois Modernism, a movement spawned by capitalist America and Fascist Germany. The corridors in the MÉMOSZ were deemed too wide, more reminiscent of a

Stripped Classicism: conventional forms denuded of ornament. The Applied Arts University in Buda.

gentlemen's club than of a place where serious business was discussed. The Ministry of the Interior was 'too expensive', and looked just like a shoebox that was being used to house a child's insect collection, with holes cut in the sides to allow the bugs to breathe. The bus station had walls placed at an incline, reminiscent of a cowboy ranch in the 'Wild West'. And all of them committed the crime of crimes: their outer form did not reflect their function. A good example of the kind of stripped Classicism that the Socialist Realist pundits of the early 1950s approved is the **second district municipal headquarters** on Mechwart tér (*map p. 260, B4*). Built in 1952, the building earned its architect, József Körner, the Ybl Prize. The **Applied Arts University** at Zugligeti út 9 (Zoltán Farkasdy, 1953, *map p. 260, B1*) is another good example, with its minimalist take on a classical portico. There is also the **Ferenc Puskás Sports Stadium** (popularly known by its old name, Népstadion, People's Stadium), at Dózsa György út 1-3 (Károly Dávid and associates, 1953, *map p. 259, C4*).

Happily toiling workers adorn the façade of the former Architects' Trades Union building.

Organic Architecture

Organic architecture is, once again, an attempt to find a Hungarian style; and once again it draws on ancient folk forms. Its most famous exponent is Imre Makovecz (b.1935), whose finest work in Budapest is the **mortuary chapel at Farkasréti Cemetery** (Németvölgyi út 99, *map p. 261, D2*), built in 1977. This zoomorphic work, with its ribbed ceiling and strange, interior-of-a-whale atmosphere, is a good example of the organic style. There is also a less successful office block at **Szentkirályi utca 18** (*map p. 263, D4*) where Makovecz has added an organic-style structure to the top of a 19th-century building.

A Handful of Heroes

Some of the major figures who shaped Hungarian history:

St Stephen (c.975-1038) - Born a pagan and later baptised, Stephen (István) was the first monarch to unite Hungary's disparate tribes and form a homogenous nation. He was canonised in 1083.

King Mátyás Corvinus (1443-1490) - During his reign (1458-1490), Hungary reached the zenith of her mediaeval power and influence. Mátyás, both knight and humanist, is widely regarded as Hungary's bridge between the Middle Ages and the Renaissance.

Count István Széchenyi (1791-1860) - This progressive-minded nobleman played a large part in dragging Hungary from feudalism into the modern age. He built some of the city's most distinctive landmarks and was the driving force behind much of its growth. Disillusioned and semi-insane, he committed suicide in Austria.

Lajos Kossuth (1802-1894) - Lawyer, journalist and nationalist, Kossuth was a prime figure in the anti-Habsburg struggle of 1848-9. After the Hungarian defeat he escaped into exile, dying in Italy.

Ferenc Deák (1803-1876) - A wise and moderate politician, he was largely responsible for engineering the Compromise agreement with Austria in 1867.

Count Lajos Batthyány (1806-1849) - Prime Minister of Hungary after she declared herself independent of Austria in 1848, he was later tried and executed by the Habsburgs.

Sándor Petőfi (1823-1849) - Hungary's most celebrated romantic poet, he was a fervent Hungarian freedom fighter and died fighting for the Hungarian cause. As his body was never found, his death was - and still is - much disputed.

Count Gyula Andrássy (1823-1890) - Andrássy was Hungary's Prime Minister after the Compromise Agreement with Austria. Handsome, dashing and fiercely patriotic, he was shrewd enough not to make Vienna his enemy, and his government paved the way for the great boom years in Budapest.

Franz Joseph (reigned 1848-1916) - the Habsburg Emperor and King of Hungary was never a hero in Hungarian eyes, but his reign spanned an important time in Hungary's recent history and saw Budapest's greatest period of glory.

BATHS

Budapest is a city of spas. The Romans first developed the area's abundant thermal springs, and Buda's Jewish community made use of the waters for ritual baths. King Mátyás Corvinus also enjoyed them, maintaining a private bathhouse at the foot of Castle Hill. But it was the Ottomans who really exploited Budapest's greatest natural resource. Islamic law decrees that a body should never be immersed in still water, and the traditional hammam has no pools of any kind. Here in Budapest, far from the imams of Constantinople, the Ottomans were able to indulge their love of water and sybaritic pleasures to the full. Fabulous domed baths with steam rooms, hot and cold pools and quiet chambers to rest and relax sprang up along the Buda banks of the Danube. The only public bathhouse in Pest, the Széchenyi (*see p. 93*), was not built until the early 20th century, when thermal bathing had become a craze. Men who invested in the bathing complexes or bottling plants got rich on water as Budapest became a well known centre of curative springs. Today the city is again encouraging spa tourism - but you will still find that most of the baths are full of locals, swapping news and gossip in the steam.

MAJOR PUBLIC BATHS

Ottoman-era Baths

Budapest's surviving Turkish baths are arranged on a similar pattern, with a central warm pool surrounded by steam room, sauna, and hot and cold plunge pools. Of the original Ottoman structures only the central, domed bathing halls remain, but they are enough to conjure up an Oriental atmosphere. There is a distinct bathing etiquette, which most of the older regulars follow: start with the dry sauna, shower, then plunge into the cool pool. Next, relax in the warm central pool until you are ready for the steam room, followed by the shock-to-the-system cold plunge pool. It's best to stay as still as possible in this, but some irrepressibles make it difficult by bouncing up and down, or even performing handstands. Rub yourself down if you want to use the dry sauna again - your body should not be wet when you enter. If you've paid for a massage, don't be daunted - the massage rooms often look a bit like something out of a Crimean War hospital, but though the masseuses seldom resemble Florence Nightingale, they do know how to loosen you up. Don't forget to tip her (or him) a couple of hundred forints afterwards. Drink plenty of water to rehydrate yourself when you finally finish.

Király - This bathhouse has stood here since Ottoman times. It was built at the behest of Sokoli Mustapha Pasha in 1565. Against the back wall of the central bathing hall are two brick plinths supporting enamel basins. Thermal water (*termálvíz*) flows into one, and municipal city water into the other. Taste the difference! The steam chamber is scented with chamomile. *Open for women Mon, Wed, Fri 7am-6pm; for men Tues, Thur, Sat 9am-8pm. Last tickets 1 hour before closing. Buda II, Fő utca 84. Map p. 262, A2. NB: On men's days the clientele is mainly gay.*

Rudas - This beautifully preserved 400-year-old Turkish bath is for men only (though there is also a separate swimming pool for both sexes). The apertures in the central dome are covered with stained glass, so that when the sun shines, shafts of coloured light streak down to the marble pools beneath. This is especially atmospheric on a cold day, when the light penetrates the billowing steam. *Open Mon-Fri 6am-5pm; Sat-Sun 6am-1pm (last entry midday). Buda I, Döbrentei tér 9. Map p. 262, E3.*

BELLE EPOQUE BATHS

Though the springs that feed these baths (with the exception of the Széchenyi) have been known and exploited since ancient times, the bath houses themselves date from the 19th and early 20th centuries, when spa bathing had become a craze all across Central Europe, and anyone and everyone from butcher's wives to crowned heads was taking the curative waters.

Gellért - Part of the hotel of the same name, this huge spa complex was built in 1918. The Art Nouveau foyer is studded in glazed tiles and mosaics. Queue for tickets on the right. The left-hand line is for people with doctors' certificates, coming to take specific cures. Steam baths are separate for men and women, and there is a communal, colonnaded indoor pool where middle-aged ladies in frilly bathing caps swim languidly round in circles. Everyone congregates at the shallow end when the bubble machines are switched on. In summer there is a large outdoor swimming pool with a wave machine.

Enjoying the indoor swimming pool at the Gellért baths.

Open Mon-Sun 6am-6pm. Buda XI, Kelenhegyi út 4. Map p. 262, E3.

Lukács - The current building dates from the 1920s, though the baths themselves are much older, and were greatly prized by the Ottomans. The sulphurous waters are particularly good for rheumatism and arthritis, as well as for muscle and nerve complaints, and the leafy main courtyard contains plaques bearing thanks in many languages for cures received. As well as an indoor thermal complex, there are also two all-weather outdoor swimming pools, a sun terrace and a sauna. Sweat it all out, then shower and plunge into the bubble pool. The bubble pool also contains a whirlpool, which is so powerful that it literally sweeps you off your feet. Beside the main street entrance is an old-fashioned marble drinking hall where you pay next to nothing for a beer mug of foul (but health-promoting) water. All baths and pools are mixed. *Open Mon-Sat 6am-7pm; Sun 6am-5pm. Buda II, Frankel Leó út 25-29. Map p. 260, B4.*

Széchenyi - This huge baths complex, the largest in Europe, was opened in 1913. Neo-Baroque in style, it has an all-weather mixed swimming area as well as single-sex steam baths. Everything about this baths looks splendid, including the foyers, which preserve the aura of the great spas of Central Europe. The Széchenyi is most famous for its chess-players, who congregate around stone chessboards in the large open-air pool. The best time to wallow out of doors is in winter, when steam rises picturesquely from the surface of the warm water. *Open Mon-Sun 6am-7pm. Pest XIV, Állatkerti körút 11. Map p. 258, B3.*

NEGOTIATING THE SYSTEM

At most baths, you choose which services you want from the list in the entrance and pay for them at the cash desk. You will get a separate receipt for each thing: mud bath, wet massage, dry massage, etc. If you just want a steamy soak with no extras, a standard entry ticket is all you need. At the Gellért, Lukács and Széchenyi you will be given the choice between a locker (*szekrény*) or a cubicle (*kabin*). If you just want a place to leave your things, and don't mind getting changed in public, a locker is all you need. If you prefer more privacy, ask for

Clouds of steam create warmth and atmosphere at the Széchenyi's outdoor thermal pool.

your own *kabin*. The attendant will lock the cabin for you and hand you a tag. Don't lose it!

What to Bring

It is best to bring your own soap and shampoo (though you can buy it on site) and a pair of flip-flops. If the bath is single sex, you need not wear a swimsuit. You do not need to take towels to the Király or the Rudas, as you will be provided with a sheet to dry yourself. (If you prefer to dry yourself with a towel, by all means take one. They are useful to sit on in the steam-room and sauna.) You will need to take your own towel to the other baths. Remember also to take plenty of loose change: the locker attendants and masseuses will expect a small gratuity (a couple of hundred forints).

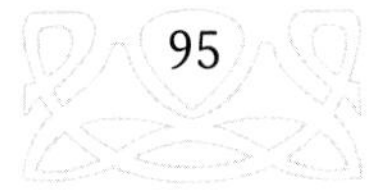

COFFEE HOUSES

Turn-of-the-century Budapest was known as 'the town of 500 cafés'. According to a late 19th-century tourist guide: *'The Hungarian cannot do without the coffee house. On Sunday afternoons the space in the fashionable coffee houses seems too limited for the accommodation of the crowds which besiege them'*. It wasn't only the fashionable who used the coffee houses, though. Artists and writers who could not afford to heat their tiny attic flats had regular tables there, and would spend all day writing, smoking, making assignations and talking animated politics. Powdered ladies and moustachioed swells would eye each other up; aspiring poets wrote masterpieces on napkin corners.

The famous New York coffee house, built in 1884 at Erzsébet körút 9-11 as a showcase for the New York Insurance Company, epitomised the Budapest coffee house. Amongst a spectacular glut of marble, gilt and glass, intellectuals

Early 20th-century scene in the Café Central (see following page).

and artists occupied their regular tables in the gallery alcoves while other visitors sat in the 'deep end', the lower floor. One evening, to ensure that the café would never shut, the novelist and playwright Ferenc Molnár and his friends threw its keys into the Danube. In those days the 'writer's dish' was introduced: bread, cheese and cold cuts offered for a song, but only to writers. Regulars were even provided with pens and paper, and could sit for whole days, hardly spending a thing. The maitre d' during the period, Gyula Reisz, allowed endless credit to his chosen literary elite - he may not have had much of a head for business, but he should go down as one of the most faithful patrons of Hungarian literature.

Budapest's network of coffee houses also became famous as a hotline for news, gossip and the dissemination of ideas. The humorist Frigyes Karinthy once decided to measure how quickly it would take a joke to travel across the river. He told his joke in a coffee house in Buda, then an hour and a half later strolled into Pest's Centrál (*see below*), where the same joke was promptly told back to him. According to Ferenc Molnár, it was this phenomenal capacity for underground communication that made the coffee houses so unpopular with the Communists: when they came to power in 1948, they had every coffee house in the city closed down. Times change, however, and today the coffee houses are flourishing again. The old New York, once the doyenne of Pest cafés, is reclaiming her old title as the most glittering of them all, with a luxury hotel now occupying the former insurance company's office space.

Belle Epoque-style Coffee Houses

Astoria - The coffee is no more than tolerable and the cakes are a bit of a let-down, but the décor and atmosphere more than make up for that. Fat marble pillars, palm trees and gilt-framed mirrors give it an air of graceful living. The card tables at the end of the room promise more of a saloon-bar feel, but are seldom occupied. Most of the time the place is genteelly placid, and the waiters so discreet it is often hard to attract their attention. *Pest V, Kossuth Lajos utca 19-21. Map p. 263, D3.*

Centrál - One of Budapest's classics, this coffee house first opened in 1887, and by the 1890s had become a famous literary meeting place. The poet József Kiss held editorial meetings here for his daring new magazine *A Hét* ('The Week'). After the First World War, the place was home to the staff of another periodical, the literary *Nyugat* ('West'), which immortalised the café in their writings. Today the renovated Centrál is once more the realm of dignified waiters in striped waistcoats serving dainty cups of coffee and thimblefuls of Magyar schnapps. *Pest V, Irányi utca 29. Map p. 263, D3.*

Gerbeaud - Famed in the last century as the most elegant café in town, this sumptuous place came into being as a result of a partnership between two patissiers: Henrik Kugler, a Hungarian, and Emil Gerbeaud, a Swiss, whom Kugler met in Paris. Elisabeth, Empress of Austria, once came here to gratify her sweet tooth, accompanied by her Hungarian ladies-in-waiting. The place's fame has meant that it is now on every tourist itinerary, and service can be frustratingly slow. But the interior makes up for that, with its faded velvet wallpaper and high stuccoed ceilings, tiny marble-topped tables, heavy curtains and old-fashioned pastry counter. Though the elderly ladies with their fur wraps and tangerine rinses have deserted it, it is

Waiting to be served at Gerbeaud. It can sometimes take a while, but the surroundings are good to loiter in.

A tranquil afternoon coffee in the Astoria.

still worth visiting for the aura of days long gone. *Pest V, Vörösmarty tér 7. Map p. 262, C3.*

Hauer - Newly restored to a semblance of its former self, the Hauer is a famed for its vast series of rooms and its enormous pastries. Originally founded in 1890 as a tiny shop, it was expanded by Rezső Hauer, a master pastry chef trained at Gerbeaud (*see previous page*). Today it is making a gallant bid to revive the elegant atmosphere that made it one of the choicest coffee houses at the turn of the last century. *Pest VIII, Rákóczi út 47-49. Map p. 263, C4.*

Lukács - This was once the coffee house of the Communist Police, set up in a confiscated patrician mansion. Now restored, its twinkling chandeliers and Venetian-lookalike glass still whisper faintly of days gone by, although the wall-to-wall carpet betrays Lukács's status as a modern re-creation. *Pest VI, Andrássy út 70. Map p. 263, B4.*

Művész - Not much has changed at the Művész since it first opened its doors over a century ago. It still attracts smoke-stained writers and powdered ladies who leave their lipstick behind on their coffee cups. It

Staff in the Ruszwurm at the turn of the 20th century.

doesn't serve the best coffee or cake in town, but its muted golds and greens and tarnished mirrors give it a wan appeal. *Pest VI, Andrássy út 29. Map p. 263, C3.*

Ruszwurm - The oldest café in the city (founded in 1827), the Ruszwurm is tiny and cosy, furnished with marble and Biedermeier. The elderly lady in the picture (*on the facing page*) is Róza Ruszwurm, the daughter of a pastry chef imprisoned for his part in the 1848 uprising against Austria. While in prison he met one of the commanders of the Hungarian forces, Rudolf Linzer, after whom he later named the Linzer biscuit: two rounds of shortcake sandwiched together with apricot jam and sprinkled with icing sugar. *Buda I, Szentháromság utca 7. Map p. 262, C1.*

Other Cafés

Auguszt - The Auguszt name has been in the confectionery business since the late 19th century. This quiet little upper-floor enclave above an over-the-counter cake shop is a delightful breath of refined air near fume-filled Moszkva tér. The coffee is good, the cakes are excellent, and the atmosphere the epitome of gentle civilisation. If you order a mineral water, make sure it's Parádi: subtly fizzy Hungarian spa water. *Buda II, Fény utca 8. Map p. 262, B1.*

Déryné - The famous Auguszt family of pastry chefs first set up a cake shop here in 1870, but in 1951 it was confiscated and nationalised. The Auguszts have moved on (*see above*), and this café is now named after early 19th-century actress and entertainer Mrs Déry (Déryné), who was so famous that painted Herend porcelain figurines of her, with ringlets and guitar, were once a staple ornament of bourgeois mantelpieces. The atmosphere is unpretentious and cosy, and the cakes are good. *Buda I, Krisztina tér 3. Map p. 262, C1.*

Café Eckermann - This pleasant little café (big bowls of café au lait are its speciality) is housed at the Goethe Institut, a cultural centre funded by the German government. It occupies the space one tenanted by the Három Holló ('Three Ravens') coffee house, a famous literary spot and a favourite haunt of early 20th-century poet Endre Ady. In the main doorway to the building there is a memorial to him. A Socialist Realist male nude pilots a small vessel, engraved with a line from one of his poems: 'Fly, little boat,' goes the quotation, 'you've got tomorrow's hero on board.' For the complicated, blustering, syphillitic Ady, that heroic tomorrow never came. For the young intellectuals who crowd the Eckermann today, though, it just might. *Pest VI, Andrássy út 24. Map p. 263, C3.*

Eklektika - The concept of retro is quite new in Budapest, as the immediate post-Communist decade was spent trying to avoid the past rather than fetishise it. But nostalgia is gaining appeal, and a reflection of this is Eklektika, which celebrates the 1960s. Booths, low tables and squashy vinyl chairs make the clientele feel at home, and there's an old upright for the musically inclined. Lesbian-run, straight-friendly. *Pest V, Semmelweis utca 21. Map p. 263, D3.*

Király - Cakes are sold at the counter on the ground floor. You can either buy a couple to munch as you wander, or choose what you want and go upstairs to sit with it and a cup of coffee in the intimate, vaulted upper room. In summer it is stiflingly hot; in winter it makes an admirable retreat from the cold and ice. *Pest VII, Király utca 19. Map p. 262, C4.*

Szalai Cukrászda - Once upon a time every café in Budapest looked like this. This is one of the only survivals, a bitter-sweet hark-back to somewhere around the middle of the 20th century. Three large, gilt-framed mirrors and an old-fashioned pair of scales set the tone. The coffee is good, the cakes are home-baked, fresh orange juice and lemonade is available, and there is ice cream in summertime. *Pest V, Balassi Bálint utca 7. Closed Mon-Tue. Map p. 262, B3.*

Cream cake from Auguszt.

Hungarian Cakes & Pastries

Count István Széchenyi once remarked that: 'Things are only going well in a country if the tailor, the soap-maker and the patissier are firmly convinced that the happiness of the nation depends on their skill'. As far as cakes are concerned, his opinion still stands.

Cakes are a vital part of Hungarian life. Late on Sunday mornings the streets in residential areas will be deserted except for a steady file of people carrying home carefully wrapped pastries from the corner *cukrászda*. Here are a some of the best examples of the Hungarian patissier's art:

Dobos Torta: A rich confection of chocolate sponge with a chocolate cream filling, topped with crunchy caramel.

Esterházy Torta: A delicious soft cake, made of layered ground walnuts and vanilla cream.

Francia Krémes: A puff pastry base crowned with a tall square of light vanilla custard, another of whipped cream, then topped with sticky caramel icing.

Gerbeaud Szelet: A layered slice made of chocolate, apricot jam and ground walnuts. Topped with chocolate icing.

Pogácsa: A savoury scone made usually with cheese (*sajtos*) or pork cracklings (*tepertős*), and sometimes with potato (*burgonyás*).

Ischler: Two round shortcake biscuits sandwiched together with jam and coated in melted chocolate.

Rétes: This is the Magyar name for what the Austrians call strudel. Hungary claims to have invented it, and certainly Hungarian strudel is good. It typically comes with fillings of apple (*almás*) and cinnamon (*fahéjas*), poppy seed (*mákos*), sour cherry (*meggyes*) or sweet curd cheese (*túrós*).

Rigó Jancsi: A chocolate and vanilla sponge square filled with chocolate fondant. It is named after a famous 19th-century violinist who eloped with a French countess.

Túrós Táska: A puff pastry shell filled with sweet curd cheese and raisins. Perfect for breakfast or a mid-morning snack.

Types of Coffee

Cappuccino: Gone are the days when Hungarian cappuccino was lukewarm Nescafé topped by a glob of spray-can foam. Now you can order one and breathe easy, although occasionally the Viennese influence appears with a dollop of whipped cream instead of the expected frothed milk.

Tejes kávé: A large, milky espresso, which usually comes ready mixed. If you like your coffee stronger, ask for a double espresso with hot milk.

Presszó kávé: The typical shot of espresso (if you want a double, ask for a *dupla*). If you just order 'coffee', without specifying what kind, this is what you will get.

Hosszú kávé: Espresso coffee made weaker with the addition of hot water (it is fairly similar to American coffee, although not as weak as filter coffee). Specify whether you want it with milk or not, and if you want the milk to be hot, it is always worth saying so.

MUSEUMS & GALLERIES

Once upon a time Hungarian painters were as likely to haunt the salons of Paris as any Picasso or Modigliani. Decades of being locked away behind the Iron Curtain pushed the country into obscurity, and Communist ideology set up road blocks in the path of artistic progress. But Hungarian fine art is gradually making a name for itself again. A number of good exhibitions in recent years has brought Hungary back into the world's eye. Works are being taken out of storage and Hungarians are rediscovering home-grown masters such as József Rippl-Rónai, István Csók or Philip de László, all of whom were internationally renowned in their day.

Few visitors know what to expect from Budapest's museums. There are wonderful surprises in store. The Fine Arts Museum has one of the best early Spanish collections outside Spain; the Ludwig has a splendid Picasso. And the Hungarian National Gallery is where you'll discover those home-grown masters.

The Madman of Syracuse (1930) by István Farkas (see p. 110).

MAJOR ART GALLERIES

The Hungarian National Gallery

(Magyar Nemzeti Galéria) Buda I, Budavári Palota
Entrance from Wing C, the Danube-facing façade.
Open Tue-Sun 10am-6pm. Map p. 262, D2.

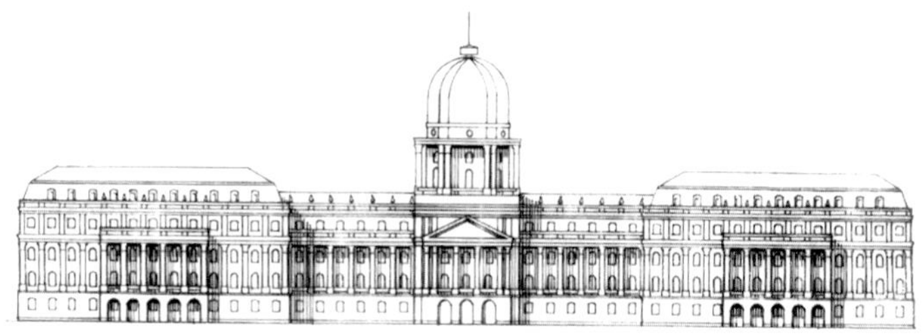

Taking up the main wing of the former Royal Palace, the collection here covers Hungarian art from the middle ages to the 20th century.

Permanent Collections

Ground Floor

Mediaeval lapidarium: a collection of stone fragments recovered from mediaeval and Renaissance Buda and elsewhere in Hungary.

First Floor

Mediaeval art: The best piece is the beautiful *Visitation* (1506), by the artist known only as Master MS. Once part of an altar triptych, its exquisite combination of human figures, landscape elements and wild flowers will stun anyone who thought that late mediaeval art stopped at the Alps. In the former throne room of the palace, next to *The Visitation*, is a collection of carved, painted and gilded winged altarpieces, salvaged from the woodworm and the damp that would otherwise have destroyed them in parish churches all over Hungary and its crown lands.

Baroque painting: The finest works here are Jakab Bogdány's (1660-1724) still lifes with birds.

Carved altar of the Passion from the mediaeval collection.

19th-century painting: As soon as you reach the top of the stairs, you enter the epic world of Hungarian history painting. **Gyula Benczúr**'s *Recapture of Buda* (1896) dominates the atrium space with all the assertive confidence of its age. The Ottoman Pasha Abdurrahman lies dead, a victorious trumpet is sounded from stage right, and Turkish captives are led off stage left. And in the centre the commanders of the Christian armies, Eugene of Savoy and Charles of Lorraine, look haughtily down from their white chargers as a fanatical Franciscan friar brandishes a crucifix. More paintings in a similar dramatic vein are exhibited in the halls to right and left of this.

Also part of the 19th-century collection are the whimsical, boudoir creations of **Károly Lotz** (1830-1904). Lotz, the public artist par excellence, contributed more to the 19th-century face of the city than any other painter. His romantic Historicist style (also adopted by his contemporaries Bertalan Székely and Gyula Benczúr, who share wall space with him here)

'Bathers' by Károly Lotz, typical of his sensual salon style.

can be found in frescoes in the Opera House and Parliament, as well as in countless villas around town.

Other artists include **Pál Szinyei Merse**, best-known voice of the Hungarian pastoral idyll. More important is **Mihály Munkácsy** (1844-1900), who began life as a poor peasant boy from a village now in the Ukraine and went on to fame and riches in Paris, marrying a Belgian baron's widow. It is definitely his early pictures, filled with suffering and doubt, that are worth looking at. Acclaimed in his lifetime as the greatest Hungarian artist, after his death his body lay in state on a ceremonial bier in Heroes' Square for all to pay homage to. Wanamaker, the US department-store tycoon, bought his *Christ Before Pilate* for a fantastic sum. But success made Munkácsy vain, and in the end Paris and the salons ruined him with their easy money and elegant ways. He contracted syphilis at an early age, which contributed to his brooding outlook. Sadly, he mixed bitumen with his paint and his canvases are getting darker and darker as a result - and nothing can be done about it.

Early works of the **Nagybánya School** are also on this floor. The rural landscapes of Nagybánya in Transylvania (now Baia Mare, Romania) inspired a whole school of

'The Condemned Cell' (1872), one of the most famous of all Munkácsy's sombre canvases.

Csontváry's 'Ruins of the Greek Theatre at Taormina' (1904-5).

painting at the turn of the 20th century. Plein-air artists flocked to what became a well-known colony to produce their own version of Impressionism, and the painter Simon Hollósy transferred his art school from Munich to Nagybánya in 1896. As in France, the new painters were reacting against the prevailing Historicist and salon-painting styles, but in Nagybánya they were also seeking a Hungarian mode of expression. Painters to look out for include István Réti, Béla Iványi Grünwald and István Csók.

Second Floor Landing

Maverick painter **Tivadar Csontváry** (1853-1919), whom Picasso recognised as a fellow genius at the beginning of the 20th century, dominates the second floor landing with three paintings, including his huge canvas of the Greek theatre at Taormina. This strange man, who started life as a pharmacist and only turned to art after a vision which he had in his twenties, was wholly unrecognised in his own lifetime. He travelled extensively in the Balkans and the Holy Land, as his output reflects. Totally unafraid to use colour, he also experimented strikingly with different types of light: moonlight, firelight and electric light.

Second Floor

20th-century painting: Perhaps the styles which were to find most resonance in early 20th-century Hungarian art were Art Nouveau and Symbolism. As the century progressed, the vision became darker and more grimly burlesque. **János Vaszary** (1867-1939) is a good example to chart the way painting developed over the decades. Vaszary was born just as Hungary was forming the Dual Monarchy with Austria. He died as the Second World War broke out. His oeuvre begins with the innocent, Eden-like idealism of his *Golden Age* (*'Aranykor', pictured below*), and progresses through fast, frenetic, neon-lit city scenes to the corrupted, worn out escapism of *La Morphiniste*. A refreshing counter to both ends of this spectrum are the folk-genre works of **Adolf Fényes**. There is also a collection of bronze medals, a genre at which Hungary has traditionally excelled. Other important artists on this floor are:

'Golden Age' (1898) by János Vaszary, an example of his idealistic early flirtation with Art Nouveau.

'My Father and Uncle Piacsek over a Glass of Wine' (1907), one of the best-loved works by József Rippl-Rónai.

József Rippl-Rónai (1861-1927): Hailed as the Father of Hungarian Art Nouveau, Rippl-Rónai was at once painter, draughtsman and applied artist. As part of the Nabis group in France he knew Bonnard and Bernard, but his use of flat colour and clear lines was more for decorative purposes than impressionistic ones. His huge body of work covers everything from tea sets to tapestries, but perhaps his greatest works are the small-town interiors and garden scenes, and intimate portraits of the people he loved, his family, lovers and relations.

Lajos Gulácsy (1882-1932): Gulácsy was subject to Symbolist visions all his life, and created his own fantasy world of Na'Conxypan, a land peopled with the strange, phantom-like figures you can see in his dreamy, deceptively innocent, subtly disturbing works. He also compiled a dictionary of Na'Conxypan words, which included poems about this wraith-like land in a language only he could decipher. He spent the last thirteen years of his life entirely in psychiatric hospitals suffering from severe schizophrenia.

The Later Nagybánya School: In the colony's heyday, folk motifs and a use of colour which was almost Gauguinesque in its daring brightness became popular. Look out particularly for works by **Oszkár Glatz**. Perhaps the greatest artist of all the Nagybánya group, however, was **Károly Ferenczy** (1862-1917), who soaks his canvases in carefree sunlight. Some of the works will seem derivative, but Ferenczy's *October* (*pictured below*) or *Sunny Morning* (1905), as well as Glatz's *Boys Wrestling* (1901) stand on their own as great works of art. The Nagybánya School operated until the mid 1930s.

István Farkas (1887-1944): Born into a well-to-do Jewish family, Farkas lived in Paris in the 1910s, meeting and impressing Apollinaire and living next door to Rilke. Thrown out of France as an enemy alien at the beginning of World War I, he worked as a war artist on the front, returning to Hungary in 1919 after a short spell in an Italian prisoner-of-war camp. During the inter-war years his work became increasingly tense and disturbing, as reflected in his *Madman of Syracuse* ('*Szirakuzai bolond*', *pictured on p. 103*) or *Fate* ('*Végzet*'). As the anti-Jewish laws began to take effect from 1937, his life became ever more constrained. He was well enough connected to have been able to hide or even escape, but in his last recorded message, in June 1944, he declared that 'if human dignity is so debased, then it is no longer worth living'. He was murdered in Auschwitz.

'October' by Károly Ferenczy (1903), one of his finest and most atmospheric plein-air works.

The Fine Arts Museum

(Szépművészeti Múzeum)

Pest XIV, Hősök tere

Open Tues-Sun 10am-5.30pm. Closed Mon. Map p. 263, A5.

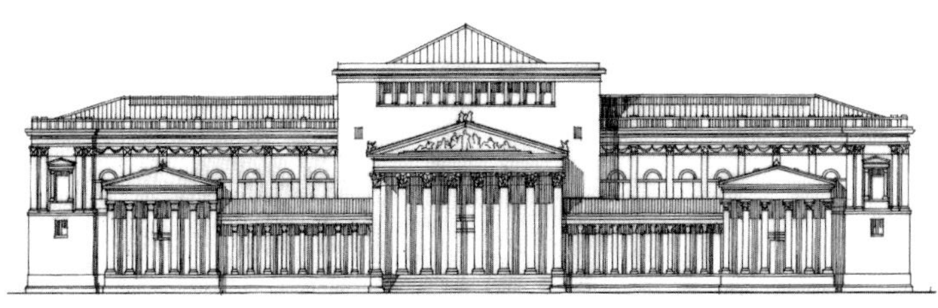

Housed in an austerely grand building, its main hall as massive and imposing as a Victorian railway station, this gallery boasts one of the best collections of Spanish art outside Spain: a total of seven El Grecos are to be found in the Old Masters collection on the first floor. Overall the museum's collection gives the impression of having been deliberately and painstakingly put together, with every major artist represented by at least one work (Van Gogh seems to be a notable exception to this rule), even if not always a great or characteristic one. The result is that the museum works brilliantly as a lightning, teach-yourself tour of European art history.

The Permanent Collection

Basement

The basement is home to three small collections: antiquities from ancient Egypt; a collection of mediaeval ecclesiastical sculptures, mainly statues from altarpieces; and a smattering of 20th-century works, including a Kokoschka, an Utrillo, a Chagall and a Le Corbusier. There are also a handful of works by contemporary artists, including a sculpture by Anthony Caro. The basement also houses cloakrooms, the garderobe, and the museum shop and café.

Ground Floor

Antiquities from ancient Greece and Rome; church frescoes by mediaeval Umbrian masters; 19th-century painting including the **French school** (a representative selection, including several Courbets, a Renoir, a Gauguin, a Cézanne), and the **German school**, including Böcklin.

Prints & Drawings: This collection is probably the finest in the museum. Sadly it is not on permanent view, owing to the fragile nature of the prints. The prints and drawings gallery on the ground floor at the back hosts temporary exhibitions: it is worth going to see what's on.

First Floor

The Old Masters Collection: This is the museum's major collection. It is divided into the following sections:

The Italian School: This, the largest of the Old Masters collections, includes some superb works, including a Sassetta (*St Thomas Aquinas at Prayer*, 1423), two Giorgiones, works by Raphael, Correggio, Titian and Veronese, and a splendidly erotic Bronzino: *Venus, Cupid and Jealousy*, 1545, the companion work to the Bronzino in London's National Gallery.

'Penitent Magdalene' by El Greco (c. 1580).

The Spanish School: The highlights of this collection are the El Grecos - all seven of them. Velázquez, Murillo and Goya are also represented.

The Netherlandish & Dutch Schools: A rich and varied collection, including works by names known (Jordaens, Rubens, van Dyck and three Brueghels) and unknown.

The German School: Look out for a wonderful Dürer (*Portrait of a Young Man*), plus works by Lucas Cranach the Elder.

The British School: A tiny collection of minor works by some major names: Lely, Reynolds, Constable and Raeburn.

Ludwig Museum

Buda I, Budavári palota

Entrance from Wing A. Open Tue-Sun 10am-6pm. Map p. 262, C2.

Founded by German chocolate millionaire Peter Ludwig, this collection comprises works by contemporary Hungarian artists as well as a scattering of world names, for example Roy Lichtenstein, Warhol and Rauschenberg. There is a single Picasso, *Musketeer with Sword* (1972), cleverly framed in an elaborate Renaissance-style frame. Look out for Yoko Ono's all-white chess set (*Play it by Trust*). The museum café offers a lunchtime menu. (Don't let Daniel Spoerri's assemblage of stale food displayed nearby put you off.)

NB: At the time of going to press the Ludwig Museum was planning to move premises to a site in south Pest. The National Gallery will expand into the present space.

Temporary Exhibition Spaces

MEO - The name is the Hungarian acronym for 'Quality Control Department', an apt name for a contemporary show space housed in a 19th-century leather factory in the northern suburb of Újpest. It is worth a visit for the building alone. Local artists show here, along with some major international names.

How to get there: take blue metro line to Újpest Városkapu. Bear left out of the station until you come to Árpád út; cross it, then turn left and then right into Attila utca. Walk a few blocks through the housing estate until you come to József Attila utca. To the right, on the corner of Berzeviczy utca, is the area's old synagogue, founded - as was the leather factory - by the Lőwy family. The MEO's main entrance is on your left. Pest IV, József Attila utca 4-6. Map p. 5, A3.

Műcsarnok - A grand Hellenistic façade and entrance hall give way to large, high, well-lit spaces. International contemporary art is the focus here. *Pest XIV, Hősök tere. Map p. 263, A5.*

MAJOR MUSEUMS

National Museum

(Nemzeti Múzeum) Pest VIII, Múzeum körút 14-16
www.hnm.hu
Open Tue-Sun 10am-6pm. Map p. 263, D4.

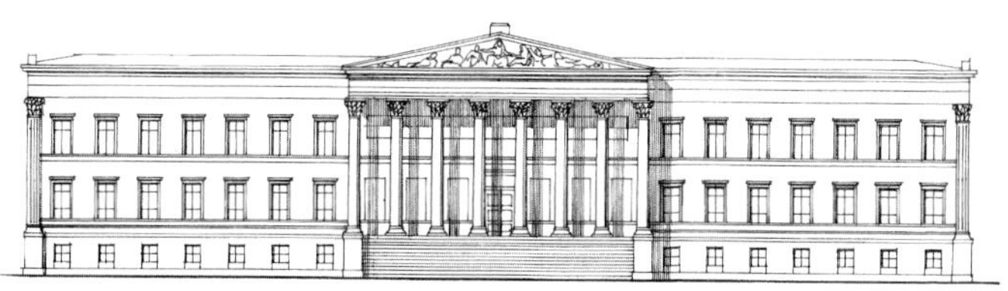

The museum is housed in Budapest's grandest and most perfect Neoclassical building (*see p. 76*). Its most valuable exhibit is the Hungarian coronation mantle, housed in a darkened room on the ground floor. The silken mantle is in fact a bishop's cope, made for the bishop of Székesfehérvár in 1031 and embroidered in golden thread by Queen Gizella (wife of King Stephen, *see p. 63*) and her ladies. It was only in later centuries that the kings of Hungary came to be crowned in it.

The main exhibition is the second floor collection, which traces the history of Hungary from the founding of the nation in 1000 up to the fall of Communism and the start of a new era in 1990. An enfilade of themed rooms contains exhibits aplenty, best of which are a portrait of Suleiman the Magnificent (*reproduced on p. 16*), some exquisite early 16th-century choir stalls, personal articles belonging to Count István Széchenyi

PHOTO: BENCE KEPESSY/HUNGARIAN NATIONAL MUSEUM

Lajos Kossuth.

(*see p. 88*), and the printing press that was used in 1848 to print revolutionary leaflets, including the famous *People's Twelve Demands*, which were read out in front of this very building to massed crowds in March 1848. The demands included freedom of the press, a yearly parliament in Pest, a national bank and an end to serfdom.

Most interesting are the later rooms, which deal with the First and Second World Wars and their aftermath. There are some superb propaganda posters, from both political sides, plus a reconstruction of a Second World War air-raid shelter, complete with piped music from the husky-voiced Katalin Karády (Hungary's answer to Marlene Dietrich), singing after-lights-out melodies to boost morale. Most moving of all is the letter, never received and never opened, returned to sender stamped 'Addressee in the ghetto'. The Communist years are represented by personal effects belonging to Imre Nagy (his pince-nez and travelling chess set), plus the door of the prison cell where he spent his last days. There is also a recreation of a 1960s council-flat living room, with János Kádár speechifying endlessly on an old bakelite TV set.

Applied Arts Museum

(Iparművészeti Múzeum) Pest IX, Üllői út 33-37
Open Tues-Sun 10am-4pm. Closed Mon. Map p. 263, E4.

In 1872, inspired by the example of the Victoria & Albert Museum in London and the Museum für Angewandte Kunst (MAK) in Vienna, the Hungarian Parliament voted to set aside money for the purchase of applied art objects, and the decision to found a museum followed close behind. The result, architecturally speaking, is perhaps the most fantastic of all Budapest's museum buildings, a fabulous concoction designed by Ödön Lechner (*see p. 78*) and his partner Gyula Pártos. It was deliberately intended to be Eastern rather than Western in its atmosphere, to reflect the supposed origins and cultural heritage of the Magyars. The permanent collection, for reasons best known to the museum management, is no longer displayed, and the bright white arabesque halls stand empty. A trip here offers little except an architectural experience, but that is magnificent enough. Temporary exhibitions are still hosted here. At the time of going to press there was an exhibit on Zsolnay ceramics (*see box on following page*), running until mid-2005.

Zsolnay Ceramics

Eosin-glazed vase with a pattern of vines (1898-9). Purchased from the Paris Exposition Universale of 1900.

The Zsolnay name became famous in the late 19th century, when a former earthenware and stoneware factory in Pécs in southern Hungary turned its attention to decorative ceramics. Vilmos Zsolnay, with his designer daughters Júlia and Teréz and marketing manager son Miklós, turned the Zsolnay name into an international brand with their tea services and ornamental objects. In the late 19th and early 20th centuries, Zsolnay regularly won prizes at international exhibitions, including the great Exposition Universale in Paris in 1900. Zsolnay also produced architectural ceramics, and invented pyrogranite, a clay-like substance resistant to heat and frost. Covered in coloured glaze, it was used to adorn many a fine Budapest building, including the Gellért baths and the Liszt Music Academy. The architect Ödön Lechner (*see p. 78*) insisted on the use of Zsolnay materials for his buildings, and his Applied Arts Museum is an excellent example of its application: the roof tiles and glazed brickwork of the exterior, and the eosin-glazed walls and majolica-clad banisters in the entrance porch. At the Zsolnay café on the first floor of the Radisson Hotel (*Pest VI, Teréz körút 43, map p. 263, B3, open from 2pm*), you will be served coffee in Zsolnay cups. Pieces similar to that are for sale in china shops. For antique Zsolnay pieces, visit Falk Miksa utca (*map p. 262, A3*). One particularly good source is the Mű-Terem, at Falk Miksa utca 30.

Ethnographic Museum

(Néprajzi Múzeum) Pest V, Kossuth tér 12
Open Tue-Sun 10am-6pm. Map p. 262, B3.

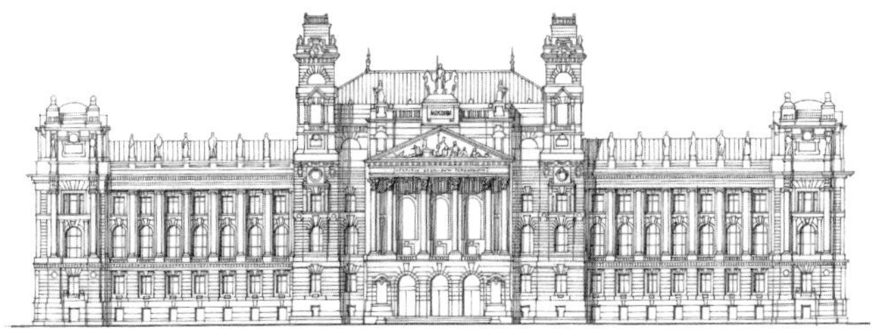

This magnificent pile right opposite Parliament is worth a visit for its entrance hall alone. It was built in 1897 to house Hungary's Constitutional Court. Go up the steps past the ticket desk and you find yourself in an expansive hall, decorated with marble and alabaster, lit by two huge semi-circular glass windows and topped by an allegorical frieze of Justice. The building is famously unsuited to its present role, and locals maintain that it is only really any good as a film set (it was used repeatedly in Alan Parker's *Evita*). The permanent exhibition on Hungarian peasant life and folk traditions is on the first floor. Exhibits include agricultural implements that seem to date from the middle ages, though in fact they are almost all from the 19th and early 20th centuries; regional costumes, including the heavy, embroidered sheepskin cloak, the *suba*, which kept the Great Plain shepherds warm; and some striking and memorable photographs of daily life, work and (very little) play: village life is traced through birth, marriage, child rearing, cooking, toiling in the fields, and death.

Village baby in an 'állóka', a wooden frame that both supports and confines.

OTHER MUSEUMS

House of Terror (*Terror háza*) - A museum dedicated to those who perished in the dictatorships (both Fascist and Communist) that controlled Hungary for almost the entire 20th century. It is housed in a building where both the Arrow Cross (the Hungarian Fascist party) and the ÁVH (the Communist State Security Authority) operated. Here both groups extracted 'confessions' and sentenced people to death - often for crimes that they and their torturers knew full well they hadn't committed. The Arrow Cross made Budapest Jewry its target over the winter of 1944-45. Men, women and children were either lined up and shot into the freezing Danube or herded into detention centres awaiting deportation to Auschwitz. After the Communist takeover in 1948, the ÁVH spied on and arrested anyone whom they deemed politically undesirable. They came to be so hated that during the 1956 uprising a crowd stormed the building, captured anyone working inside and lynched them on the spot. The plaque on the outside wall reads: '*Though you may forgive the murderers, never forget the horror of the terror, and remember the victims*'. The museum is a chilling reminder of what human beings can do - and have done - to each other. *Pest VI, Andrássy út 60. Open Mon-Fri 10am-6pm. Map p. 263, B4.*

Reconstruction of an interrogation cell in the House of Terror.

Postal Museum (*Postamúzeum*) - Housed in what was once a sumptuous town residence, this museum is most interesting for the curtain it raises on the lives of Budapest's late 19th-century plutocracy. The metal template initials of the

The original brand of mineral water bottled and sold by Saxlehner. Still available in pharmacies and health food shops, it has to be tasted to be believed - but its health-giving properties are said to be prodigious.

building's owner, Andreas Saxlehner, and his wife Emma (AS and ES) can still be seen on the street door. The entranceway is splendid, decorated with frescoes by Károly Lotz, the foremost fresco artist of his age. The Saxlehner wealth came from bottled mineral water, and tribute is paid to that noble trade by the friezes in the entranceway. One shows the god Mercury dispatching bottles to earth to cure mortal ills, another shows a sick man having the water administered to him, and a third shows nubile women bathing in it. Apartments and living quarters were at the front of the building, and the mineral water company had its offices across the central courtyard at the back. A small natural stream runs underground here; in former centuries it was used as a Jewish ritual bath. Andreas Saxlehner stored his merchandise in the cellar just above it, but quality controls assured the public that his water was sourced elsewhere, from the thermal springs of Kelenföld in south Buda. The Postal Museum, upstairs on the first floor, is housed in what used to be the old Saxlehner apartment. Almost oppressive in its luxury, the wooden panelling, English silk wallpaper, Murano crystal chandeliers and Carrara marble fireplace are all the originals, and the cameo female heads on the ceiling of the main salon are said to be portraits of Emma Saxlehner herself. Before her marriage she was an opera singer. *Pest VI, Andrássy út 3 (press 10 on the bell panel). Open Tues-Sun 10am-4pm. Map p. 263, C3.*

RÓTH MIKSA MUSEUM - A little museum dedicated to the work of glass painter and mosaicist Miksa Róth (1865-1944). Responsible for much of

Revolutionary Socialist worker in full throttle at the Statue Park.

the late 19th and early 20th stained glass in the city (in the Postal Museum, Parliament and Liszt Academy), Róth used glass like paint, creating sinuous designs in luminous colours with techniques to rival Tiffany. His former home now houses a small collection of his work, with some rooms reconstructed in the heavy pre-Raphaelite style so beloved at the time, with items of Róth's original furniture and belongings. *Pest VII, Nefelejcs utca 26. Open Tues-Sun 2pm-6pm. Map p. 263, C5.*

STATUE PARK (*Szoborpark*) - After the collapse of Communism in 1989, Budapest began gleefully toppling its sculpted Lenins and Stalins from their cast iron and marble perches. Realising that an episode of history was fast being rubbed out, two enterprising young Hungarians decided to set up a museum dedicated to all this discredited Communist iconography. The result is the Statue Park, where you will find Marx and Engels, Hungarian Communist leaders and Workers' Movement heroes, joyful factory workers and broad-hipped mothers, all in fine Socialist Realist style. The park also boasts a tongue-in-cheek shop where you can buy 'Molotov Cocktails' and CDs of rousing proletarian songs. Gyula Illyés's poem *One Sentence on Tyranny* is beaten onto the huge gates: 'Where there is tyranny, Everyone is a link in the chain'. *Buda XXII, on the corner of Balatoni út and Szabadkai út. Open 10am-sundown every day. The easiest way to get there is by taxi (see list of reputable companies on p. 246). Otherwise take bus 7 (from Blaha Lujza tér, Astoria, Ferenciek tere or outside the Gellért Hotel) to the last stop, Etele tér. From there take the yellow coach service Volán Busz from platform 2-3. It leaves every 15 minutes, and the journey time to Szoborpark is 15 minutes. Ask the driver to let you off. Map p. 4, E1.*

MUSIC & DANCE

Hungary has a rich musical tradition, deriving from the many and various peoples that inhabit this part of the Carpathian Basin: Magyars, Slavs, Roma Gypsies and Jews, to name just the largest groups. This mix brings with it a certain exoticism: Hungary's music has always diverged from the European mainstream. Hungary is also one of the foremost folk music nations of the world, and though its folk tradition is no longer truly living, it definitely exists within living memory and exerts a powerful influence on contemporary musicians. Many of the familiar sounds are being given a new lease of life, not just by traditional bands, but by fusion groups and electronic outfits who play the club circuit. Hungary's classical music heritage is also rich. The voluptuous piano of Franz Liszt fills concert halls the world over, and the operettas of Kálmán and Lehár are still popular. Hungary has also produced one of the undisputed geniuses of 20th-century classical music: Béla Bartók (*see p. 125*).

Lobby of the Liszt Academy, with the Art Nouveau mural 'Fountain of the Muses'.

CLASSICAL MUSIC

THE LISZT ACADEMY

(Zeneakadémia) Pest VI, Liszt Ferenc tér 8
Map p. 263, C4.

The Art Nouveau Liszt Academy, built in 1907, is one of the great musical venues of the world. The exterior is square-built and sober, giving no hint at all of what lies within. The reason for this oyster-shell approach is because government pressure forced the architects Korb and Giergl to shift from their original Art Nouveau designs to the Historicism which the Emperor Franz Joseph so loved. However, the government watchdogs were only concerned with exterior façades. The interior shimmers in green and gold, and is one of the Art Nouveau masterpieces of the city. Frescoes, mosaics and stained glass by leading masters adorn the concert hall and its foyers. The hall itself has erotic quasi-Nubian girls holding up the roof, and the ceiling is covered in golden leaves. As an institute, the Liszt Academy is Budapest's premier centre of music teaching and has turned out some great conductors, including Sir George Solti. In its heyday it had Bartók teaching piano and Kodály (*see p. 125*) teaching composition. And although the teaching side of the Academy has fallen, it still attracts its fair share of top-class performers. A good concert here is an experience not to be missed. The staple repertoire is Brahms, Bartók and Liszt, but

Detail of the Liszt Academy interior.

György Kurtág.

early music makes it onto the programme occasionally, as do the works of contemporary composers. Hungary's best known contemporary masters are György Ligeti (1923 -) and György Kurtág (1926 -), whose difficult, atonal work is grounded in Bartók and Webern. Kurtág studied in Paris under Milhaud and Messiaen, although his career began at this very academy.

For concert programmes, check in the free Koncertkalendárium, available at the ticket office at Vigadó utca 6 (Map p. 262, D3). Tickets can be bought from the Liszt Academy box office itself (Mon-Fri 10am-8pm, Sat-Sun 2pm-8pm) or from the ticket office at Vigadó utca.

The Opera House

(Magyar Állami Operaház) Pest VI, Andrássy út 20
Map p. 263, C3. www.opera.hu
Box office open Tue-Sat 11am to performance time;
Sun and holidays 4pm to performance time.

The quality of the acting and singing may be inconsistent, but the sheer grandeur of this building makes a trip to the opera a must for all visitors to Budapest. The Opera House's list of musical directors is distinguished: Gustav Mahler, Otto Klemperer and János Ferencsik have all been among them. Ferencsik died in 1984, and since then the Opera has never regained its musical brilliance. The brilliance of the gold chandeliers and marble statues, however, remains, and a night here is simply fun. And ticket prices are still so reasonable that it is possible to cultivate the belle époque attitude: the point of going to the opera is not for the music but for the social occasion. Reserve yourself a box, step down to the buffet for a glass of dry Tokaj in the first interval and a restorative *pálinka* (schnapps) in the other, and slip out before the third act, when the voluminous heroine breaks into a caterwaul prior to stabbing herself to the heart.

Dress rehearsal in the Opera House.

Bartók & Kodály

Interior of Bartók's house in the Buda Hills, now a museum.

The musical achievement of Béla Bartók (1881-1945) had a profound influence on the whole of 20th-century music. One of his chief sources of inspiration was the folk music of Hungary, and he was one of the earliest ethnomusicologists, travelling around the country making field recordings of village musicians. The most perfect expression of his restless, questing, yet curiously light, resolved and intimate style are probably the string quartets, pieces which go some way towards fusing the verve of Stravinsky, the brittle tension of Debussy and the homely cadences of folk song. Yet for all his love for his country, when the Jewish Laws were introduced he wrote a public letter expressing his disgust and sadness that Hungary was capable of such infamy, and left the country in 1940, despairing at the rise of Fascism. He emigrated to New York and never set foot on European soil again. The Bartók Béla Emlékház is a small memorial museum housed in the villa where Bartók lived from 1932 until he left Hungary. It contains a reconstruction of his study, with original furnishings and personal effects. (*Buda II, Csalán utca 29. Open Tue-Sun 10am-5pm. Map p. 260, A1*). Close to the Applied Arts Museum, at Hőgyes Endre utca 3, is the Unitarian church (*map p. 263, E4*) where Bartók once worshipped. To view the pretty interior, press the bell for the *templom gondozó* (caretaker).

Zoltán Kodály (1882-1967), like Bartók, was a keen collector of folk songs. His output as a composer includes the rousing *Psalmus Hungaricus* and *Budavári Te Deum* (the first was composed to celebrate the 50th anniversary of the union of Buda and Pest; the second to commemorate the 250th anniversary of the Turkish surrender of Buda Castle). But Kodály is best known as a great pedagogue, developer of the famous Kodály Method of music teaching. A small memorial museum exists at Pest VI, Kodály körönd 1, in the apartment where the composer lived. (*Open Weds 10am-4pm; Thurs-Sat 10am-6pm; Sun 10am-2pm. Map p. 263, B4.*)

MODERN DANCE

Contemporary dance is a relatively new phenomenon in Hungary, though dance definitely has a place in the Hungarian soul. In Budapest, a city where so much that the visitor witnesses is a testimony to faded glory, dance is an area where the present and the future are the focus. Perhaps the best-known name is Pál Frenák, who has made a name for himself across Europe with his France-based Compagnie Pal Frenak. Born in Budapest to deaf and dumb parents, Frenák's main mode of communication from birth was physical rather than verbal. Orphaned at an early age, he spent much of his adolescence in an institution. Both these circumstances play an important role in his choreography and in the atmosphere of his pieces. Though based in France, he performs regularly in his home city. Other Hungarian names include Árvay György, known for his performance-based work; Tamás Juronics's Szeged Contemporary Dance Company; and the Central Europe Dance Theatre. The styles are always theatrical and intense. Budapest also plays host to a lot of foreign companies and choreographers, many of them top names in experimental forms of dance. **Best venue:** *Trafó, Pest IX, Liliom utca 41. Map p. 259, E2.*

FOLK MUSIC & DANCE

Hungarian folk music is rural in its origin. Village bands composed of violin, viola and double bass would accompany weddings, harvest festivals, pig-killings and Sunday mass; shepherds on the Great Plain would while away the loneliness and fill the empty sky with their flute-playing. The music is completely unlike any other in the region. Recognising this, and in response to a growing interest in national culture and identity, early 20th-century scholars and musicologists scoured the country to collect these melodies and folk lyrics for posterity, bringing them back to town to be adopted and enjoyed by the urban population. Much of that music is from Transylvania, which for historical and cultural reasons is a region where traditions have altered little. Under Communism, while so many countries found their folk traditions hijacked by the diktats of feelgood fakelore, Hungary remained robust, and its folk music survived largely unscathed. In the 1970s the *táncház* (dance house) movement was formed as a forum for young urban Hungarians to listen to the music of their forefathers

Whirling on the dance floor at a Budapest dance house (táncház).

and learn the dance steps. Some of the stars of that movement, such as Muzsikás and Márta Sebestyén, are now such supernovas that they rarely play the home circuit. But their apotheosis gives others the chance to shine. Sándor Csoóri, former fiddler with Muzsikás, has founded Ifjú Múzsikás ('Young Muzsikás'), bringing talented young musicians together, some of whom have Transylvanian roots. Csoóri also includes female musicians in his band, an entirely new and exciting development in a genre where the woman's contribution is traditionally confined to the vocals. Experiments at fusion are also happening. Deep Forest demonstrated that it could be done with Márta Sebestyén, while folk singer Irén Lovász teams up with with esoteric, Indian-inspired László Hortobágyi on the excellent album *Világfa/Roses in a Stoneyard*. Most Magyar roots music, though, is still presented in the raw, and by far the best way to experience it is live. *Táncház* evenings are regular events, and sitting with a thimbleful of plum *pálinka* as the musicians fiddle away and girls with braids and boys with beards dance a flawless *csárdás*, is as close to a Transylvanian village as you'll ever get in the capital city.

Best Dance Houses

Fonó - This traditional dance house offers a varied concert programme, with a live act or teaching session at least two evenings a week. A bar area with tables and chairs, space to dance, a larger hall for concerts and an excellent CD shop complete the offering. The CDs are mainly of Magyar folk, a lot but not all from Fonó's own label. *Buda XI, Sztregova utca 3. Map p. 4, D2. www.fono.hu*

Aranytíz Ifjúsági Centrum - The Kalamajka *táncház* takes over this renovated 19th-century office block every Saturday evening. Béla Halmos and his band - Halmos was the founder of the *táncház* movement in the early 1970s - produce a superb sound. Dance steps are taught earlier in the session. After that the dance-floor is dominated by people who really know how it's done. It makes a great spectator sport, but your attempts to join in, however bungled, will be more than welcomed, too. The musicians often sing an impromptu couple of numbers between sets. The *pálinka* flows freely from the makeshift bar outside the main hall. Soak it up with *zsíros kenyér* (bread and dripping sprinkled with powdered paprika). *Pest V, Arany János utca 10. Map p. 262, C3.*

ROMA GYPSY MUSIC

Budapest Gypsy bands have played in restaurants since at least the 19th century, when they entertained diners with popular tunes called *nóta*, usually either sorrowful love ditties or merry drinking songs. The tradition still endures today, but the music that they played was never strictly from the Roma tradition. In fact Márk Rózsavölgyi, friend of Sándor Petőfi, who lent his name to Budapest's most famous music store (*see p. 132*), although one of the most famous 'Gypsy' fiddlers of the 19th century, was Jewish. For an experience of dinner in Budapest as it might have been in the city's belle époque heyday, go to Rézkakas (*see p. 234*), where Róbert Kuti and his band bring tears of nostalgia to the eyes of returnee exiles. Lajos Sárközi plays in Kárpátia (*see p. 233*), an old-style Magyar restaurant decorated to look like the Mátyás Church.

But Gypsy music in Budapest goes beyond reinforcing the cliché of the dusky-faced fiddler in an embroidered waistcoat. Though Hungary's Roma are still fighting for social acceptance, their music is taking off in exciting directions, fusing with other traditions and demanding to be heard. Budapest-based Fekete Vonat sing Hungarian and Romany lyrics to rapper beats. Kálmán Balogh plays traditional *horas* on his dulcimer, tapping the strings with amazing cat's-paw precision, while his band goes wild around him, taking the tunes off into the realms of free jazz, Latino ballroom and bossa nova. Mitsou (Mónika Juhász Miczura), best known as the voice of Ando Drom, explores the Romany journey from the Indian sub-continent, across the Arabian desert and into Central Europe.

Best venues for Roma music

Millenáris - This 19th-century factory building right in the heart of Buda has been converted into a stunning concert venue. There are two main concert halls. The smaller *pódium* is an intimate, informal space just next to the bar: you can get up and replenish your drink between songs. The large *teátrum* is a housed in a vast brick hangar, with a high

Gypsy fiddlers in brocaded waistcoats are still a familiar sight in old-style restaurants.

ceiling into which music can swell and soar. *Buda II, Fény utca 20-22. Map p. 262, A1. www.millenaris.hu*

Roma Parliament - This dilapidated apartment block in the heart of Pest's traditional gypsy neighbourhood is home to the Roma Assembly (an organisation aimed at safeguarding Roma identity and giving the Roma people a voice), and it has an atmosphere all its own. The main room is fitted out as a concert hall, with tables and chairs, sagging sofas, Roma art all over the walls, moody lighting highlighting the twirls of smoke from the audience's cigarettes, and a raised stage at one end. *Pest VIII, Tavaszmező utca 6. Map p. 263, D5.*

WORLD MUSIC, JAZZ & THE ETHNIC CLUB SCENE

It was only a matter of time before Hungarian folk music was blended with other traditions and a good ladleful of jazz. One of the main people on the ethno-jazz scene is saxophonist Mihály Dresch, whose best albums are the beautiful, lyrical *Zeng a lélek* and *Mozdulatlan utazás*, from the early 1990s. A prodigal former band mate of Dresch's is also causing serious waves. Folk violin maestro Félix Lajkó, whose hypnotic, frenetic playing has made him a star, has now moved on to a successful solo career, with a number of albums to his credit, of which the best is perhaps the wild, galloping *Lajkó Félix és Zenekara*. Gyula Babos's Babos Project Romani blends the gypsy music he heard as a child with pop and jazz influences from his later years.

More straightforward jazz is played by Aladár Pege, a jovial Santa Claus of a double bass player who's a great favourite in Hungary and adept at creating an intimate mood. Classically trained jazz pianist Béla Szakcsi Lakatos is from a famous dynasty of gypsy musicians and is credited with bringing fusion jazz to Hungary. A veteran of numerous collaborations, he's passed his talent on to his son, Béla Szakcsi Lakatos Jr, who now has his own trio.

Ghymes, a band formed by ethnic Hungarians from Slovakia eighteen years ago, have had huge success on the local scene with their folk-based music, which blends fragments of Central European folk heritage with modern song-writing. The more recent Djabe calls its genre 'jazz/world fusion', with typical 'world music' sounds and a slick, professional package. New favourites Besh o

Millenáris Park, one of the city's best folk and world music concert venues.

droM take Gypsy and Balkan beats and rev up the tempo to a fast and furious pace, while Hungary's new immigrant community is represented by bands like Djoliba 2000, with members from Guinea, Cameroon and Rwanda. For world music in its best multi-culti, minestrone sense, look no further than the acclaimed Anima Sound System, stars of the ethnic club scene. Anima uses snatches of Gypsy music, Magyar folk, Yiddish tunes and anything else that takes their fancy, putting it all together into a moody compendium.

Best venues for World Music & Jazz

A38 - This boat, moored on the Danube in southern Buda, has been fitted out as a music venue and restaurant. The permanent concert hall is below deck. In summertime the music emerges above the hatches as well. When there's a star turn, it tends to get packed. *A38 Állóhajó. District XI (Buda). Close to Petőfi Bridge. Map p. 259, E2. www.a38.hu*

Millenáris (*see p. 129*).

Concert Information

Classical concerts are listed in the free *Koncertkalendárium*, available at the Vigadó utca 6 (*map p. 262, D3*) ticket office. The best events listings magazine is the (Hungarian-language) weekly *Pesti Est*, which comes out on Thursdays, available free in cinemas, shopping centres, hotels and restaurants across town. Look in the section entitled *Könnyű*, where events are listed alphabetically by venue and artist. If the language is too impenetrable, try *The Budapest Sun*, an English-language weekly newspaper, or *Where Budapest*, a free magazine available in most hotels, though neither has fully comprehensive listings.

Where to Buy Music

The best selection of sheet music, classical CDs, second-hand records, and Hungarian folk (in the basement) is the Rózsavölgyi music store at Szervita tér 5 (*map p. 262, D3*). Another good store is the large Zeneszalon at Deák Ferenc utca 19 (*map p. 262, C3*). Concerto, at Dob utca 33 (*map p. 263, C4, open from midday every day*), has a superb trove of second-hand records, as does Rockin' Box at Paulay Ede utca 8 (*map p. 263, C3*).

RELIGIOUS MONUMENTS

Roman Catholicism may be Hungary's main religion, but the face of Budapest is by no means uniformly papist. In fact the city is home to an exceptionally varied tradition of worship.

We cannot know how deep King Stephen's religious convictions were. Born into the traditional totemistic religion of the Hungarian tribes, he was nevertheless given a Christian education, married the sister of the Holy Roman Emperor, and was quick to spot the advantages of turning Hungary into a Christian state: it meant the cessation of warring with the German principalities and also put an end to the internecine disputes between the Magyar tribal chiefs. In effect, Stephen completed the process started by his chieftain father, Géza, and within two generations a complete transformation of Hungarian society had taken place. With the accession of Stephen as a Christian king, he became leader

Central dome of St Stephen's Basilica, the grand neo-Renaissance cathedral dedicated to the monarch who Christianised the Magyars.

of all the Magyars, ruling by the authority of his apostolic crown and with succession decided on the basis of primogeniture, instead of through the consensus of the chieftains.

After Stephen's reign (1001-1038), Hungary remained a bastion of the church of Rome in a region of Orthodoxy and Islam - until Islam triumphed in 1541 and Buda fell to the Turkish sultan. For 150 years most of Hungary remained part of the Ottoman Empire. By the time it was recaptured for Christianity in 1686, the Reformation had passed it by, and it fell under the sway of Catholic Austria. Pockets of Calvinism existed, however, particularly in the east of the country, where Vienna's influence was weaker. The princes of Transylvania had traditionally done deals with the Ottoman sultans, retaining a measure of autonomy in return for tribute. When the house of Habsburg gained

Bishop Gellért (see p. 209) brandishes the cross over Budapest. King Stephen, with Gellért's help, turned Hungary from a land of polytheistic tribes into a Christian kingdom, paving the way for its future mediaeval power.

control of Hungary, Transylvania was loath to give up its semi-independence, and continued to seek protection from the Sublime Porte. It is no coincidence that many of Hungary's most prominent anti-Habsburg freedom-fighters from the 18th and 19th centuries were Protestants: Lajos Kossuth, to name the most famous. István Bocskai, who united the Protestants of Transylvania to fight against Habsburg-enforced Catholicism, and who was elected prince of the region in 1605, is one of the sculpted figures on Calvinist Geneva's 'Mur des Reformateurs'. The Protestants' ultimate survival was due not to Turkey, however, but to the 'enlightened despot' Joseph II, son of Maria Theresa, who passed his Edict of Tolerance in 1781, giving freedom to Protestants and Jews to worship as they pleased. The Budapest Protestants had never known such freedom, while the Jews had not known it since Ottoman times. Protestant churches and synagogues, forbidden within the city confines since the recapture of Buda, suddenly began to spring up in central Pest and Buda. Orthodox Christian communities - Serbian, Greek and Armenian - also built places of worship.

Statue of Calvin in Kálvin tér in Pest, the site of the city's first Protestant church.

And despite all this turbulent history, and all these overlays of culture upon culture, Hungary has never completely forgotten its origins, somewhere deep in the misty and mystic East. The allure of a return to the traditions of the past has encouraged the growth of new groups embracing shamanism, despite the lack of detailed information on just what made up the religion of the ancient Hungarians. In addition, the spiritual trends of the New Age and the imported religions of Asia have made as much headway here as anywhere else in the West, as you can see by occasional lines of Hari Krishna chanters.

CHURCHES

Pest Churches by András Mayerhoffer

András Mayerhoffer (1690-1771) was born in Salzburg. As a young man he entered the service of Prince Eugene of Savoy, and his talents quickly became noticed. Of all the crown lands ruled by Austria, it was in Hungary that he had his greatest successes. He settled permanently in Pest, becoming a citizen in 1724.

The University Church - This central Pest church is one of the prettiest in town, and retains most of its original Baroque atmosphere. A mediaeval church formerly stood on this site. It was converted into a mosque under the Ottomans, and when the Ottomans were overthrown, was rebuilt entirely in the Baroque style. The present building dates from 1722-42, and though it was renovated twice since, and had to be restored following damage in World War II, the restoration was sensitively and faithfully carried out. In the 18th and 19th centuries, the church belonged to the Paulines, the only monastic order of Hungarian origin, who occupied the adjoining monastery and teaching centre. (The street retains its old name,

Sumptuous Baroque interior of the University Church.

Façade of the Church of St Michael.

Papnövelde utca or Clerical Seminary Street.) The west façade has statues of the two hermit saints of 3rd-century Egypt, St Anthony and St Paul: the latter gave his name to the Pauline order. Be sure to notice the beautifully carved main door, showing a pelican plucking her breast to feed her chicks (symbol of Christ's sacrifice) and a phoenix rising from the ashes (symbol of the Resurrection). These carvings were the work of a Pauline monk called Brother Felix, also responsible for the choir stall doors and possibly for the pulpit as well, though this is more doubtful. The church was completed in 1742, but the Paulines lost it less than half a century later, when the Emperor Joseph II dissolved their order and gave the church to the University. *Pest V, Egyetem tér. Map p. 263, D3.*

The Church of St Michael - This church was originally built for the Dominican order, hence the altarpiece with its romantic white-robed St Dominic. The Dominicans received the church and adjoining seminary in 1747, but were to enjoy it for only a few brief decades. The Emperor Joseph II's Edict of Tolerance, aimed at weakening the power of Rome within the Hungarian Church, dissolved all the mendicant orders and gave this church complex to an obscure order of nuns, commonly known as the Virgines Anglicanae (English Maidens), after their foundress, an Englishwoman called Mary Ward, who established the order for teaching and charitable purposes in 1609. She and her nuns were invited to Hungary in 1628, allowing them to escape the English Civil War and the anti-Catholic legislation of Cromwell. The order was finally disbanded by the Stalinist regime in 1950, and the church and nunnery were only given back after Communism collapsed in 1989. The church is a fine example of Mayerhoffer's easy but decorative style: a sort of fusion of the Austrian Baroque with provincial Hungary. During the day the door is usually open, so you can get a glimpse of the interior. *Pest V, Váci utca 47. Map p. 263, D3.*

The Serbian Orthodox Church - Before 1914 Budapest was a mass of different communities; the streets of the city would have clamoured with German, Serb, Croat, Slovak, Czech, Romanian, Yiddish and Ukrainian, as well as Hungarian. As the second city in the Habsburg empire, it attracted people from all over the crown lands, and had been a home to German and Serb communities since the middle ages. Serb merchants traded in this part of Pest in mediaeval times, but the first major wave of immigration came when the Ottomans invaded Serbian lands. Great numbers of refugees came up the Danube, their possessions loaded into boats, to settle here in the early 16th century. Budapest was also one of the first

Wall-niche mosaic of St George outside the Serbian Orthodox Church.

points of refuge for those fleeing the Balkan wars of the 1990s when, in an echo of history, Serbian was once again heard in these streets. This lovely little church of St George, on the corner of Veres Pálné utca and Szerb utca, is enclosed in its own pretty garden. Film buffs may recognise it from István Szabó's film *Sunshine*: this is where the fencer converts to Christianity in the 1930s. A church has stood here from the mid-16th century at least, but the present one dates from 1750. It is kept locked, but can be visited on Sundays during the service, which starts at 10am. *Pest V, Szerb utca 4. Map p. 263, E3.*

CHURCHES ON & NEAR BATTHYÁNY TÉR

The Church of St Anne - This church was built in 1762 in the Italian Baroque style, following the plans of Kristóf Hamon, and was completed by Matthias Nepauer. Nepauer, born in present-day Slovakia, married Hamon's widow, and became a citizen of Buda in 1749. He ran a large workshop, which undertook a number of simultaneous building projects on and around Castle Hill. The church's former presbytery has been turned into a coffee house, with a weekday morning clientele of elderly local ladies. Apart from their chatter, the place is pleasantly subdued and peaceful. Full meals are also served in the glassed-in inner-courtyard restaurant section. A beer garden operates outside in summer. *Buda I, Batthyány tér 7. Map p. 262, B2.*

The Church of St Elizabeth - Opposite the church of St Anne is a striking, dark red building. Formerly a Franciscan friary, it was converted into a hospital for the poor in the mid-18th century, run by nuns of the order of St Elizabeth. Today it is an old people's home. The church that adjoins the hospital complex was originally known as the Church of the Wounds of St Francis, hence the carving over the main entrance of two crossed hands bearing the stigmata. It is the oldest and best preserved of the Baroque churches in Buda. The present building dates from 1757, and its interior furnishings from 1777. Its most prized possession is St Elizabeth's staff: perhaps the very stick with which her cruel confessor, Conrad, used to beat her for every minor transgression. Born into the royal house of Hungary in 1207, Elizabeth dedicated herself to the service of others after her husband, Ludwig IV of Thuringia, died of pestilence on crusade. She is remembered particularly for her charitable work, and for the protection she offered to children and to the sick. The church today functions as the parish church of Budapest's German-speaking Catholic community. *Buda I, Fő utca 41. Map p. 262, B2.*

The Uniate Church - This pretty church was built by Matthias Nepauer in 1760 with money donated by a master baker from Buda. Originally it was a small hospice and chapel, dedicated to St Florian, patron saint of firefighters. It was given to the Uniate Church in 1920. Uniates use the Greek Orthodox liturgy, but recognise the Pope, not the Patriarch, as supreme pontiff. On the left of the entranceway is a shrine to the miracle-working Madonna of Máriapócs: it was believed to be thanks to her divine intervention that the Turks were beaten back from the gates of Vienna in 1683. *Buda II, Fő utca 90. Map p. 262, A2.*

A Successful Modern Church

Church of the Sacred Heart - Built by the father and son team of Aladár and Bertalan Árkay in 1936, this reinforced concrete assemblage of cubes and hemispheres is a stylish modern take on Gothic ecclesiastical forms. Traditionalists hated it, and dubbed it 'God's garage'. The entrance porch has a wide archway carved with repeated reliefs of the Lamb. Inside, a wide nave is separated from north and south aisles by slender, unarticulated columns. Between each hang simple globe lamps, suspended on long wires. The minimalist version of a coffered ceiling is decorated with frescoes by Vilmos Aba-Novák, one of a number of Hungarian inter-war artists to be influenced by a study trip to Rome. The main east window of the Sacred Heart was designed by the architect's wife, Lili Stehló. The free-standing campanile is connected to the north side of the church by a simple colonnade. *Buda XII, Csaba utca 5. Map p. 260, C3.*

SYNAGOGUES & JEWISH MONUMENTS

The Jews in Budapest: A Short History

Tablets of the Law over the entrance to the great Synagogue on Dohány utca.

Jews were first given the right to reside in Buda in the 13th century, under the terms of a charter granted by Béla IV. Here they enjoyed the protection of the monarch, and presided over the state mint and the court's finances. They were briefly expelled in 1350, when the zealous king Lajos I failed to convert them to Christianity. Fifteen years later they were allowed to return, and settled in the area around Táncsics Mihály utca on Castle Hill, where a prayer house still stands (*see p. 155*). Most of the early Jewish families in Buda were German (Ashkenazi) Jews, who had fled pogroms elsewhere in Europe. They did not flee the Ottoman advance.'The cowardly denizens of Buda realised that the Lord of the world was approaching and scattered like the stars of the Great Bear,' wrote Suleiman the Magnificent scornfully. Only the Jews remained, and came out to meet him dressed in white burial robes. Suleiman took the women and children and the able-bodied men with him and resettled them in Turkey and his Balkan domains, where their skills as craftsmen and traders were much valued. Gradually, as the fighting died down and the occupying Ottomans settled in, Buda's Jewish quarter was resettled by Jews from all over the Ottoman empire. Some were returning Ashkenazis, but the majority were Sephardim. Their Turkish overlords allowed them freedom to worship and to trade, and in 1686 the Jews helped the Ottomans defend Buda against the Christians. When the

Christians triumphed, the Jews were either executed as collaborators with the enemy, or taken into captivity. The Jews of Pest were mainly merchants and innkeepers, living on and around Király utca, in today's seventh district. This area was (and still is) the Jewish heart of the city. Many of Pest's Jews grew very prosperous, particularly during the manufacturing boom of the late 19th century. For the most part they were assimilated into the greater community, and their position became assured as members of the haute bourgeoisie, or even of the nobility. Some of the greatest Jewish financiers and industrialists received hereditary titles, and built grand town palaces on Andrássy út, the most fashionable address in town. By 1930 almost a quarter of all Budapest citizens were Jewish (tellingly, this dropped to just 9% after the Second World War). The 1930s was the decade of the so-called Jewish Laws (*numerus clausus*), regulations that restricted the number of Jews permitted to enter universities and the professions. As the decade wore on, these laws became more and more stringent. In 1939, Hungary entered the war as an ally of Germany. Though officially the Hungarian administration did not sanction the deportations, Jews were nevertheless transported in their thousands from the Hungarian countryside to the death camps of Germany and Poland. It was only the Budapest Jews who survived, at least until Admiral Horthy was overthrown and the Fascist Arrow Cross seized power and turned a part of the seventh district into an enclosed ghetto. Of a population of around 825,000, over half a million Hungarian Jews lost their lives in the Holocaust. Today, however, Judaism is enjoying a renaissance in Budapest, and

HUNGARIAN NATIONAL MUSEUM

Budapest Jew wearing the yellow star, doing forced labour in the city streets.

where once only a few elderly people celebrated the high holidays and even fewer regularly observed *shabbat*, the city now boasts Jewish newspapers, secondary schools and community centres.

What to See

NB: Budapest's major temple, the Dohány utca Synagogue, is described on *p. 65**. The Sephardic prayer house on Castle Hill is featured on* *p. 155**.*
Tours of Jewish Budapest can be booked from Chosen Tours, Tel: 355-2202 (not Saturdays).

The Rumbach Sebestyén utca Synagogue - This fabulous building was completed in 1872 for the city's Conservative community. Designed by the great Viennese architect Otto Wagner, the building, with its two slender minarets and horizontal bands of red, as well as the Moorish-style decoration running under the tablets of the law at roof level, is reminiscent of the great mosque in Cordoba. During the Second World War, the synagogue was used as a detention centre for Jews awaiting deportation. It has never been reopened since, and was allowed to fall into total disrepair. Although restored fairly recently, it is still disused, and no one is sure what its fate will be. One idea has been to turn it into a Jewish study centre and library; another (which the Jewish community vehemently rejected) was that Yoko Ono would buy it and use it as a rock concert venue. *Pest VII, Rumbach Sebestyén utca 11. Map p. 263, C3.*

The Orthodox Synagogue - Built in 1911-13 by the Löffler brothers, followers of Béla Lajta (*see p. 82*), this building seamlessly meshes modernity with tradition. Designed to house a school, civic buildings, a restaurant and apartments, as well as a temple, it is now being restored and is very much in use. The inscription on the façade reads, '*This is none other than the house of God, and this is the gate of Heaven*'. Enter by the iron door to the right of the main entrance, following the sign to the Hanna Restaurant. You can peep into the synagogue itself through the small door just inside the gateway, and see its sky blue ceiling. The synagogue is only used for high holidays, but the Shas Chevra prayer house, just inside the gateway to the right, is used regularly. The gate is open from 7am to 3.30pm every day except Saturday, when it does not open until 11am. Go through into the courtyard and admire the stained glass at the back of the building, and the wrought iron *huppah*, or wedding canopy. Orthodox Ashkenazi communities hold their wedding ceremonies under the open sky, and the inscription is from Jeremiah: '*The voice of joy and the voice of gladness, the voice of the bridegroom and the voice of the bride*'. *Pest VII, Kazinczy utca 29-31. Map p. 263, C4.*

Béla Lajta's Schmidl family mausoleum (1903).

The Kozma utca Cemetery - Many of the great names from 19th and early 20th-century Budapest lie at rest here. In the centre stands Alfréd Hajós's stark 1949 memorial to the Holocaust victims, whose names are inscribed on stone tablets, ranged according to where they died. Many names omitted by the original compilers have been added in in handwritten scrawls. Around the cemetery perimeter stand the grand mausoleums. Until relatively recently they were overgrown and untended, offering shelter to derelicts, and unvisited by the descendants of the families who built them. Many still are, but increasingly they are being restored. Most famous is the hump-backed cerulean ceramic mausoleum (*pictured above*) of Sándor Schmidl, a grocer who kept a shop near Deák tér. The ceramics are by the Zsolnay factory (*see p. 116*) and the mausoleum design, incorporating stylised Hungarian folk motifs, is by Béla Lajta (*see p. 82*).

To get to the cemetery, take tram 37 from Népszinház utca (*map p. 263, D4*) to the final stop. Tram 28 from the same place also works, though it terminates one stop short of the cemetery entrance. Trams run every 10 to 15 minutes, and the journey takes just over half an hour, taking you past the bustling Chinese market on Kőbányai út and Ödön Lechner's ceramic-decorated Kőbánya Church on Szent László tér. *Pest X, Kozma utca 6. Open Sun-Fri 8am-2pm. Visitors are requested not to enter bareheaded, so take a hat or scarf with you to cover yourself. Map p. 5, D5.*

A RELIC OF OTTOMAN RULE

Gül Baba's Tomb

Buda II, Mecset utca 14. Map p. 262, A2.

Very little remains to tell of the Ottomans' century-and-a-half in Buda. There is the tomb of Abdurrahman Pasha on Castle Hill (*see p. 156*) and a few scattered gravestones on the hill's southern slope (*see pp. 39-40*). The most complete survival is the tomb of Gül Baba. Though not strictly a place of worship, Muslims have traditionally regarded this place as holy. Gül Baba was a Dervish who came

Interior of Gül Baba's tomb.

to Buda with the Ottoman invaders in 1541. He then died of over-excitement at the victory thanksgiving ceremony held in the Mátyás Church-turned-mosque, and was buried in the place where his tomb now stands. Just outside the railed-off precinct is a statue of him - or, at least, an artist's impression. Legend remembers him as a great horticulturalist, responsible for introducing cultivated roses into Hungary (his name roughly translates as 'Rose Daddy'). Though his sojourn in Buda would barely have given him time to prune a single rosebush, the story caught on, and has become part of his legend. His tomb and the ornamental garden around it were restored in 1997 with money given by the Turkish government. The tomb is a small octagonal, domed building, built between 1543 and 1548. It was turned into a Christian chapel by the Jesuits in 1690, but this was the only break in an otherwise continuous Muslim tradition. Inside, the walls have been hung with modern ceramic dishes inscribed with Koranic verses, and Gül Baba's sarcophagus lies draped in a green cloth embroidered with gold. The view from the garden's colonnaded parapet is good: the tiled rooftops of lower Buda, Margaret Bridge, and a shining sliver of the Danube. And there are roses planted in the garden.

Hungarian Nobel Prizewinners

Albert Szent-Györgyi (1893-1986) - Chemist who discovered Vitamin C. He writes that sometime in 1932, his wife gave him some bread and butter and green paprika for tea, but instead of eating the paprika he whisked it away to the lab. He found it to contain massive amounts of Vitamin C, or hexuron acid, which he had been trying to isolate for some time. He was awarded the prize in 1937.

György Békésy (1899-1972) - Physicist who won the prize in 1961 for his work on human hearing, particularly for his discovery of the stimulus mechanism found in the cochlea. For his research he needed to dissect a great number of heads. He once remarked that he was grateful to many people, especially to the police officer who informed him in retrospect that he could have been arrested at any time on suspicion of murder, given that he carried human heads about in his briefcase.

Dénes Gábor (1900-1979) - Physicist whose interest in electron optics led him to discover the holograph. He realised in the late forties - twenty years before the invention of the laser - that information not only about the intensity of refracted light waves, but also about their phases, must be employed to create a complete (*holo*) and spatial image (*graph*).

Jenő Wigner (1902-1995) - Physicist who received the prize in 1963 for the proposal and application of the modern symmetry-based theory of fundamental physical forces. He was one of those who, in 1939, drew Einstein's attention to the fact that the Germans might use atomic energy for military purposes. This realisation resulted in the Manhattan Plan, which allowed for the development of the atomic bomb, something that sorely distressed Wigner until the end of his life.

Imre Kertész (1929 -) - Novelist who won the prize for his book *Fateless*. First published in Hungary in 1975, it received little or no recognition at the time. Reissued in German in 2000, it went on to win Hungary's first ever Nobel Prize for Literature. Kertész was deported from Budapest at the age of fifteen. He writes of his experiences in Auschwitz, Buchenwald and Zeitz, describing unimaginable horrors with a child's baffled and sometimes dispassionate incomprehension.

PART III

GUIDED WALKS

Each of these five city-centre walks is designed to take about an hour. Visiting museums, cafés and restaurants along the way will stretch them out to occupy a whole morning or afternoon.

GUIDED WALKS

Typical Castle District streetscape.

WALK ONE

MARGIT
Pengő u.
Fény u.
Vars. udv.
Bajvívó u.
Varsányi Irén
Kacsa
Vitéz u.
Vitéz
Csapl. u.
Nagy I. tér
BEM
Széna tér
Csalogány
Hattyú
Ostrom
Fiáth J.
Kapás
Fazekas
Medve
Toldy F.
Batthyány
Mária tér
Gyorskocsi
Fő
Batthyány tér
BATTHYÁNY TÉR
HÉV
M2
56
4,6
59,61
Moszkva tér
MOSZKVA TÉR
Batthyány
Várfok
Szabó Ilonka
Jácint
Kagyló
Donáti
Iskola
Markovits I.u.
Aranyh.u.
19
Mátray
Linzi
Hunfalvy
Anjou bástya
Bécsi kapu tér
B.M.
Táncsics
Franklin
Lovas
Körm. u.
Mil. Hist. Mus.
Peterm. bíró u.
Mus. of Music Hist.
Vám
Székely
Szilágyi D. tér
KRISZTINA
KRT.
ATTILA
Logodi
Tóth Á.
Kapisztrán tér
Országház
Kard
Fortuna
Hess A.tér
Toldy
Don.
Budai Vigadó
Jáv.S.
Árpád
Úri
Lant
Fort. k.
Szeder
Corvin tér
Korlát
VÁR
MÁTYÁS CHURCH
FISHERMEN'S BASTION
Donáti
Halász
Magyar jakobinusok tere
Szenth. tér
Bugát
Nőegy.
Szenth. u.
Balta k.
Ponty
Hunyadi
Szalag
DÉLI PU.
Tárnok
Csónak u.
Hunyadi J.
Szőny.
Pala
Vérmező
DÉLI STATION
Krisztina
Gránit
Anna u.
Háj. u.
sétány
Palota
Mag.
Jégv.
Szalag
Király
Kosciuszko
Móra F.
Dísz tér
A.P.
Clark Ádám tér
RAKPART
Tábor
Palota út
Feszty Á.u.
Mikó
Pauler
Zerge
Szt. György u.
Színház
Hunyadi J. u.
KRISZTINAVÁROS
krt.
Palota
Szt. György tér
Funicular
Várkert rkp.
Kuny D.
Tádé
Krisztina tér
Roh.
Alagút u.
Váralja
Lovarda u.
Ludwig Mus.
Sikló u.
Lánchíd
Márvány u.
Mészáros
Gellérthegy
Krisztina
ÚT
Sarló
Nat. Gallery
Győző
Pálya
Ág u.
Naphegy
Lisznyai
Győri
Róka u.
Tigris
18
ROYAL PALACE
Dózsa Gy. tér
Budapest Hist.Mus.
NAPHEGY
Mészáros
Fenyő
Orvos
Pásztor
Attila
Kemál A.
Ybl M. tér
Nyárs u.
Párd.
Naphegy tér
Fém
Dezső
S.M.
Apród u.
Döbrentei
Kap. u.
Avar
Tibor
Kőműves l.
út
Szarvas tér
TABÁN
B.Ö.F.
Bán u.
Zsolt
Czakó
krt.
Rác baths
Kereszt
Hadnagy u.
Táltos u.
Derék
Piroska u.
Galeotti
Czakó
ÚT
ALKOTÁS
Győri
Csörsz
Aladár
Csap
Sánc
HEGYALJA
Szirtes
Orom
Berényi
Antal
Szirom
61

CASTLE HILL

This is the most scenic district of Buda, where solidly prosperous Baroque town houses mingle with vestiges of mediaeval splendour and the constant reminders of battles lost and won. In its time Castle Hill has been fought over by Ottomans and Christians, Habsburgs and Hungarians, Soviets and Nazis.

This walk starts in Szentháromság utca, in the **Ruszwurm café**. The oldest café in the city (founded in 1827), it is tiny and cosy, non-smoking, and renowned for its pastries (*see p.* 99). You are in the heart of Castle Hill, a limestone outcrop rising steeply on the western bank of the Danube, and chosen as the site for the Royal Palace in the 13th century, when King Béla IV retreated here, to escape the marauding Mongols. Buda was captured by the Turks in 1541: most of Hungary remained part of the Ottoman Empire until 1686, when Buda was recaptured for Christendom by the Habsburg armies. The siege

The 'flying nun' commemorates a long-disbanded convent of Poor Clares.

Plague monument outside the Mátyás Church, celebrating Buda's deliverance from the dreaded black death in 1713.

was a destructive one. Most of Buda's buildings were razed to the ground, and only a few hundred people were left alive out of a population of thousands. The city was rebuilt in the Baroque style, but it never regained its mediaeval prosperity. Hungary was ruled from Vienna; and without a royal court, Buda was forsaken by the aristocracy. Instead it became home to a mainly German-speaking community of shopkeepers, merchants and artisans. Though the patricians returned in the 19th century, it was the old burghers' houses that accommodated them, and it is mostly those houses that line the Buda streets today.

Come out of the Ruszwurm now and turn left. The street takes you out into **Szentháromság tér** (Holy Trinity Square), which is marked by a votive monument erected in 1713, after a series of plagues had swept through the city. In front of you is the **Mátyás Church and Fishermen's Bastion** (*see p. 41*). On your left is the restored neo-Gothic Kulturinnov, a cultural institute, archive and hostel. Before the Second World War it was Hungary's Finance Ministry. Keeping it on your left, turn left towards the **Hilton Hotel**. A modern structure preying on two fine old buildings, it was cobbled together by Béla Pintér in 1976 out of the remains of a 13th-century Dominican friary and a former Jesuit College built in the Zopf style. The lower part of the friary's church tower still stands, and part of its cloister is preserved too. To see it, go into the hotel and turn left. A plate glass window overlooks it from the hotel bar. Back outside the hotel again, look at the old **monastery tower** with its relief (allegedly a faithful portrait) of King Mátyás Corvinus (reigned 1458-1490), hailed as Hungary's greatest ruler. A true Renaissance prince, he was at once bibliophile and hunter, scholar and sovereign. Children are still told of how he roamed the country in disguise, intervening in village arguments and using his wit and patience to pacify his quarrelsome subjects. It was during his reign that the following Italian saying was coined: 'Europe has three pearls of cities: Venice on the Water, Buda on the Hill and Florence on the Plain'. Mátyás was only 47 when he died, and his death is shrouded in mystery. Some say he died at the hands of his duplicitous queen Beatrice, others that a palace uprising struck him down in his prime. But these are probably just more examples of the thousands of fables that surround him, or the conspiracy-theorising of people unwilling to accept that such an exceptional man could have succumbed to something as banal as a virus. Whatever the cause of Mátyás's death, he died leaving Hungary a dominant force in Europe, with control over Bohemia, Silesia, Moravia and even lower Austria, including Vienna itself.

Opposite the Mátyás relief, in the centre of a little square, is a **statue of Pope Innocent XI**, on whose initiative the pan-Christian army joined forces against the Ottomans in 1686. It is in this very square that the last Pasha of Buda, Abdurrahman, is said to have fallen. On the Pope's right, across the street, is a large yellow building with an open entranceway. Tucked inside its courtyard is the **Litea bookshop and tearoom**. Their selection of foreign-language titles is quite good. Behind Pope Innocent is the old **Vörös Sün (Red Hedgehog) inn**, with a red plaster hedgehog above its main entrance. This was the first inn in Buda, later home to the architect Matthias Nepauer, who worked on much of the restoration work here.

Take the road to the right of the inn now. This is **Táncsics Mihály utca**, probably the most attractive street in all of Castle Hill, with its unbroken line of colour-wash Baroque façades, each with its own peculiarities of detail and ornament. In many cases ancient stones are incorporated into the walls, telling tales of how the 17th-century Baroque town was erected over Gothic and Ottoman rubble, or how the mid 20th-century town, rebuilt once again after the devastation of the 1945 Battle of Buda, put back together what the Allied bombs had cast down.

Each house has a steeply pitched roof with storage space inside as well as deep cellars that plunge down into the limestone caverns beneath the hill. The cellars all had a well for drinking water, a wine cellar and a grain store. No. 5 on the right used to be the ice-chamber of the Turkish janissaries. The fine **mid-18th century building at No. 7** was built by Matthias Nepauer, the architect who lived in the Red Hedgehog inn, and the male heads on the pilasters supporting the first floor balcony are said to be self-portraits. Formerly it was the town palace of the Erdődy family, patrons of Beethoven, who invited the composer here as their guest in 1800. Today it is home to the Music History Museum, where you will find the Bartók archives as well as collections of ancient instruments. In the summer, concerts are held in the courtyard, and there is a lovely garden at the back with views over the river into Pest. At No. 9 next door, formerly the **city gaol**, you will see the likenesses of Lajos Kossuth and Mihály Táncsics, Hungarian heroes of the war of independence from Austria, imprisoned here in the 1840s for their subversive activities. Originally a barracks, this building, with its two-metre-thick walls, became a prison for so-called 'status prisoners' in the period leading up to the 1848 revolution. Táncsics, a weaver-turned-pamphleteer, famous for his excoriating delivery and radical passion, was loathed by the authorities on account of such declarations as: '*Patriots, my worker brothers! Listen well to my words: there are no more lords and peasants, there are no serfs, people will not be beaten any more; we are all equal citizens and brothers*'.

Walk on up the street now, passing No. 17, formerly home to **Albert Apponyi**, a liberal politician who was thrown out of

Patterned cobbles and Baroque detailing in the courtyard of the former Erdődy Palace, now the Music History Museum.

Parliament in 1912 when he and his supporters rioted against the Prime Minister. A great patriot, his pet project was to make the Austro-Hungarian Empire more visibly Hungarian. When his campaigns extended to Magyarising the non-Hungarian ethnic minorities within Hungary, however, he met with resistance and resentment. A generation later, his son was taken from this house to Mauthausen (a concentration camp close to Dachau) by the Nazis.

The green building at No. 20 opposite is an experiment at a modern structure that blends in colourwise. When the Red Army finally drove the Nazis from Buda in 1945, only four houses were left in a habitable condition. Where possible all the bombed-out hulks were rebuilt in their original form, but some were too badly damaged and had to be replaced.

No. 26, a little further on, contains a **Sephardic prayer house** (*open May-October 10am-5pm, daily except Mondays*), established in the mid 16th century by Sephardic Jews who came to Buda in the wake of the Ottoman conquest. This street was then known as Jew Street (*Zsidó utca*), and a small Sephardic community lived and traded here for one and half centuries, along with the Ashkenazi community, the original Jewish settlers of Buda, whose larger synagogue still remains, buried underground at No. 23 on the opposite side of the street. Until such time as it can be uncovered again and opened to public view, the tiny Sephardic prayer house is all that remains of Jewish life in the Castle District. When on September 2nd, 1686, the armies of the Holy Roman Emperor took back the Buda Castle, four and a half centuries of Jewish life in Buda were wiped out. Jewish elders issued rat poison to their community on the eve of the battle, so terrified were they of the Christian onslaught. Many Jews fought alongside the Ottomans, who had allowed them to trade freely and had not restricted them to usury as many previous reigns had done. A contemporary general, Johann Dietz, writes that the women were rounded up and taken to Berlin where they were married off to the German nobility. Jews were not allowed to settle in the Castle District again until nearly two centuries later.

Leaving the prayer house, go straight ahead until you come out into a wide square. This is **Bécsi kapu tér** (Vienna Gate Square), dominated by the lugubrious neo-Gothic National Archives. In fact the building is so gloomy that when the Soviet tanks rolled in in 1956 to suppress the anti-Stalinist revolution, they mistook the place for a barracks and bombarded it. It was built in 1913 by Samu Pecz, who designed Pest's Central Market Hall (Vásárcsarnok, *see p. 69*). The owls guarding the Archives' entrance testify to its serious intent. The tiles on the roof represent medals slung from Hungarian tricolor ribbon. Flanking the further side of the square is a row of pretty Baroque buildings. In the 18th century, Nos. 5 and 6 were home to a family of blacksmiths - possibly the very smiths who created the wrought ironwork in front of so many ground-floor windows in this district. The two houses have a common roof because, as tradition says, the son of one house married the daughter of the other, and their parents decided to unite the two families under a single roof.

Climb up to the top of the **Vienna Gate** to admire the view towards Moszkva tér and the tree-covered Rózsadomb (Rose Hill), Buda's most exclusive residential area. It looks a lot better from a distance - much of its original charm was lost when faithful cadres, scrambling for a good address in the 1960s and 1970s, coated it with concrete blocks. Turn left across the gate now, go down the steps and along the path that leads behind the Archives, along the **old city ramparts**. Follow the line of the fortifications until you come to a turban-topped stone stele. This is the **tomb of Abdurrahman Pasha**, who died in 1686, '*on the afternoon of the second day of the last month of summer. A valiant foe, peace be with him*'. When he fell, it was from these walls that the victorious Hungarians hoisted their standard: it still flaps from the corner bastion straight ahead.

Carry on towards the flag, past the ancient cannons and gun carriages. Turn left at the corner, to come out in front of an imposing white-painted building: the **Military History Museum**. The cannonballs embedded in its outer wall are said to date from

Wrought ironwork on Bécsi kapu tér.

On a desolate north-facing stretch of rampart, rarely blessed by sunshine, stands the white turban-topped stele of Abdurrahman, last Pasha of Buda, who fell in battle in 1686.

the 1849 battle in which the Hungarian rebel forces attempted to capture Buda from its Habsburg liege lords. It was a difficult battle to win, especially in Buda, where the ethnic German majority was not particularly supportive of the Magyar cause. Turn left round the Military History Museum into Kapisztrán tér. In doing this you are doing exactly what the Christian armies did in 1686, for it was here that they at last breached the walls and streamed into the city, despite the cannons that had been set up by the Turks in the **church tower of St Mary Magdalene**, which is ahead of you to the right. This church was badly bombed in World War II, and its 15th-century tower is more or less all that remains. Originally it was the church used by the Hungarian-speaking minority - German speakers heard mass in the Mátyás Church. During much of the Ottoman occupation all churches except this one were used as mosques, and the Christian communities in Buda all came to pray here, regardless of denomination. While the Counter Reformation raged in the rest of Europe, with the Inquisition sending thousands to the stake, religious tolerance was an important feature of the reign of the terrible Turks - at least at first. Eventually wearying of repeated Christian attempts to win back the city, the pashas converted this church into a mosque as well.

Go right down **Úri utca** now. The pink and white building at No. 51 on the left looks like a Baroque church without a west door - which is exactly what it is. It was once the church attached to the next-door convent of the Poor Clares. No. 58 is the **former Royal Treasury**, and even its drainpipes have crowns on them. Today it houses the district's registry office. The façade, with its extraordinary array of symbols, some apparently masonic, others superstitious good-luck charms, dates from 1904, from the hand of the man who built the Gresham Palace (*see p. 33*). **Nos. 52 and 60** boast plaques commemorating the vindictiveness of two regimes. From No. 60 Count Antal Szigray was dragged away to Mauthausen by the Nazis. Count Zsigmond Széchényi, writer and big-game hunter, was evicted from No. 52 by the State Security Authority (ÁVH) in 1951, at a time when the Communists were sending the 'class enemy' off to do forced labour and using their homes to house apparatchiks. The house in 1951 would only have been a shadow of its former self: it suffered a direct hit during the siege of Buda in 1945. Széchényi's father, who was staying with his son at the time, wrote a diary. '*Constant heavy shelling. The sky above Pest is blood red. They say the city is burning... a heap of ruins... Apparently the Germans are going to try to break through the cordon on both Danube banks. Our house will certainly be destroyed, and with it everything we own. The souvenirs of a lifetime. And among the ashes of Pest, Hungarians are dying in their thousands - impossible to*

Café Miró brings a touch of surrealism to its Gothic and Baroque environs.

bury them. This is hell! A thousand times worse than we dared expect. Will we get through this - how will we? Once there was a Hungary. Now there's just dust and cinders. God have mercy on us!'

Those days seem almost forgotten now. At the end of the street on the right-hand corner is **Café Miró**. If you feel surfeited on the past, this place, with its Surrealist wrought iron furniture and solarium-bronzed waitresses, is guaranteed to return you to the modern world. Alternatively, turn right into Tóth Árpád sétány, where you can sit on a bench under the chestnut trees and contemplate the Buda Hills.

Hollywood Hungarians

Turbulent times sent Hungarian emigrés flocking to the movie studios of Hollywood. The story goes that a sign was hung outside the studio building in the 1930s declaring: 'Being Hungarian isn't enough; you need talent as well!'

Béla Lugosi (1882-1956) - He made a sensation as Dracula on Broadway in 1927, but always shrugged off his blood-curdling success as merely a 'living', and lamented the fact that he wasn't taken more seriously.

Michael Curtiz (1888-1962) - His best-known film is the all-time classic *Casablanca*, but he also directed *The Adventures of Robin Hood, The Jazz Singer* and *White Christmas*. Curtiz was amazingly prolific, shooting two or three films a year.

Alexander Korda (1893-1956) - As a young man Korda became an important figure in Budapest cinema, but his real fame came later for work he did in the UK and the US, both as producer and director. He was the first producer to receive a knighthood.

Peter Lorre (1904-1964) - The diminutive character actor was best known for his pitch-perfect depiction of slimy evil in Fritz Lang's *M* and *The Maltese Falcon*.

Alexander Trauner (1906-1993) - A set designer, he worked in France until the 1950s, doing the marvellous sets for Marcel Carné's *Les Enfants du Paradis*. His work on Orson Welles's *Othello* won him awards at Cannes and he received Oscars for *The Apartment* and *Irma la Douce*. He also designed Joseph Losey's sumptuous *Don Giovanni* and Luc Besson's *Subway*.

Miklos Rózsa (1907-1995) - Respected both as a classical composer and a master of film music, Rózsa worked with Korda and in Hollywood during its golden age. He continued composing until his death.

Zsa Zsa Gabor (b. 1917) - More famous for her many marriages than for her acting, Zsa Zsa has become a celebrity personality known for her quips: 'Darlink, I'm a perfect housekeeper. Venever I get divorced, I alvays get to keep ze house'.

Many children of Hungarian immigrants also went on to Hollywood success. Director George Cukor (1899-1983) is known for *The Philadelphia Story*, *A Star is Born* and *My Fair Lady*. Tony Curtis (b. 1925) was born in New York to Hungarian parents. And Hungarian success continues unabated. Producer Andrew Vajna, screenwriter Joe Eszterhas and cinematographers Vilmos Zsigmond, László Kovács and Lajos Koltai are now inspiring Hungary's younger filmmakers with dreams of fame and fortune.

Opposite: Carved west door of the University Church, with the wood carver's impression of the Egyptian hermit saint St Paul, clad in a palm-frond skirt.

WALK TWO

Batthyány
Nagymező
Lovag
TERÉZ
Aradi
Vértanúk tere
Báthory
Vécsey
Aulich
Garibaldi u.
Nádor
Perczel M.u.
Nagysándor J. u.
Szabadság tér
Zoltán
Hajós
Dessewffy
Oktogon
OKTOGON
Jókai tér
Mozsár u.
Operetta Theatre
Liszt F. tér
Szófia
Zichy Jenő
Kiss E. u.
Bank u.
ARANY J. U.
Podm. Fr. t.
Lázár
OPERA HOUSE
OPERA
Academy of Music
Hegedű u.
Dohn.E.
Kürt
Kertész
Akácfa
Csányi u.
Széchenyi u.
Tükory
Arany János u.
Vigyázó F. u.
V
Október 6.
Sas
Szt. Istv. tér
BASILICA
BAJCSY-ZSILINSZKY
Rév. k.
Révay
ANDRÁSSY
Ede
Vasvári P. u.
Paulay
Székely M. u.
Kis Diófa
Kazinczy
Klauzál tér
Klauzál
Zrínyi
Mérleg
Hild tér
H.p.
BAJCSY-ZS. ÚT
Postal Mus.
Holló
Rumbach S.
Nagy
Nyár
Diófa
Eötvös tér
JÓZSEF A.
József n.tér
Erzsébet tér
Deák F. tér
Király
Asbot
Mad. I. út
Mad.I. t.
Wesselényi
Síp
Dob
BELGRÁD
Apáczai
Dorottya
Szende P.u.
Vörösm.
VÖRÖSMARTY TÉR
Bécsi u.
Mia.
Sütő
Sz.D.t.
47 49
KÁROLY KRT.
Merlin
Vigadó tér
Vigadó
Deák
Váci
Krist. t.
Feh.Hajó
Szervita tér
Bárczy I.
BELVÁROS
Semmelweis
Gerlóczy
V. M.
Herzl T.tér
SYNAGOGUE
Dohány
RÁKÓCZI
Szentkirályi
Puskin
Gyulai P. u.
Stáhly
Vas
Vigadó tér terminal
Dunakorzó
Csere J. u.
Türr I. u.
Aranykéz
Városház
Petőfi S. u.
Kam.K. tér
Vármegye u.
Pilvax k.
Párizsi
Haris k.
Régi posta
Galamb
Petőfi tér
KOSSUTH L.U.
Magyar
M2
ASTORIA
Trefort u.
MÚZEUM KRT.
Ferenciek tere
FER.TERE
Kígyó
P.B. u.
Piar. k.
Márc.15.
Szép u.
Reáltanoda u.
Brody Sándor u.
Pollack
SZABAD SAJTÓ ÚT
Duna u.
Veres
Curia
Károlyi M.
Ferenczy I.
Károlyi kert
Literary Mus.
Henszl.
Kém.
Irányi
Sz.K.
Cukor
Papnöv.
Egy. t.
Kecskeméti u.
NATIONAL MUSEUM
M.tér
Kálvin tér
KÁLVIN TÉR
Múzeum u.
Ötp. u.
Mikszáth K. tér
Szabó E. tér
Reviczky u.
Baross u.
ERZSÉBET BRIDGE
Molnár
Nyáry Pál
Pálné
Királyi P.
Képl.
Belgrád rakpart International Terminal
Sörház u.
Pintér
Szerb
Fejér Gy.
Bástya
RAKPART
Havas
Szarka
Só u.
VÁMHÁZ KRT.
Török P.u.
Ráday
ÜLLŐI ÚT
Szentkirályi
Fővám tér
Vásárcsarnok
Pipa u.
Gönczy P.
Lónyay
Erkel
Sóház u.
Csarnok tér
Imre
IX
Markusovszky tér
Köztelek
SZT. GELLÉRT RKP.
18,19
THE CITADEL
Verejték u.
47,49
SZABADSÁG BRIDGE
Fővám tér
Mátyás
Czuczor
2,2A
Szt.
Gellért
MUSEUM APPLIED

OLD PEST: INSIDE THE CITY WALLS

This walk takes you into the narrow streets of the former mediaeval city, past Budapest's best inner city park, taking in a handsome Baroque church and one of the belle époque's most literary of coffee houses.

This walk begins in **Kálvin tér**, so named for its Calvinist church, once the focal point of the square. It was built outside the old city walls, on the site of a former Turkish cemetery, a plot of land granted to the Hungarian Reformed Church in 1801, at a time when Protestants and Jews were not allowed to build places of worship within the official city boundary. Today any religious debates have given way to arguments about two new buildings that grace (or deface, depending on your opinion) the square. On one side stands the great glass 2001 Kálvin

Kálvin tér in the 1860s, site of Pest's main haymarket.

Center and on the other side is another glass office building; both face the pink and green Corona Hotel. It is hard to believe that this once was an area of fields, vineyards and grazing land, scattered with simple mud-brick dwellings, a suburb lying beyond the city walls. The only vestige of that suburb now is the little clutch of steep-roofed houses next to the church.

Turn to face the Korona Hotel now, and go underneath the green archway that links the hotel's two halves. Immediately after the archway, on the left, is a red marble **relief of a knight in armour**, marking the spot where the old mediaeval city gate used to stand. The city of Pest in the 13th century covered a tiny area of around a tenth of a square mile, bounded by a thick stone wall. The oldest surviving parts of this wall date from before the Mongol invasion and sacking of Pest in 1241. When the citizens heard that the Mongol hordes were on their way, they apparently put up a second fortification to reinforce their wall in an amazing three days. All in vain: the whole lot was razed and the city ransacked. Three centuries later the Hungarians tried again, building more walls, this time with the added precaution of a moat and an earthwork. It still wasn't good enough: the might of the Ottoman Turks proved too much, and the wall was razed to the ground again.

Turning right into **Magyar utca** now, you will see a section of the old wall by the catering entrance to the hotel. Walk further on down the street. You are now inside the old heart of Pest. Although nothing of the old mediaeval buildings remains, the streets follow the line of the original plan and are narrow and sometimes winding as a result. **No. 28 Magyar utca** used to be the Lamacs Inn, favourite haunt of poets and writers at the time of Hungary's 1848-49 struggle for independence from the Habsburgs (*see pp. 18-19*). The most famous Hungarian freedom fighter, patriotic poet and warrior Sándor Petőfi, killed in battle at the age of 26, used to dine here frequently - on credit, we must assume, as he was famously penniless and couldn't even afford to paint the peeling walls of his nearby flat. On a less heroic note, this street was also the site of a notorious brothel, where a party of British MPs on a visit to Hungary in 1907 drank and debauched until the small hours - and then left the Hungarian authorities to pick up the tab. The Vintage Gallery at No. 26 is housed in what was once the **Molnár and Moser Pharmacy** - its old stone shopfront can still be seen, looking out over the **Károlyi kert** (Károlyi Garden), Budapest's prettiest inner city park. The restrained and elegant town houses that surround it are typical of the early 19th-century style, plainer and more modest than what was built during the explosion of wealth and flamboyance in the years leading up to the First World War.

The Károlyi kert originally belonged to the large house at its far end, the town residence of the Károlyis, one of Hungary's premier patrician families. The house continues a fine Hungarian tradition of nobility alloyed with ignominy and tragedy. It was from here that independent Hungary's first ever Prime Minister, Count Lajos Batthyány, was dragged away into captivity in 1849. Batthyány, a nobleman from the then Hungarian town of Pozsony (now Bratislava, capital of Slovakia), was proclaimed Prime Minister of an independent Hungary in 1848. He held office for just six months. Condemned to death as a traitor by the Habsburgs, his appeal for pardon was rejected, whereupon he attempted suicide by stabbing himself with his own dagger. It was the gravity of his wounds which in the end melted the Habsburg hearts and led to his

Enjoying the sunshine in the Károlyi kert.

Stylised Classicist school building (1913) on Veres Pálné utca.

sentence being commuted from death by hanging to death by firing squad. At the turn of the 19th and 20th centuries, the house was the town residence of Mihály Károlyi, known as the 'Red Count' because of his socialist sympathies. It was here that he planned and organised his National Council, which governed the newly independent Hungarian Republic after the collapse of Austria in 1918, and in which he served as Prime Minister. Károlyi was not popular with Western leaders, who found him too radical. In the event, in fact, he found himself swept away by the power of his own reforms. When Hungary declared itself a Soviet-style Republic in 1919, Mihály Károlyi resigned. Appropriately enough, the former palace of an aristocrat who led a failed socialist revolution now houses the literary memorabilia of the same Sándor

Petőfi mentioned above, who died fighting another doomed libertarian cause.

From the Károlyi kert turn left down Henszlmann Imre utca, to Egyetem tér. Straight ahead to your left is the Law Faculty building of Budapest's arts university, and next to it the **University Church** (*see p. 136*), one of the best Baroque churches in town. Under the Ottoman occupation, all the churches in Pest were converted into mosques, including this one. Just to the left of the church, connecting church and university, is a fine little structure with a Pro Patria monument of the First World War.

Coming out of the church again, turn left down Papnövelde utca, noting as you go the **secondary school at No. 4** on the right, quasi-Art Deco with stylised Classicist elements, and architecturally far ahead of its time: it was built in 1913. Cross Veres Pálné utca into Nyáry Pál utca, noting the building on the left-hand corner, adorned with statues of legendary Hungarian leaders, all sporting fabulous moustaches. On the wall of No. 11, the next building on the left, is a **plaque commemorating Katalin Karády**, who sheltered persecuted Jews in 1944. Karády, an actress and smoky-voiced singer of wonderfully slushy songs (available on CD), was arrested by the Gestapo in April 1944 and beaten severely, but released later that summer. She left the country after the Communist takeover and went to live in New York and later Brazil. She never returned, but her ashes were repatriated in 1991 and buried in the Farkasréti Cemetery.

Retracing your steps, turn left down Veres Pálné utca. The street's namesake, Veres Pálné herself (Mrs Paul Veres), was one of Hungary's first feminists and a pioneer of women's education at the end of the 19th century. It is perhaps ironic that she has gone down to posterity under her husband's name, as her real name, Hermina Beniczky, is almost entirely forgotten.

Turn right into Szivárvány köz, a tiny alley that leads into Cukor utca. You will come out just opposite the side of the school you saw earlier. Turn left, and then right at the corner, where you will emerge with the **Centrál Kávéház** on your right, with the yellow and red harlequinade cupola of the University Library rising ahead of you to the left. The Centrál is one of the landmark coffee houses in Budapest's great tradition (*see p. 96*), famous for being the place where Frigyes Karinthy, one of the greatest inter-war Hungarian humorists, heard trains steaming through his head one

March evening in 1935. '*The trains started on time, according to schedule, at exactly 7.10. I clutched my head in wonder. What's going on? There was a definite rumbling, a forceful, slow screech, like when a locomotive's wheels slowly start off, and then accelerate into a noisy clatter... The train went past us, and ran on....*' At first he thought he was going mad, but he turned out to have a brain tumour, which was later successfully removed in Stockholm by a famous Swedish surgeon. His account of this experience, *Journey Round My Skull*, deserves to be a 20th-century classic.

Finish the walk by sitting down in this airy café for a good black coffee, served on a tin tray with a little glass of water in the old-fashioned way.

Street scene in inner Pest.

WALK THREE

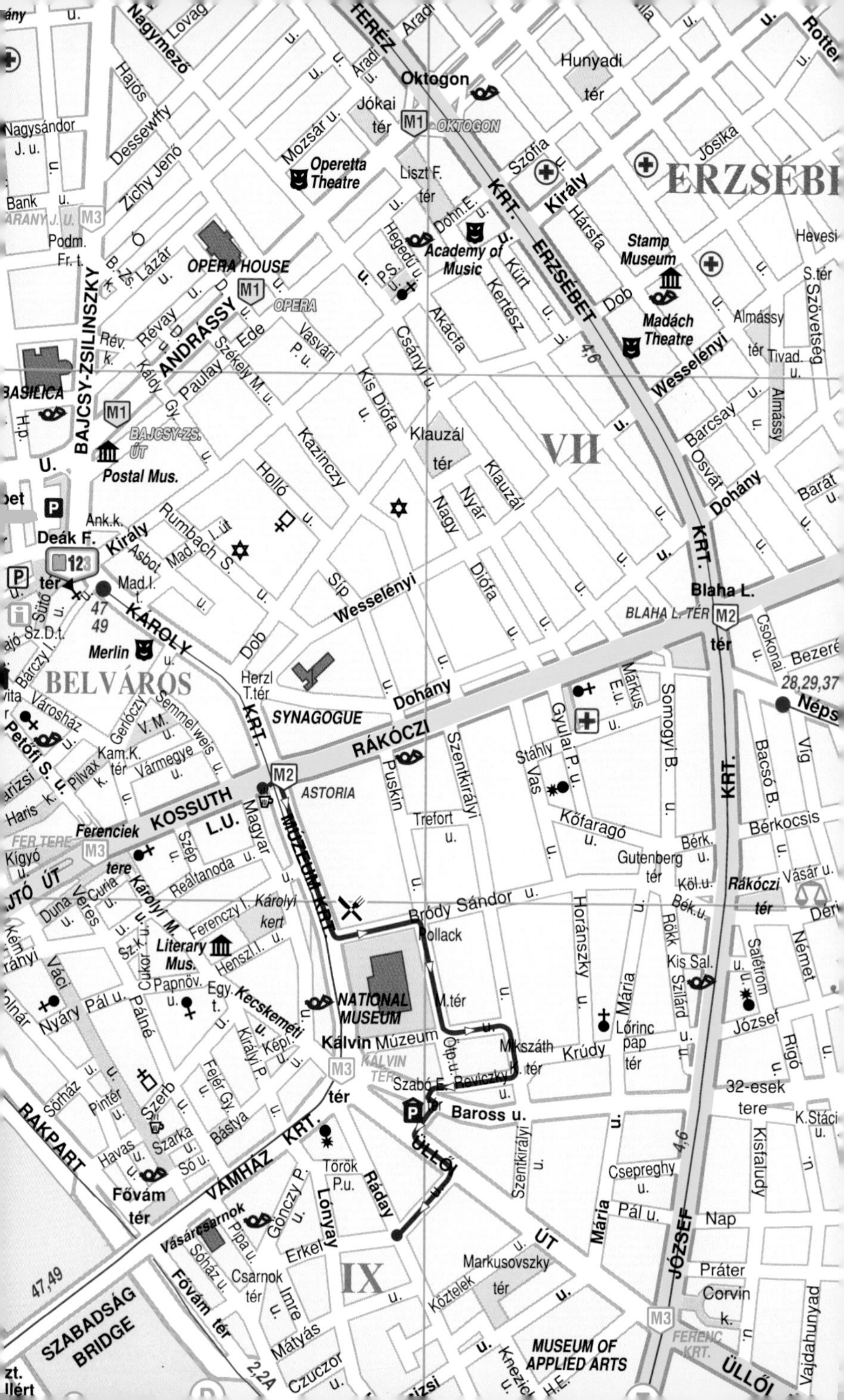

ERZSÉBET
VII
IX
BELVÁROS
Oktogon
OKTOGON
Jókai tér
Hunyadi tér
Operetta Theatre
Liszt F. tér
Academy of Music
OPERA HOUSE
OPERA
BASILICA
BAJCSY-ZS. ÚT
Postal Mus.
Stamp Museum
Madách Theatre
Klauzál tér
Deák F. tér
Merlin
Herzl T.tér
SYNAGOGUE
Blaha L. tér
BLAHA L. TÉR
ASTORIA
Ferenciek tere
FER. TERE
Literary Mus.
NATIONAL MUSEUM
Kálvin tér
KÁLVIN TÉR
Mikszáth K. tér
Gutenberg tér
Rákóczi tér
Lőrinc pap tér
32-esek tere
Fővám tér
Vásárcsarnok
SZABADSÁG BRIDGE
Markusovszky tér
MUSEUM OF APPLIED ARTS
FERENC KRT.
TERÉZ KRT.
ERZSÉBET KRT.
JÓZSEF KRT.
KÁROLY KRT.
MÚZEUM KRT.
VÁMHÁZ KRT.
ANDRÁSSY
BAJCSY-ZSILINSZKY U.
RÁKÓCZI
KOSSUTH L.U.
ÜLLŐI ÚT
RAKPART
Király
Wesselényi
Dohány
Dob
Baross u.
Bródy Sándor u.
Kecskeméti u.
Váci
Ráday
Lónyay
Mária
Szentkirályi

OLD PEST: AROUND THE NATIONAL MUSEUM

The area around the National Museum, once grazing land outside the city walls, is home to some former noble palaces. The roll-call of famous names associated with this district includes a romantic poet, an underground Communist activist later to lead the country, and a banker who encased his lovers in precious metal.

The walk begins in the **coffee house of the Astoria Hotel** (1912-1914), a fine chandeliered room with card tables and marble pillars and dainty Biedermeier chairs, where you can sit for hours over a single coffee and the waiters will never dream of pestering you. From here take the door out past the reception desk and into Kossuth Lajos utca. Once outside, look up to your left, behind the first floor balcony railings, to see a plaque

Old lithograph of the National Museum, with the Károlyi town palace visible behind it.

HUNGARIAN NATIONAL MUSEUM

commemorating the fact that Sándor Petőfi, Hungary's greatest romantic poet, once lodged in a building on this site. The printing press that helped broadcast his impassioned cries for an end to Austrian oppression had its offices in a building on this same street, and the National Museum, where Petőfi declaimed his patriotic verses and roused the rabble to revolution in 1848, is just around the corner. The Astoria has given its name to the busy traffic junction on which it stands. In the middle ages, one of three city gates stood here, leading out of walled Pest and onto the main cart road that led north-east to the town of Hatvan. Turn right, dodging past the steps into the underpass, and go round the corner into **Múzeum körút**. This busy thoroughfare, part of Pest's inner ring road (*körút*), follows the line of the 15th-century city walls. One of the best buildings is **No. 7**, designed for the Unger family in 1852, a classic example of the Rundbogenstil (so named for its rounded arches and window apertures) popular at the time. Grimy but grand, with box balconies borne by griffins and decorated with a motif of eight-pointed stars, it is an early work by the great architect Miklós Ybl (*see p.* 77), and the entranceway (open during working hours) still preserves the wooden cobbles which at one time were a feature of all these buildings (wood soaks up the noise of horses' hoofs and carriage wheels better than stone). The courtyard takes you right through to the parallel street, Magyar utca, named after the same family who commissioned this house. The Magyar family's original name was Unger. They were German blacksmiths who migrated to Hungary in the 17th century, and went on to become staunchly patriotic members of the Hungarian established order. One of them served in the imperial Austrian army. Another, an admirer of Petőfi the poet, became a champion of the cause of Hungarian independence. It was he who Hungarianised the family name from Unger to Magyar.

Continue down the körút, pausing to glance to your right down Ferenczy István utca. A little way in, on the right hand side, you will see a preserved section of old city wall. Further up the körút, in the **courtyard of No. 21**, a fine, crenellated section is preserved. If the door is locked, there is a peephole through which you can get a glimpse of it. Though Pest's city walls were not rebuilt when the town was recaptured from the Turks in the 17th century, their circumscribing aura somehow remained. Only Catholics were allowed to build places of worship within the old city precinct; Protestants and Jews were relegated to the outlying areas. So it was that the area stretching back from the other side of the street from here became the **Jewish quarter of Budapest**. The white building across the road on the corner, with the restaurant on its ground floor, once housed the offices of the Holy Cross Society, a Catholic organisation that ran religious courses for Jews wishing to convert to Christianity. During the earlier years of the Second World War, Jews who converted were awarded government protection. In the last two years of the war, however, the rules changed. Adolf Eichmann arrived in Budapest in 1944 to carry out his Final Solution, and the Jewish quarter was barricaded with a makeshift wooden fence and turned into a ghetto.

On the opposite corner from the restaurant stands the imposing bulk of the **Hungarian National Museum** (*see p. 114*). It was outside the Museum building that the anti-Habsburg revolutionaries gathered on March 15th, 1848, and the poet Petőfi recited his battle-cry: '*Hungarians arise, the homeland calls! Now is the hour, now or never! Shall we be*

Crenellated section of Pest's mediaeval city wall.

slaves or shall we be free?' Stirred to action by such rhetoric, the people set off to free the imprisoned Mihály Táncsics from the city gaol (*see p. 154*). Táncsics, a weaver by trade, became a wanted man as early as 1842 for his radical pamphlets championing the freedom of the Press, the cause of the people, and Utopian ideals in general. With a price on his head, he fled Hungary, but the Habsburg guard caught up with him in Croatia and took him back to Budapest, where he was summarily flung into prison. Freed by the mob in 1848, he spent the next ten years of his life hiding, as legend has it, under the floorboards of his wife's house, behind a trapdoor concealed by a heavy painted trunk. Despite numerous searches and the tricky business of his wife having to explain away the mysterious birth of a daughter, he was never found, and lived to a ripe old age. Now every year, on March 15th, Hungarian National Day is celebrated on the steps of the museum with speeches and patriotic songs.

Everyone from aristocrats to humble tradesmen inhabited this part of town. The wealthy chimney sweep who built himself a house at Bródy Sándor utca 15 made no secret of how he had made his fortune.

Cross the road towards the museum and go straight ahead into **Bródy Sándor utca**. Before the mid-19th century this area was little more than a marshy stretch of grazing fields, farms and brick factories. A disastrous flood in 1838 swept most of the houses and fields away, and instead of replacing what had gone before, the municipality sold the land to developers, to be used as building plots to cater for the ever-growing population. Wealthy patrician families moved down from the cramped, mediaeval streets of Castle Hill to the wider, purpose-built boulevards of Pest. Miklós Ybl was one of the architects to profit from this. He bought much of the land around the Museum, carved it up into separate lots, and gave building commissions to himself and his friends. One such friend was Antal Weber, who built the **house at No. 4** on your left (1876), with its Renaissance top storey and Classical Corinthian columns. The façade is built of real stone; behind that it is brick overlaid with stuccoed plaster, as is the case with most 19th-century Pest architecture. Weber was one of the most sought-after architects of his day and the brother-in-law of the noted artist Károly Lotz (*see p. 105*), who painted the fresco in the loggia: Eros in a chariot with two cupids, representing the triumph of Love. No. 8, the neo-Renaissance building now housing the **Italian Cultural Institute**, with café and bookshop in the entranceway, is by Miklós Ybl. If you look up to the roofline, you will see the crown of St Stephen, Hungary's symbol of temporal authority. This is because the building originally housed the Hungarian House of Representatives, which had come into being after the 1867 Compromise Agreement with Austria. The Hungarian Parliament's lower house sat here, before the vast, bi-cameral parliament on the Danube bank was completed (*see p. 44*). It is said that the local carpenters were put under such pressure to finish the fittings on time that they went on strike in protest. No hearts melted; the problem was simply solved by importing carpenters from Austria.

There are plenty of fine façades in this street. Note the owl and the rooster symbolising night and day on the balcony of No. 12. Bródy Sándor utca is also famous for being the street where the young Communist activist János Kádár lived under an assumed name (the Communist Party was illegal at the time), as a lodger with Mr and Mrs Ottó Róna. There was a romantic, not political, consequence: Mrs Róna left her husband to marry Kádár some years later.

Turn right now into **Pollack Mihály tér**. This square was once filled with the town palaces of the nobility. On its Bródy Sándor utca corner is the former Festetics Palace, now the Gyula Andrássy German-language University. Next door a building belonging to Magyar Rádió, all of glass, stands behind a magnificent pair of iron gates bearing the proud crest of the Esterházys. To the right of this is the surviving part of the former Esterházy mansion, which between 1946 and 1949 was used as the Presidential Palace of the Peoples' Republic. Now it is used by the Radio, who also occupy the modern building next on the right. It was here that shooting first began in

1956 (*see p. 24*), after a storm of protesters mobbed the building, calling for the freedom of the media. At the further end of the square is the former Károlyi family town house, with its grand carriage sweep. It was designed by Miklós Ybl to look like a French country château. Gutted by fire in 1945, it has an unloved air.

On reaching Múzeum utca, turn left. You are now in the heart of the area that came to be known as the **'magnates' quarter'**. Múzeum utca was home to some of the grandest of the grand, including plenty who were not born to riches but earned them, and learned to live in a high style. One such man was the fabulously rich banker Jenő Freystätdler, who purchased an aristocratic title as well as obtaining permission from the Shah of Persia (a personal friend) to style himself Pasha. His house on Múzeum utca contained statues of all his former lovers, coated in either gold, silver or bronze, depending on how much he valued their memory. Walk along Múzeum utca now until you reach No. 17. This was the **town residence of Count István Károlyi**, uncle of Mihály Károlyi, architect of the National Council (*see p. 166*) and nicknamed the 'Red Count' for his left-leaning politics. István Károlyi the uncle was, by all reports, a famous bon viveur. A keen sportsman, he used to hold grand shooting parties at his country estate and provide peasant girls from the neighbouring village to warm his guests' beds (one of these guests was Edward, Prince of Wales, later Edward VII of England). After the Second World War his town palace - this house - was confiscated. '*The revolutionary workers' and peasants' government*,' proclaims a plaque in the entranceway, '*wanting to promote technical development, converted this house into a modern library*'. It still functions as a library today, which means that on weekdays the doors are open and it is possible to peer inside. Miraculously the front hallway has hardly been altered, and the magnificent spiral staircase and wooden panelling survive. Dating from 1884, they are the work of a Transylvanian master carver, of whom there were several in the area.

Turn right at the end of Múzeum utca, and continue walking until you see the gleaming white **statue of Kálmán Mikszáth** (author of *St Peter's Umbrella*, a novel particularly admired by F.D. Roosevelt). Behind Mikszáth is a ruddy brick building and a buff brown one, with resonances of Morocco, perhaps, or is it Venice? This is Budapest eclecticism at its best.

With the statue on your left, turn right into Reviczky utca, and stop outside **No. 6**. This is the other side of the Károlyi Palace. On the top floor you can see how the revolutionary workers' and peasants' government modernised the facility, though recent paintwork harmonises it with the lower floors somewhat. In 1944 this building, now a students' information centre, was one of the houses used by Raoul Wallenberg (*see p. 68*), at a stage when he was constantly on the move, never staying in the same house two nights running, for fear of detection. A lot of the old aristocratic mansions in this area were turned into safe houses owned by the embassies of neutral countries, sheltering Jews and giving them diplomatic immunity.

Further down the street, the bright orange building housing a music library was originally the town house of the Pálffy family, and is another French château-style creation by Ybl. Opposite it is the entrance to the **Szabó Ervin Library**, housed in a neo-Rococo patrician mansion (1887), formerly the town residence of the Wenckheim family. Seeing the way the political tide was turning, the Wenckheims sold their house in the mid-1920s for a considerable sum - which they then imprudently left inside Hungary, so after the Second

A portly Kálmán Mikszáth dominates the square that bears his name.

The 'Justice for Hungary' fountain, in memory of the British newspaper baron who supported Hungary's irredentist claims to territory lost after World War I.

World War they lost it anyway. The library that their mansion now houses holds a collection on Budapest history and sociology, and it takes its name from fervent Workers' Movement adherent Ervin Szabó, promulgator of the teachings of Marx and Engels. Today the central courtyard contains a lively café. Either stop here, install yourself in a library chair on the 2nd or 3rd floor, where there are English newspapers and magazines, or visit the 4th floor to see what is preserved of the palace's former grandeur. When you leave, walk round the building's main façade, past the **'Justice for Hungary' fountain**. It commemorates British press baron Viscount Rothermere, who in the thirties used his newspapers to launch the 'Justice for Hungary' campaign, aimed at righting the wrongs of Trianon, the peace treaty which carved up Hungary after the First World War. Cross diagonally to the left now, into Erkel utca, at the end of which you will come into **Ráday utca**. This street has been semi-pedestrianised, and is a wonderful, muddlesome mixture of old and new, with plenty of bakeries, cafés and restaurants all along its length.

A pair of caryatids heaves aloft the portal on an Andrássy út mansion.

WALK FOUR

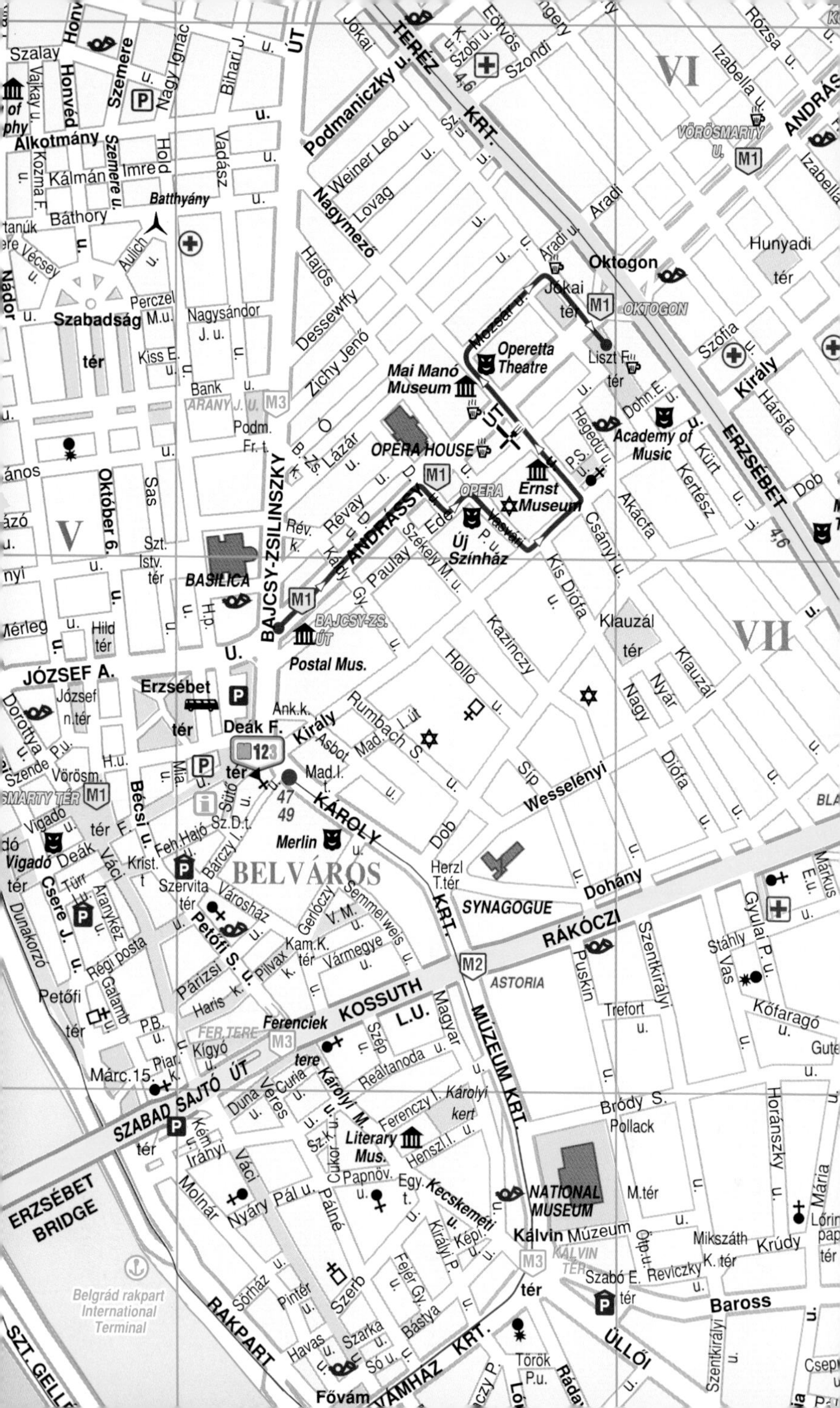

VI
VII
V
BELVÁROS
Oktogon
Operetta Theatre
Mai Manó Museum
OPERA HOUSE
Ernst Museum
Academy of Music
Új Színház
BASILICA
Postal Mus.
Erzsébet tér
Deák F. tér
Merlin
Vigadó
SYNAGOGUE
Literary Mus.
NATIONAL MUSEUM
ERZSÉBET BRIDGE
Belgrád rakpart International Terminal
Szabadság tér
Liszt F. tér
Klauzál tér
Hunyadi tér
ANDRÁSSY ÚT
BAJCSY-ZSILINSZKY ÚT
TERÉZ KRT.
ERZSÉBET KRT.
KÁROLY KRT.
MÚZEUM KRT.
RÁKÓCZI ÚT
KOSSUTH L. U.
SZABAD SAJTÓ ÚT
ÜLLŐI ÚT
Kálvin tér
Ferenciek tere
Astoria

ANDRÁSSY ÚT

This route goes up Budapest's most magnificent boulevard, a straight avenue that leads all the way from the city centre to Heroes' Square (Hősök tere). Visit a preserved 19th-century apartment, a splendid coffee house, and see the exuberant architecture of Budapest's theatre district.

'On afternoons of a fine day we may meet in Andrássy Street all the beauty and elegance in the city: it is a fashionable lounging place for the swells of the town and their admirers.' So wrote Joseph Kahn in his 1891 guide to Budapest. And if Andrássy deserved a separate mention then, it definitely still deserves one today as one of the finest streets of its period in Europe. It is named after Count Gyula Andrássy, who was one of the few anti-Habsburg Hungarians to survive the 1848 revolution (*see pp. 18-19*) and still make a career for himself. He went on to become Prime Minister after the Compromise with Vienna in

Andrássy út at the end of the 19th century.

1867 and to preside over the country's much mourned Golden Age. Rumour has it that he had an affair with the eccentric, melancholy Empress Elisabeth, though that is most likely an apocryphal tale.

This walk begins at the very **top of Andrássy út**, where busy Bajcsy Zsilinszky út roars past and the green grass of Erzsébet tér beyond provide peace and a place to sit down amid the hurly burly city. Andrássy út follows no natural contours. It is a dead straight, man-made boulevard, a perfect example of the deliberate planning that went into late 19th-century Pest. Scores of one-storey houses were demolished to make way for it, and though at first the authorities grumbled, they were argued down and work began in 1872. The result is Budapest at its showiest and most theatrical. The buildings may look massive and robust - look across the road at the bronze Hermes lording it over an eclectic confection of Ionic and Corinthian columns - but in fact the whole street went up in record time, as did most of 19th-century Pest, and all the ashlar and rustication is really plaster masquerading as stone. Plaster is an ideal vehicle for ornament, though, and the Hungarian love of ornament is manifest everywhere, in elaborate stucco work, carved

Detail from a stained glass door panel in an Andrássy út entryway.

wooden doors, stained glass windows and wrought iron gates, all of which was irresistible to the nobles and wealthy bankers and brokers who commissioned mansions here. Unfortunately, very few of the buildings are open to the public, and many of them have been irrevocably altered as old apartment blocks have been transformed into banks and offices. One building you can go inside, however, is **No. 3**, built in 1885 for the mineral water millionaire Andreas Saxlehner. His sumptuous apartment on the piano nobile is well preserved, and is now home to the Postal Museum (*see p. 118*). If you haven't got time to go up and see it, punch the number 10 into the bell console and you will be let into the entranceway, which is splendidly decorated with frescoes by Károly Lotz (*see p. 105*), all with a mineral water theme.

At **No. 9**, two Graeco-Renaissance youths heave aloft the portals of what is now ING Bank. Built originally in 1883 for the Brüll family, the building was converted into modern office space by Dutch architect Erik Van Egeraat in 1994. By covering over the courtyard and placing a glass capsule conference room on the roof, Egeraat managed to graft 21st century forms onto a conservative Historicist mansion. On weekdays you can go in and admire this spectacular transformation. A little further on, at No. 17, you pass the colourful premises of fashionable hairdresser Zsidró. Fixed to the walls of Nos. 19 and 21 are plaques commemorating great Hungarian opera singers who once lived here. And if you look ahead to your left, you will see the **Opera House** itself (*see p. 55*), built by Miklós Ybl, the most sought-after architect of his generation. Indeed all of Andrássy was something of a showcase for architects during the late 19th century, and every house has a bronze tablet sunk into the pavement in front of it telling you who built it and when. Of all the grand mansions of Andrássy út, the Opera House is unquestionably the grandest, decorative without being gaudy, and refined without being insubstantial. The vaguely erotic sphinxes at the entrances give the building an Eastern touch - something which the great architect of the next generation, Ödön Lechner (*see p. 78*), was to use much more explicitly. Lechner is responsible for the **former Ballet Institute** (1886), which stands immediately opposite the Opera, and heralds the onset of an entirely different architectural approach. Here the emphasis is not on Italian Baroque or Renaissance forms, but rather on the mystical East, the purported

The imposing eclectic Opera House, a fusion of neo-Renaissance and neo-Baroque, the great magnum opus of 19th-century architect Miklós Ybl.

ancient homeland of the Magyars. The ballet dancers have all been moved out of the building now, and the sounds of the piano and shouts of '*plié, plié, entrechat!*' no longer drift through the windows, as the whole pile is empty, and plans for a luxury hotel seem to have evaporated. A century ago there was a famous café here, the Reuter, a haunt of stout, bowler-hatted gents with standing credit and a roving eye, who would sit under its portals sucking cigars and libidinously eyeing the chorus as they came spilling out of the Opera House. The only present survival of Andrássy's great age of the coffee house is the **Művész** at No. 29 (*see p. 98*), a little further up on the same side of the street. Though tourist popularity has turned it into something of a museum piece, it still retains enough atmosphere to allow you to imagine how it must once have been. In the summer you can sit out on the pavement, with the Opera House before you, and - almost - whirl yourself back to the 1890s. If you do decide to stop here, retrace your steps afterwards, back past the Ballet School, until you reach Dalszínház utca, where you will get a view of the **Újszínház** (New Theatre) at the end of the street. Built by Béla Lajta (*see p. 82*), the leading architectural light of the 1910s, this hieratic, geometric building was initially a nightclub, but is now a modern theatre venue.

When you reach the theatre, turn left into Paulay Ede utca and then right into Vasváry Pál utca. This street is named after a heroic student leader who died in the revolution against the Habsburgs in 1849 (*see pp. 18-19*) at the tender age of 23. People still commemorate him by placing wreaths on the tablet here. At No. 5 you will find the **Pest Lubavitch Yeshiva** (Talmudic college), started by American emigré Hungarians on the site of a former Talmudic centre. Tucked discreetly away in the courtyard is a century-old synagogue, one of many such semi-hidden Jewish places of worship to be found all over the city. It regularly draws a congregation of 150. Though the Lubavitch are a hasidic sect and observe strict laws, this synagogue and the yeshiva are open to the public, and as long as you do not disturb them on Saturday or Friday evening, you can go in and look round. If the door is locked, try upstairs, where the Rabbinical students pore over their books. English is the lingua franca here, so you are bound to find somebody you can communicate with.

At the end of Vasvári Pál you come to **Király utca**. Though Andrássy may have all the pomp and circumstance, it is Király where deals are done. Originally the main thoroughfare of Pest, it was reviled by many of the 19th century's opinion-formers for being smelly, noisy and traffic-ridden. 'Vile and narrow', pronounced the radical politician Lajos Kossuth, who heaved a sigh of relief when it was replaced by the elegant Andrássy. But somehow Király utca has retained its buzz. Turn left into it and you will see that it is a mix of new design boutiques and old shabby shops, some still bearing the old signs. This is also the street where you can eat anything from Syrian to Viennese, where old traditional early 19th-century Pest houses, still with their flowering courtyards, snuggle next to grand neo-Gothic structures. No. 47 a little way up on the right, the **Pekáry ház**, is one such building: a magnificent crenellated concoction in burnt umber. Built in 1847, it was one of the first buildings in the city to use neo-Gothic elements, and caused a small sensation when it was unveiled. It was once home to one of the country's most popular writers, Gyula Krúdy, who wrote about the influx of people from all over the

Habsburg empire who came to Budapest to seek their fortunes.

On the other side of the street you can see the **Terézváros parish church**, built in 1801-11. It has recently been restored to Maria Theresa yellow, the colour Maria Theresa decreed all public buildings throughout her empire should be painted. The spire was designed by Miklós Ybl (*see p. 77*). Beside it is a little pedestrian walkway with benches, part of the city's programme to create open spaces for its citizens. If you choose to rest here you will probably hear scales or broken chords wafting through the windows of the building next door, the Bartók Béla Music Secondary School, which also has practise rooms for students at the Liszt Music Academy.

Turn left now into **Nagymező utca**. This street, known as the Broadway of Budapest, is home to several galleries, cafés and theatres. This particular section was an artists' quarter at the end of the 19th century, and there are a number of plaques commemorating the artists and their achievements. In No. 8 lived painter Adolf Fényes, one of the principal exponents of the Hungarian folk genre - his colourful still lifes and peasant scenes were a breath of fresh air after the heavy academic history painting that characterised much Hungarian art throughout the 19th century. Next door lies the **Tivoli Theatre and Ernst Museum**, designed by Gyula Fodor in 1911. Ferenc Flau's Art Deco theatre lobby has been beautifully restored, and it is worth wandering in even if you don't wish to catch a performance. The Ernst Museum next door was built to house Lajos Ernst's art collection. Wanting to create a *gesamtkunst* showcase for modern Hungarian art, Ernst enlisted Lechner to design the balustrade and the benches in the lobby, and József Rippl Rónai (*see p. 109*) to design the stained glass window on the stairs. Outside, note the replica cameos of King Mátyás Corvinus and his wife Beatrice on either side of the main entrance.

You can stop for a coffee or light lunch at the **Két Szerecsen**, just up past the Ernst Museum on the corner of Paulay Ede utca. Otherwise cross over Andrássy út, and stay on Nagymező, where at No. 20 on your left you will find the **Mai Manó House of Hungarian Photography**. This magnificent building was once the Arizona nightclub, patronised by swells and nobles from all over Europe, including Britain's King Edward VIII. Go into the entranceway and you will see a ceiling fresco of chubby cupids shooting love darts at each other, with a handful of red roses added in for good measure. The club was famous in the twenties and thirties for its lavish floor shows . In *Between the Woods and the Water* Patrick Leigh Fermor describes it: '*(We) whirled downhill and across the Chain Bridge to plunge into the scintillating cave of the most glamorous night-club I have ever seen. Did the floor of the Arizona really revolve? It certainly seemed to. Snowy steeds were careering round it at one moment, feathers tossing: someone said he had seen camels there, even elephants...*'. But its glory was doomed to die. Its Jewish owner and his wife, 'Miss Arizona', were deported by the Nazis and the club was closed by order of the Gestapo. Today it functions as Hungary's biggest photography museum, with exhibitions ranging from the great old Hungarian masters (*see p. 190*) to contemporary photographers. Next to the Mai Manó is the plushly refurbished Thalia Theatre and opposite, at No 17, the blushing pink, splendidly neo-Rococo **Operetta Theatre**, built in 1898. Operetta is something the Hungarians practically invented, and a night at the *Queen of the Csárdás* is a frothy affair of lost plots, mistaken identities and masses of ruched lace. If that is not enough

Két Szerecsen, a cosy little bar-restaurant just off Andrássy út.

high farce and melodrama, try a revue at the Moulin Rouge next door. Between the wars Budapest vied with Berlin for cabarets. The famous Barrison Sisters - a motley crew of cheeky soubrettes who passed themselves off as English, danced the can-can in flesh-coloured bodystockings and performed striptease routines on horseback - had all the girls in Budapest imitating their hairdos and the men telling fibs to their wives, plus one young nobleman blowing his brains out for love. The cabaret tradition is trying to revive itself, though it has been long buried - you only have to glance across the road to the huge blue and neon-bulb sign on the Socialist Realist No. 28, which announces the **'18th Lawyers' Work Collective'** to see how Stalinist design would have no truck with all that naughty nineties nonsense.

Sugar-icing pink and gilded female beauty: the Operetta Theatre on Nagymező utca in Budapest's theatre district.

Turn right down Mozsár utca now and walk past the bright pink Kolibri Theatre at the end into **Jókai tér**. Facing you as you enter is the Vörös Oroszlán (Red Lion) teahouse, a relaxing little place that makes a nice change from endless cups of strong coffee. Glance down Jókai utca to your left and you will see the Buda Hills rising in the distance, lending a sense of space to the densely packed streets. At the other end of the square you come back into Andrássy út. The square is named after the prolific novelist Mór Jókai (1825-1904), the Victor Hugo of Hungary, who scandalised the country by marrying a young showgirl at the age of 74 - although the statue of him sitting solemnly in an armchair gives no hint of this sprightliness (in fact, he seems to be staring rather disapprovingly into the underwear shop on the right-hand corner).

Cross over into **Liszt Ferenc tér** now, a pedestrian square given over to pavement cafés (*see box on p. 237*). On the right hand corner is the **Írók Boltja** (Writers' Bookshop), which has a selection of foreign-language books and Hungarian works in translation. Here you can help yourself to tea from the samovar and browse the shop, or pass on to one of the many bars or restaurants on the square itself.

Hungarian Photographers

During the first half of the 20th century, Hungary produced some of the world's finest photographers. They include:

André Kertész (1894-1985) - As a young man Kertész took part in and photographed World War I. He was invalided out and sent to a sanatorium where there was an exercise pool, and it was then that he began work on his great series of swimmers. He was primarily interested in the way the water distorted the body, and later, in his studio in Paris, where he settled until World War II, he even set up a distorting mirror, and photographed reflections of his models. Throughout his long life he continued to be fascinated by the idea that there is a dissonance in even the most harmonious subjects.

László Moholy-Nagy (1895-1946) - One of the great avant-garde artists of his day, Moholy-Nagy invented the photogram, an image produced by placing objects on light-sensitive paper and exposing them to various degrees of light. He left Hungary when the Soviet-style commune was declared in 1919, and went to work in Berlin, becoming a colleague of Walter Gropius. Fleeing Hitler's Germany, he eventually settled in Chicago, where he set up the New Bauhaus.

Georges Brassaï (1899-1984) - Famed for his fabulous 1930s *Paris by Night* series, Brassaï, a native of Brasov in Transylvania, also took photographs of Picasso, Matisse and the beau monde of his time. His candid shots of street life and spontaneous roving photos - for example his image of two lovers in a swingboat - influenced generations of young photographers.

Lucien Hervé (1910 -) - Hailed as a photographer with the soul of an architect by Le Corbusier, for whom he served as official photographer, Hervé is most famous for his beautifully-realised shots of buildings and architectural details. These range from mediaeval cathedrals to stark, half-constructed modern designs. Like Kertész, he left Hungary for Paris in the 1920s, and met and photographed many of the great artists and thinkers who flocked there in the early 20th century.

Robert Capa (1913-1954) - One of the founders of modern documentary photography, Capa spent the thirties roaming Europe, and earned his name for his depictions of the Spanish Civil War. He then went on to work as a US Army photographer during World War II, taking some extraordinary pictures of the liberation of Paris. In 1947 he set up the Magnum Photographic Agency with Henri Cartier-Bresson, only to be killed on assignment to Vietnam in 1954, when he accidentally stepped on a land mine.

The Mai Manó House of Hungarian Photography, at Nagymező utca 20 (map p. 263, B4), has collections of these photographers' works. Open Mon-Fri 2pm-7pm; Sat-Sun 11am-7pm.

Opposite: Exterior view of the grand Dohány utca synagogue.

WALK FIVE

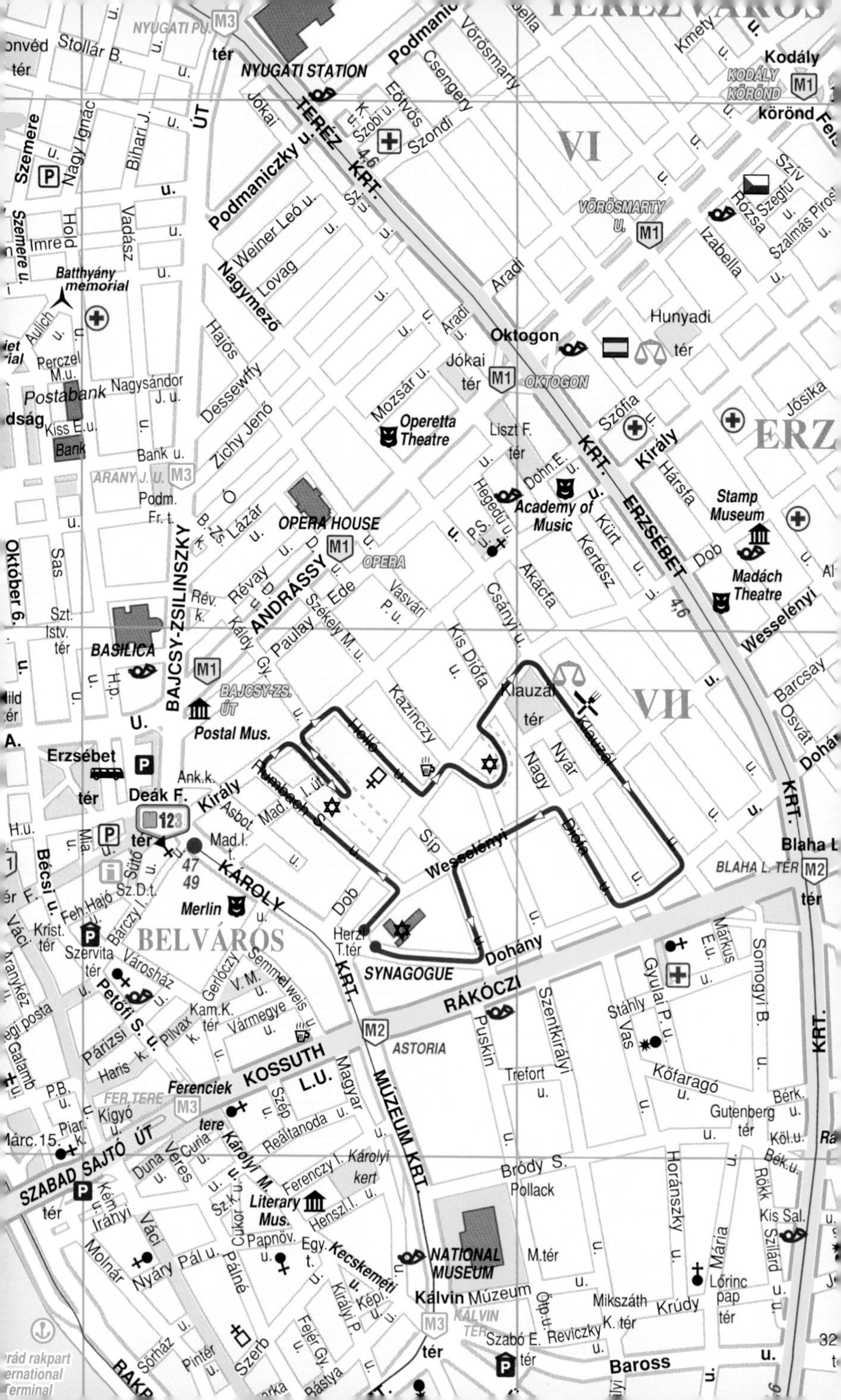

NYUGATI STATION
NYUGATI PU.
M3
tér
Stollár B.
Szemere
Nagy Ignác
Bihari J.
ÚT
Jókai
TERÉZ KRT.
Podmaniczky u.
Podmaniczky
Vörösmarty
Csengery
Eötvös
Szobi u.
Szondi
Kmety
Kodály
KODÁLY KÖRÖND
M1
körönd
VI
Szív
Szegfű
Rózsa
Izabella
Szalmás Piroska
VÖRÖSMARTY U.
Hold
Imre
Vadász
Weiner Leó u.
Lovag
Nagymező
Batthyány memorial
Aulich
Perczel M.u.
Postabank
Nagysándor J. u.
Kiss E.u.
Bank
Bank u.
ARANY J. U.
Hajós
Dessewffy
Zichy Jenő
Mozsár u.
Aradi
Oktogon
OKTOGON
Jókai tér
Hunyadi tér
Operetta Theatre
Liszt F. tér
Szófia
Király
Jósika
ERZ
Dohn.E.
Academy of Music
Hegedű u.
Podm. Fr. t.
Lázár
OPERA HOUSE
OPERA
ANDRÁSSY
Révay
Székely M. u.
Ede
Vasvári P. u.
Kürt
Kertész
Akácfa
Csányi
ERZSÉBET KRT.
Hársfa
Stamp Museum
Dob
Madách Theatre
Wesselényi
Október 6.
Sas
Szt. Istv. tér
BASILICA
BAJCSY-ZSILINSZKY
BAJCSY-ZS. ÚT
Paulay
Kazinczy
Kis Diófa
Klauzál tér
Klauzál
VII
Barcsay
Osvát
Dohány
Postal Mus.
Erzsébet tér
Deák F. tér
Király
Asbót
Rumbach S.
Holló
Nagy
Nyár
Síp
Wesselényi
Diófa
KRT.
Blaha L.
BLAHA L. TÉR
M2
Bécsi u.
Váci
Mad.I. t.
KÁROLY
47 49
Merlin
Sütő
Sz.D.t.
Feh.Hajó
Barczy I.
BELVÁROS
Herzl T.tér
SYNAGOGUE
Dohány
RÁKÓCZI
Márkus E.u.
Somogyi B.
Szervita tér
Városház
Petőfi S. u.
Semmelweis
Gerlóczy
V. M.
Kam.K. tér
Vármegye
Pilvax k.
Párizsi
Haris k.
KOSSUTH L.U.
M2
ASTORIA
Puskin
Szentkirályi
Stáhly
Gyulai P. u.
Vas
Kőfaragó u.
Trefort u.
Gutenberg tér
FER. TERE
Ferenciek tere
Kígyó
Márc.15.
SZABAD SAJTÓ ÚT
Duna
Veres
Curia
Károlyi M.
Reáltanoda
Szép
Magyar
MÚZEUM KRT.
Ferenczy I.
Károlyi kert
Literary Mus.
Henszl.I.
Bródy S.
Pollack M.tér
Horánszky u.
Mária
Rökk Szilárd
Kis Sal.
Kecskeméti u.
Képl.
Irányi
Molnár
Nyáry Pál u.
Cukor
Pálné
Papnöv.
Egy. t.
NATIONAL MUSEUM
Kálvin Múzeum
KÁLVIN TÉR
Ötp.u.
Mikszáth K. tér
Krúdy
Lőrinc pap tér
Szabó E.
Reviczky
Baross
Sörház
Pintér
Szerb
Fejér Gy.
Bástya
Királyi P.
Irányi

THE JEWISH QUARTER

This route takes you into the heart of the Jewish quarter, with three splendid synagogues, a crumbling series of interlocking courtyards and a warren of old-fashioned sidestreets.

This walk starts in front of the **Dohány utca Synagogue**, the largest in Europe, built in 1862 (*see p. 65*). It stands on the outermost fringe of an area of Budapest that has been home to the city's Jewish community since the 18th century. In a house that once stood on the site, Theodore Herzl, founder of the Zionist movement and campaigner for a Jewish homeland in Palestine, was born in 1860. After the 1867 Compromise between Austria and Hungary (*see p. 19*), Jews received full civic status, and during the latter half of the 19th century the Jewish urban middle class played a large part in driving Budapest's burgeoning prosperity. Their tenancy in the main professions seemed secure, and the

Orthodox Jewish children play in the Klauzál tér playground.

most obvious choice for many was assimilation. Herzl thought otherwise. Writing to a friend in the 1890s, he maintained that it was impossible to be both Jewish and Hungarian; that in times of prosperity it might work, but that if times grew hard Jews would instantly be attacked and used as scapegoats - a prophecy not much heeded in those comfortable times.

With the Synagogue on your right, bear up Wesselényi utca, where a small plaque on the Synagogue colonnade announces that *'Here stood one of the ghetto gates knocked down by the Soviet Army on January 18th, 1945'*. Just up from here on the right hand side is a small **garden of remembrance**, which was designated as a burial ground during the two-month existence of the ghetto. One of the most heartbreaking stones reads, *'Évike Bernfeld March 1944 - January 1945. By your birth you saved your mother and grandparents. We will always remember you'*. The wooden barricade that surrounded the ghetto was erected in December 1944 after Eichmann arrived in Budapest to put the 'Final Solution' into practice. The ghetto was bounded to the north and south by Király utca and Dohány utca, and to the west and east by Károly körút and Kertész utca. Although anti-Jewish laws had first been passed in 1920 with the *numerus clausus* (restricting Jewish entry to universities and white-collar jobs), and despite a series of more restrictive decrees that appeared from 1938 onwards, Budapest had a reputation for tolerance, and until the outbreak of the war acted as a refuge for Jews fleeing more oppressive regimes elsewhere in Eastern Europe. Although Hungary was a German ally, Admiral Horthy's government tried to hold out against deportation. In the countryside he failed entirely, but Budapest remained fairly safe for

Gravestones commemorating those who died in the ghetto in 1944-45.

a long time. There are even accounts of Jewish families holidaying by Lake Balaton in the summer of 1944, and of Jewish cabaret acts parodying Horthy and his laws right up until his government fell to the ultra-nationalist Arrow Cross in October. After that the Budapest deportations began.

Turn left down Rumbach Sebestyén utca and continue down the street until you come to Dob utca. Look to your right and you will see, against a plain white wall, a **statue commemorating Carl Lutz** (1895-1975). Honoured by the Jews as one of the 'righteous gentiles', Swiss Consul Lutz had started the war helping German citizens who were stuck in Palestine, a British protectorate where Germans were regarded as enemy aliens. This meant that he was on good terms with the German authorities, and he used this to good effect by helping to organise passages to Palestine for Budapest Jews, as well as setting up seventy-six safe houses around the city. Lutz stayed on even after December 1944, when most diplomats left, trying as best he could to arrange papers and refuge. The Jacob's Ladder monument was put up in 1991, together with a quote from the Talmud, which reads: '*He who saves but one man is as if he had saved the whole world*'.

Retrace your steps to Rumbach utca and carry on along it. You might see men pushing hand carts up and down here, as a few doors down at No. 10 is a paper recycling point. Cartloads of used cardboard are brought in by the city's homeless in exchange for a few hundred forints. Just a little further down on the right hand side is a fabulous **synagogue** (*see p. 143*), completed in 1872 for the city's conservative community to designs by Viennese architect Otto Wagner.

Walk on past the synagogue, crossing over Madách út, and look left to see the **Madách complex**, a monumental mass of offices and apartments with a wide, yawning archway, built in 1937-40 (overall design by Gyula Wälder) as the gateway to a proposed boulevard which would lead right up to the Nagykörút. The project as a whole never left the ground, and the complex remains incongruously massive in these small streets.

Carry on up Rumbach utca until you come into **Király utca** and turn right. In the early 19th century this was the site of a Jewish market, where a brisk trade was done in textiles, leather and wool. Nothing is left of the market now, but the bustling character of the street remains. Go on a short way until you reach No. 13 on

The Gozsdu udvar, a series of interlocking courtyards between Király utca and Dob utca.

the right, and turn into the echoing corridors of the **Gozsdu udvar**. This forlorn series of interconnecting courtyards was built in 1904 by Győző Czigler, and was once home to a multitude of Jewish family businesses. Using German housing projects for his model, Czigler placed seven interlocking courtyards over a long, narrow lot between Király utca and Dob utca, creating what was once a light, airy environment. It was a model project in its day but was left too long to rot, though now at last plans and money have been found to save it. Luxury apartments are planned and the whole will be restored to its former, central role in the life the city. The gates at the far end are locked, but take a look at its musty courtyards. Then walk on to Holló utca and turn right. Here the old and the new rub tentative shoulders, with crumbling condemned buildings, still retaining traces of wrought iron and stucco ornament, giving way to bright new apartment blocks. At No 4 on the right you will find the **Goldziher House**, once home to the university lecturer and Orientalist Ignác Goldziher (1850-1921). The house was also lived in by Chief Rabbi Sámuel Kohn (1841-1920), whose tome *The History of the Jews in Hungary* is still a valuable work of reference. (Unlike Herzl, Kohn was a firm believer in Hungarianisation for Budapest's Jews.) You will see plaques commemorating Kohn and Goldziher on either side of the main entrance. The house itself was built in 1840 and is a typical Neoclassical Pest town house.

You are now right in the heart of former Orthodox Budapest. In its heyday more than twenty synagogues and prayer houses, a hospital, a doctor's surgery, kosher shops and religious schools dotted this area. After World War II very few of them remained.

At the end of Holló utca turn right into Dob utca. At No. 22 you will find the **Fröhlich café**, famed for its *flódni*, a wonderful wadge of walnut, poppy seed and apple. Family-run and very friendly, this kosher coffee shop is closed from Friday afternoons until Monday morning. Carry on up Dob utca until you come to Kazinczy utca on the right. Turn into it and you will see, on the left, the **synagogue of Budapest's Orthodox community** (*see p. 143*). Go into the courtyard and walk right round, coming out through the Dob utca gate and stopping to admire the Dob utca façade with its lovely Hebrew clock. Then turn right into Dob utca and walk on until you come to **Klauzál tér**, a large park and playground where locals go to walk dogs, play cards and relax. Walk up to the top of the square and turn right. Halfway along this top end you will find the old covered market hall, built in 1897 and now occupied by a supermarket. A little further on at No. 9 you will find the **Kádár Étkezde** (*open Tues-Sat*), a non-kosher, Jewish-run lunch place serving huge portions of traditional home cooking, and specialising in boiled meat. A plaque on the wall further up commemorates Attila Gérecz, a poet-martyr of the 1956 revolution. He was originally buried here, and in fact Klauzál tér was a designated burial ground during the ghetto period.

Walk on down Klauzál utca now. At No. 17 an old bomb site now functions as a car park, a fairly

'60 kg of paper, the life of one tree': Dob utca's old paper and cardboard collection point.

common phenomenon in the city. Many people remember returning from the war to find their apartment block no longer standing. When the Jews were deported, people took over their flats, and many of the Jews who survived found themselves displaced. The Nobel Prize-winning novel *Fateless* by Imre Kertész tells of returning from a concentration camp as a young boy to find someone else living in his home.

Turn right into Dohány utca and walk a few metres down, past the pot-bellied window-display of outsize gents' outfitters Mr XL, to No. 44 to see the entrance to the former **Hungária Baths**, with its languidly crumbling bathers over the main door. Built in 1909 by Emil Ágoston, who also designed part of the Astoria Hotel (*see p. 242*), the building was bought by a bank in 1920 and merged with the Hotel Continental next door to become a fashionable spa hotel. The hotel building is now condemned, but the baths have a preservation order on them, although no clear future has been planned. Stories of Nazi atrocities carried out in the building during the war, when the empty pools were used as torture pits, also wreathe the building in grisly mystery.

Walk on down Dohány utca, crossing Nyár utca, and turn right into

Bathing belles who have seen better days, above what was once the entrance to the Hungária Baths.

Nagydiófa utca. Before the Second World War this area was rife with small businesses. A zip-fastener repair shop is the only survival in this street - and although the area still does boast glove-makers, milliners, cobblers and tailors, who all work out of tiny, street-fronted workshops, these old trades are fading fast as Budapest society becomes more affluent and throwaway, and as rents on shop space become more expensive. Turn left down Wesselényi utca. A **shop at No.**

19 proudly claims to be the last small-size ladies' shoemakers in the city. It is in an appropriate place, as the City Cobblers Guild was housed next door, in a wonderful mosaic-clad building built at the turn of the last century. Turn left off Wesselényi utca into Síp utca, where the Hungarian Jewish communities association headquarters are found at No. 12. At the end of the street, on the corner of Dohány utca, stands the glorious but dilapidated **Árkád Bazaar toyshop**, built by József and László Vágó in 1909. The façade is adorned with reliefs of toys and of children playing. Crumbling and empty like so much in this part of town, it is now begging to be done up.

From here turn right into Dohány utca once more and walk up to No. 10-14, a building which functioned for many years as the Budapest University Press printworks. Now newly clad, it has been turned into offices and has lost much of its mighty Monumentalism (it was built in 1913). The loss of the press was a heavy blow, as it was the only printer in Hungary with the technology to print on the fly-weight paper necessary for prayer books and Bibles. Let's hope, however, that the new money coming into the area will have a knock-on effect for the whole district. Just past here you will find yourself back in front of the Dohány utca Synagogue again.

PART IV

OUTSIDE THE CENTRE

Five slightly farther-flung places to visit, each in its own way integral to the spirit of the city.

MARGARET ISLAND

'The Margaret Isle is Budapest's cameo, a gem in itself, made yet more precious by cutting', wrote the 19th-century novelist Mór Jókai. He was exaggerating a bit, though in early summer, when the leaves are still fresh and the horse chestnuts are in flower, it is a pretty place to wander. In winter, when the refreshments kiosks are shut up and only solitary ladies brave the sleet and winds to pray at the shrine of St Margaret, it has a distinctly romantic feel. In high summer its lawns fill up with sunbathers, and the stone embankment where the Danube laps its shore is covered with semi-naked bodies, sprawled like seals: an oglers' paradise.

In the early Middle Ages the island was known as Rabbit Island and was stocked with game for royal hunting parties. Later it boasted churches,

The Bishop of Esztergom celebrates open-air mass in the ruins of the Dominican convent, where St Margaret lived her brief life.

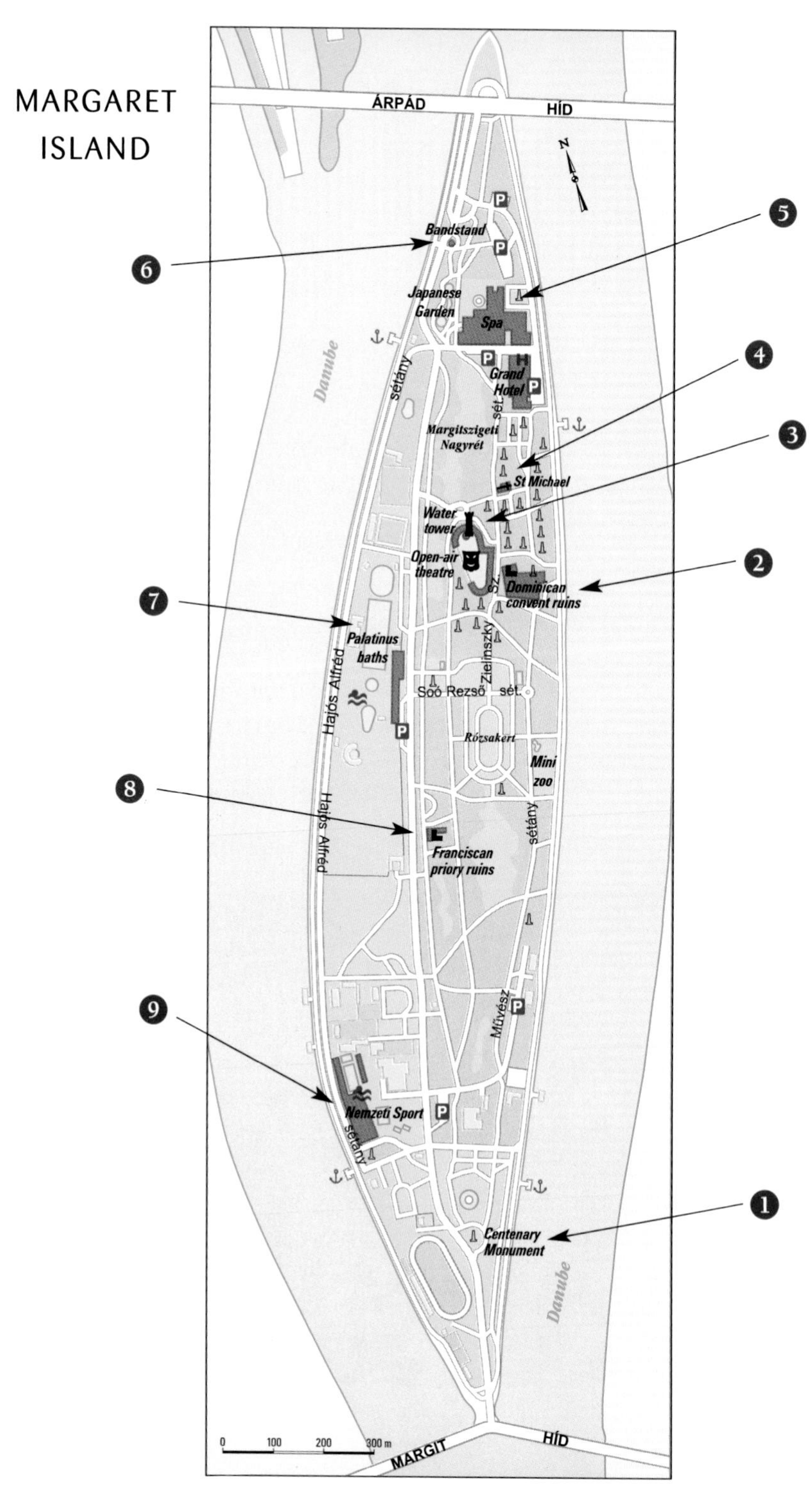
MARGARET
ISLAND
ÁRPÁD
HÍD
N
Bandstand
Japanese
Garden
Spa
Danube
sétány
Grand
Hotel
sét.
Margitszigeti
Nagyrét
St Michael
Water
tower
Open-air
theatre
Sz.
Dominican
convent ruins
Palatinus
baths
Hajós Alfréd
Zielinszky
Soó Rezső
sét.
Rózsakert
Mini
zoo
sétány
Hajós Alfréd
Franciscan
priory ruins
Művész
Nemzeti Sport
sétány
Centenary
Monument
Danube
0
100
200
300 m
MARGIT
HÍD
1
2
3
4
5
6
7
8
9

nunneries, a monastery, the Archbishop of Esztergom's manse and a royal residence - until the Ottomans came and razed everything to the ground, converting the island into a harem for a succession of priapic Pashas. Under cover of dusk, many a lusty Hungarian lad would swim out to the island (this was in the days before bridges) to spy on the women. For most of the 19th century the island was a favourite strolling place for well-to-do families. The melancholy and much-beloved romantic poet János Arany came here every summer to take the medicinal waters for his gall stones and write increasingly awful verse. Since 1908 the island has been a public park, boasting swimming pools, snack bars, ornamental gardens, lawns and fountains, and benches to sit on and soak up some sunshine and fresh air.

What to See

1 THE CENTENARY MONUMENT (*Centenáriumi emlékmű*): This bronze sculpture is the first thing that greets you as you walk onto the island. It was set up in 1972 to commemorate Budapest's centenary. The united capital was formed in 1873, an amalgam of Pest, Buda and Óbuda. The monument is shaped like a tulip bud just coming unfurled. Inside, it looks like a collage of *objets trouvés*, except that everything is fashioned from the same bronze. Medals, coins, daggers, tokens for crossing the Chain Bridge, helmets, mortar shells, cogwheels and a battered teddy bear all trace the history of Budapest from the days of the mediaeval guilds through the age of steam and iron to the wars and revolutions - and ultimate peace - of the late 20th century.

2 RUINS OF THE DOMINICAN CONVENT (*Domonkos kolostor*): It was here that Princess Margaret, the island's namesake, lived out her brief life - a red marble slab marks the spot where her tomb once lay (it and her remains were smuggled to Bratislava after the Ottoman invasion), and a little shrine dedicated to her, filled with plastic flowers and grateful plaques, testifies to her enduring popularity. The story goes that Margaret's father, King Béla IV, whose reign was plagued by the threat of Mongol invasion, pledged that if he managed to keep the marauders at bay, he would dedicate his child to God. He won his bet, and Margaret entered the nunnery as a child novice at the age of four. At the age of 12 she took her binding monastic vows. Convent life took its psychological toll, turning her into a fierce ascetic and mortifier of the flesh. But 'her rough woollen garments were not sufficient concealment for her extraordinary charms', we are told: King Ottokar of Bohemia offered to marry her in 1262. Margaret replied that she was the bride of Christ and no other, and went back to her punishing routine of scrubbing the nunnery corridors and tending the victims of diseases so nauseating that other nuns had been frightened away. She refused to wash above her ankles and dressed herself in rough hair shirts which she secured at the waist with hedgehog skins. As a result of these unhygienic practices, the stench of her sanctity was legendary and the decline in her health rapid. She died at the age of 29, a martyr to her country's cause. Shortly before her death she gave the keys of her trunk to the Mother Superior. Crowds gathered to witness the trunk's opening, convinced that it contained precious treasure. All they found were two rough-woven shifts, an iron belt studded with pointed nails, a leather whip, and two pairs of stockings lined with iron spikes. Margaret was finally canonised in 1943. They say that if you stand at a certain point on the island on the day of her death (February 15th), a marvellous light suffuses the air, coupled with a delicious perfume and the sound of high-pitched singing, while flickering blue flames guide you to buried treasure. The treasure has never been found, though the island did at one time fall prey to a rash of hopeful excavators.

❸ WATER TOWER (*Víztorony*): Built in 1911 by an architect who had just discovered the joys of reinforced concrete, this is one of the most decorative structures built from the material. In the summer an open-air theatre functions at its base, with a festival held in August. The tower itself has a look-out gallery offering superb panoramic views of surrounding Pest and Buda.

❹ CHAPEL OF ST MICHAEL (*Szent Mihály kápolna*): This is all that remains of a 12th-century monastery of Premonstratensian (Augustinian) canons. With the arrival of the Dominican nuns in the 13th century, constant squabbling broke out between the two religious houses concerning land rights and to whom the serfs should owe allegiance - and, presumably, food. The chapel was completely destroyed during the Ottoman invasion, though its ancient bell was found buried under a tree stump nearby, and rehung when the chapel was rebuilt in 1932.

Main lawn and water tower on Margaret Island.

❺ SPA (*Thermal Szálloda*): In the early 20th century the Budapest city council bought Margaret Island from the Habsburgs and turned it into a public park. It rapidly became a fashionable resort, known for its polo ground, restaurants and sports facilities, as well as for its hot springs and spa. In its heyday in the 1920s and 1930s, the spa was one of the most beautiful in the city. Sadly, it was badly damaged in the Second World War and again by flooding in the 1950s. Now it is housed in a 1970s construction, linked underground to the Grand Hotel, which was rebuilt in the 1980s to designs by Miklós Ybl, and which has a large outdoor bar terrace in summer. To the left of the spa, as you face towards Árpád híd, you will find the 'Japanese Garden', a collection of small rockeries with a string of artesian-fed thermal pools, home to terrapins and goldfish.

❻ BANDSTAND (*Zenélő kút*): This ornamental bandstand and drinking fountain is a 1930s copy of an 1820s design. Its dome is crowned by a statue of Neptune, and there are marble basins and spigots on three sides. Recorded brass-band music issues from its roof at five-minute intervals, allowing you to imagine ghostly uniformed trumpeters, playing aubades to trysting couples, matrons in their Sunday best, and sailor-suited children.

❼ PALATINUS STRANDFÜRDŐ: The Palatinus swimming pool and thermal baths complex is fronted by a lean, streamlined late 1930s building with turnstiles and a sculpture of a similarly lean and streamlined female nude. Inside is a variety of pools, the best of which is the large swimming pool, 50 by 100 metres. On a hot summer's day it is hard to think of anything more inviting, but be

Chinese immigrant families enjoying the Budapest custom of a Sunday afternoon on Margaret Island.

warned! After dining out on hot dogs and candy floss, which is about all the refreshment stalls and restaurants offer, you will probably pile on many more pounds than you shed swimming.

8 Ruins of the Franciscan Priory (*Ferences kolostor*): This was the earliest monastery on the island, founded in the 13th century. With the advent of the powerful Dominican sisters, however, the Franciscans' influence began to wane, and their territory on the island was gradually whittled away. The priory was destroyed by the Ottomans. In the late 18th century, the Habsburg Archduke Joseph, Palatine of Hungary, built himself a summer villa over what remained. The villa was later turned into a hotel, and some of Budapest's greatest writers took rooms here. With all their bodily needs cared for, they could concentrate their energy on deathless prose and verse. The building was damaged beyond repair in the Second World War and demolished in 1949.

9 Nemzeti Sport Swimming Pool: Though this handsome, red-brick building is a public swimming baths and not a visitor attraction as such, it has a claim to fame as an important monument of modern architecture. It was built to designs by Alfréd Hajós in 1935. More than just an architect, Hajós was also an Olympic swimming champion. At the age of 18 he won the 100m and the 1200m events at the first modern Olympic Games, in Athens in 1896. The Nemzeti Sport was Hungary's first indoor swimming pool. Hajós went on to design a number of Bauhaus-influenced buildings in Budapest, among them the Andrássy Hotel (*see p. 242*) and one of the houses in the Napraforgó utca estate (*see p. 84*).

GELLÉRT HILL

The Citadel on top of Gellért Hill (*map p. 262, E2*) is the best vantage point in the city. The Habsburgs were well aware of this, which is why they built a fortress here after the suppression of the 1848 revolution. Gun shafts point at the Danube and down into Pest, as well as to the Buda Hills behind. But it was more for show than anything else, and to remind a rebellious population who was in charge. It worked: the Hungarians called it the Budapest Bastille, and it was universally loathed. It was finally handed over to the City Council in 1897, but somehow never got knocked down.

A similar story is attached to the Liberation Monument in front of it. This enormous female statue was designed originally to carry a propeller blade, to commemorate the death in an air crash of the son of Admiral Horthy, Hungary's inter-war Regent. The statue did not go up until 1947, however, by which time historical events had overtaken Horthy. The propeller blade was substituted for a palm frond, stalwart Soviet soldiers were added around the base, and the whole sculpture was dubbed the Liberation Monument, the 'liberation' in question being that of Budapest by the Red Army. Though almost all the city's other Soviet monuments have been taken down from their plinths and re-erected in the edge-of-town Statue Park (*see p. 120*), this statue was granted a reprieve. The names of the Soviet soldiers who died fighting the Nazis have been chiselled off, but still, like the Citadel, the statue remains, and has been absorbed into the cityscape, despite connections to a hated regime.

Gellért Hill has a tarnished reputation in other ways, too.

Gellért Hill's Liberation Monument, the city's most familiar skyline silhouette.

Twilight view from across the water of Gellért Hill and the Gellért Hotel and baths.

According to folk tradition, it was the spot where witches from all over the country used to convene, summoned by the devil in the form of a raven or black crow. It is also the site of the murder of Bishop Gellért, the Venetian primate who had helped King Stephen to convert his people to Christianity and who acted as tutor to Stephen's pious son Imre. Gellért was clubbed to death by jealous pagan chieftains, who then rolled his body into the river below. Legend says that it took seven years to wash the stones clean of his blood. His statue now presides over the hillside overlooking Elisabeth Bridge, with an ornamental waterfall trickling downwards from it.

On an outcrop opposite the entrance to the Gellért Baths is a large natural cave, burrowing deep into the dolomite. It was inhabited in the early middle ages by a charitable hermit called Iván, who used to heal the sick with the aid of curative waters that bubbled up from a spring near the cave entrance. In the mid-1920s the cave was turned into a chapel, modelled on the one at Lourdes, and run by the Paulines, the only monastic order of Hungarian origin. The order takes its name from Paul, a 3rd-century Egyptian hermit who fled into the desert to be closer to God. There he led an anchorite's life of total seclusion, with only a raven for company. (The raven also brought him food: half a slice of bread a day.) The Communists seized the cave chapel in the 1950s, dissolved the order, executed the Father Superior and walled the chapel up. When the Church got it back in 1989, they preserved a great lump of reinforced concrete from this wall, which you can see at the cave entrance. Inside, the cave is composed of a string of natural and man-made hollows, each containing a small chapel. In the central chapel there is a little statue of St Paul, with his raven sitting on his shoulder.

Where to Eat near Gellért Hill

The coffee house (*kávézó*) in the Gellért Hotel does coffee served the old-fashioned way, in gilt-edged porcelain on a metal tray, with a glass of water beside it. Their walnut-filled *extra kifli* (a sweet, sticky croissant) is excellent. The hotel beer garden (*söröző*) is an old Hungarian family favourite. It is a bit noisy on the outdoor terrace, and the food won't win any Michelin stars, but it is an authentic Budapest experience. Otherwise stroll across Szabadság Bridge to the Pest side of the river. For a delicious long, leisurely lunch, go to Képíró, at Képíró utca 3 (*Tel: 266-0430. NB: closed Sun. Map p. 263, E3, K. u.*). For a quick snack, there is always the Vásárcsarnok market hall, where you can treat yourself to fried chicken or sausage and mustard on a paper plate from one of the upstairs stalls.

THE CHILDREN'S RAILWAY

Snaking through the Buda Hills on a narrow-gauge track, the red and white engines of the Children's Railway (*gyermekvasút*) are a friendly and familiar sight, particularly at weekends, when family parties take to the hills to toboggan and drink mulled wine, to gather the first violets of spring, or just to wander among the leafy forest pathways. A trip on the little railway is an excellent way to spend an afternoon. (*NB: From Oct-April the railway does not operate on working Mondays.*)

The engine driver is an adult, but all other staff, from the guard to the ticket inspector to the station master, are children between the ages of ten and fourteen. To be allowed the privilege of working on the railway, children have to have top marks at school, plus a letter of permission from their parents. The scheme was masterminded in 1948 by one of the old guard Soviet-educated Communists, Ernő Gerő (at that time Minister of Transport), and the first section of track was laid in the same year. The rest came as part of Hungary's first Five Year Plan. The

Uniformed guard checking the platform before blowing her whistle.

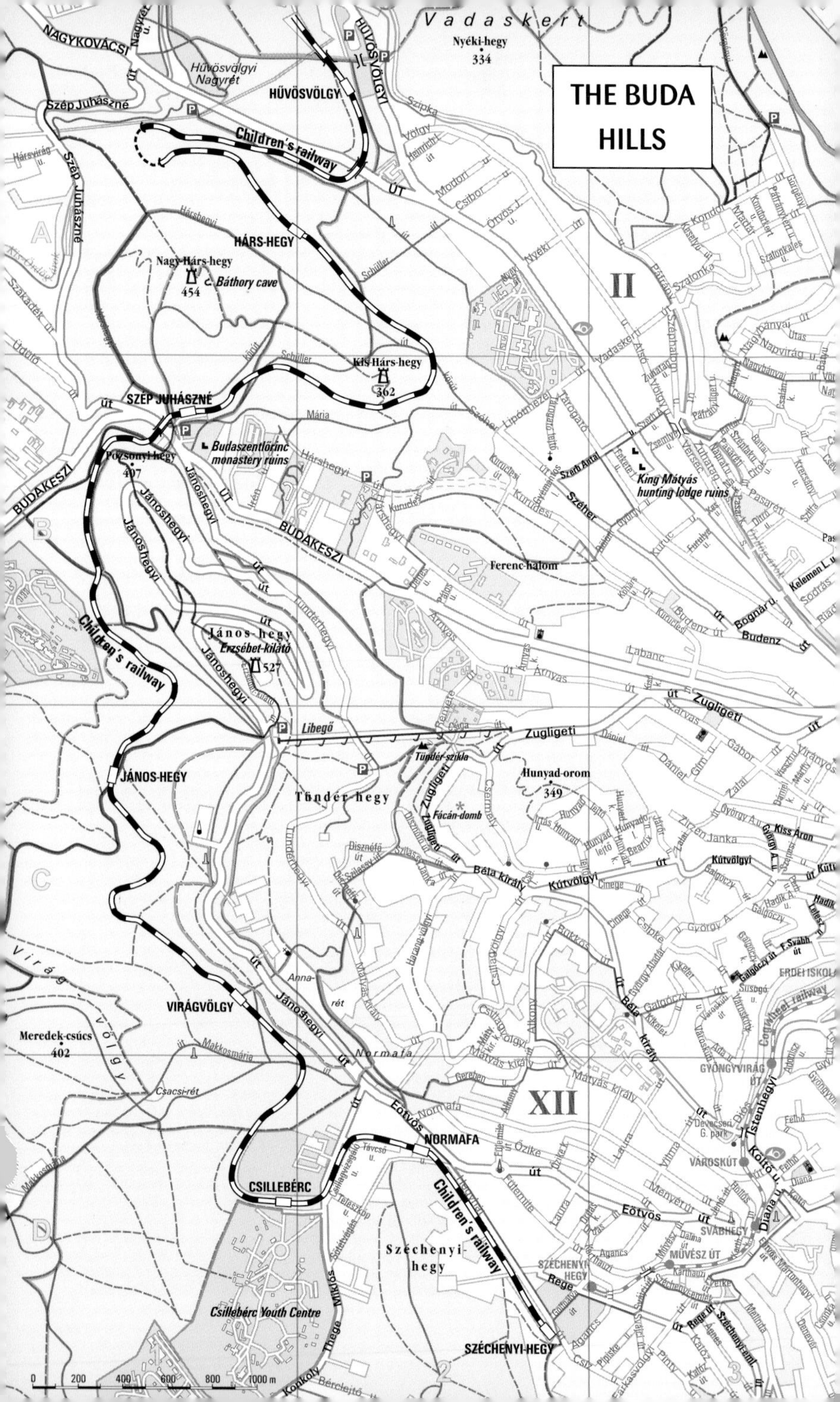
THE BUDA HILLS
Vadaskert
Nyéki-hegy
334
HŰVÖSVÖLGY
Hűvösvölgyi Nagyrét
NAGYKOVÁCSI
Szép Juhászné
Children's railway
Hárs-hegy
Nagy-Hárs-hegy
454
Báthory cave
Kis-Hárs-hegy
362
SZÉP JUHÁSZNÉ
Budaszentlőrinc monastery ruins
Pozsonyi hegy
407
BUDAKESZI
Jánoshegyi
János-hegy
Erzsébet-kilátó
527
Libegő
Tündér-szikla
Tündér-hegy
JÁNOS-HEGY
Ferenc-halom
King Mátyás hunting lodge ruins
Szeher
Zugligeti
Hunyad-orom
349
Fácán-domb
Béla király
Kútvölgyi
Virágvölgy
VIRÁGVÖLGY
Meredek-csúcs
402
Csacsi-rét
Anna-rét
Normafa
NORMAFA
Eötvös
CSILLEBÉRC
Csillebérc Youth Centre
Széchenyi-hegy
SZÉCHENYI-HEGY
GYÖNGYVIRÁG ÚT
VÁROSKÚT
SVÁBHEGY
MŰVÉSZ ÚT
ERDEI ISKOLA
Cogwheel railway
II
XII
0
200
400
600
800
1000 m

railway was run by the 'Pioneers', a sort of Communist scout club that aimed to 'prepare children to enter society'. The uniform worn by the mini-personnel has changed little since then: white knee socks and navy blue skirts for girls, navy blue jackets and trousers for boys, navy caps and bright red neckerchiefs for all. And though Communism has long been swept under the carpet, the children's railway lives on, proof that a good idea is a good idea, no matter the ideology behind it.

The locomotives are all diesel except for a single steam engine, built in 1950, which still runs an occasional route (marked on the timetables). Carriages are open-sided in summer, closed in winter. The railway runs for twelve kilometres from Széchenyi-hegy (*map D2*) to Hűvösvölgy (*map A2*), with six stops in between. Buy your ticket at the station ticket office or on the train itself, for as many stops as you like. Timetables are posted at each station. At the **Normafa** stop there is a buffet serving cold beer in summer and mulled wine in winter, a restaurant with a covered outdoor terrace, and lovely walks in the woods around. The spot has a story behind its name: in the mid 19th century, Normafa ('Norma Tree') was much beloved by a group of opera singers, who came here

Original 1950s mosaic adorning the Csillebérc railway station building.

The steam locomotive runs occasional routes. Built in 1950, it is lovingly maintained.

for fresh air and exercise, to stretch their legs and lungs. One of their number, the soprano Rozália Klein, once found herself so carried away by the beautiful views that she stood under a beech tree and broke into an improvisation of the grand aria from Bellini's *Norma*. The area around the tree has borne the name Normafa ever since, though sadly the venerable beech itself blew down in a gale in 1927.

At **Jánoshegy** (527m high at the summit) there is a lookout tower, the Erzsébet kilátó, built in 1910 by Frigyes Schulek, who also designed the Fishermen's Bastion. From the top on a clear day you get stunning views not only across Budapest itself, but far beyond, to the Mátra Hills in the north-east and the Bakony range to the south-west. Close to the lookout tower is the end station of the *libegő*, a 1970s chair lift that whirrs you down to almost the bottom of the hill. At the next railway stop, **Szépjuhászné**, there is a little restaurant, particularly pleasant in warm weather, when you can sit at the outside tables beside the track and watch the trains come and go. Close by the restaurant are the ruins of the Budaszentlőrinc monastery, which is said to have had a fine wine cellar. King Mátyás Corvinus, whose hunting lodge was in the woods nearby, often came to slake his thirst here after a hard day at the chase.

KEREPESI CEMETERY

(Kerepesi temető) Pest VIII, Fiumei út 16
Map p. 259, D3-4. Open 7am to 5.30pm (8pm in summer).
Red metro line to Keleti Pályaudvar, from where it is a few minutes' walk up Fiumei út. More detailed maps than the one below are available from the information window inside the main gate on the left.

There is nothing remotely gloomy about this beautiful place; its tranquillity and its greenery make it arguably the best 'park' in the city. Whether you want to seek out the graves of the famous or infamous, or simply wander among the unknown dead, the architecture of the mausoleums and headstones makes it well worth the effort to get there.

You can gauge political affiliations and the mood of the nation by the flowers on the graves. The contrasting gardens of remembrance for those who died in 1956 have a tale to tell: the urns of those who fought for the Soviets can be found at plot **15**. 'Eternal gratitude and honour to the heroes who fell in the

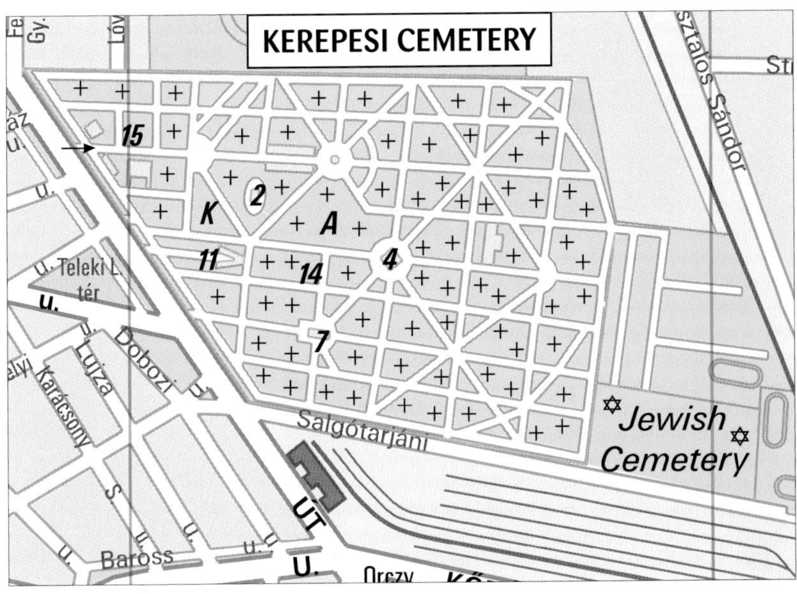

struggle against the counter-revolution,' reads the legend on the central sarcophagus. Despite this grandiloquence, the place feels abandoned, quite at odds with the flowers you will find at plot **14**, a living garden in memory of those who fought against Red Russia.

The enormous Pantheon to the Workers' Movement (**11**) is another must. Once gleaming white, it is now dusty and dishevelled like a closed-down clubhouse. 'They lived for the People and for Communism,' blares the bold black lettering. But no one cares, least of all the People. Some of the graves are still tended, but most are forgotten and overgrown. An air of dereliction hangs over the whole place, and grass and weeds are slowly breaking up the paving stones.

Very near here is the red marble grave of Hungary's last Communist premier, János Kádár (**K**), who died in 1989. He competes in floral tributes with József Antall (**A**), first Prime Minister of a democratic Hungary (d. 1993), who lies in splendid isolation in the middle of his plot. Antall generally wins the contest, but Kádár is by no means unremembered or unloved. The grandest monuments of all are those to Ferenc Deák (**4**, *see p. 88*), Count Lajos Batthyány (**2**, *see p. 88*) and Lajos Kossuth (**7**, *see p. 88*). Kossuth's is the best: a triumph of majesty and vainglory in limestone and bronze, guarded by two crouching pumas.

Round the back of the cemetery, on Salgótarjáni utca, is the entrance to the Jewish Cemetery (*open Sun-Fri 8am-4pm*), which served wealthy families before the Second World War. Wonderful tombs designed by Béla Lajta (*see p. 82*) for industrialists such as Weiss and Goldberger are to be found here, and Lajta also designed the entranceway. With few family members left alive to care for the graves, today the cemetery is sadly overgrown and tangled.

Where to Eat near Kerepesi

Rosenstein at Mosonyi utca 3 (*map p. 259, C3*) is an unpretentious, family-run place serving hearty meals. The décor is uninteresting, but there are plenty who swear by its cooking, which evokes pre-war Jewish Pest (*Reservations recommended. Tel: 313-4196*). At Keleti railway station (*map p. 259, C3*) the former station restaurant, the Baross Terem, has been restored to a semblance of its sometime grandeur, and serves homely fare in marble-pillared surroundings.

ÓBUDA & ROMAN BUDAPEST

Modern-day Buda was not a major settlement in Roman times. Pest, on the east bank of the Danube, belonged to a land of barbarian tribes, and was unconquered territory that wedged apart the Roman provinces of Pannonia and Dacia. The Danube itself, however, was more than just a boundary line between Rome and its enemies; it was an important Roman trading route. To safeguard the vessels that sailed it and to patrol its frontier, a garrison town was set up in around AD 89 around the site of present-day Flórián tér in Óbuda. The six thousand imperial soldiers that were quartered here were not officially allowed to marry, but this did not prevent them from entering into liaisons with local women. Those women, and their children, also lived in the garrison town. About five kilometres upriver from the military settlement was the civilian town of Aquincum, which began life as a cluster of tradesmen and artisans who earned a living selling their wares to the soldiers and their unofficial families. Later, in AD 107, Emperor Trajan split the province, creating a separate region of Pannonia Inferior, with its own governor who ruled from Aquincum. The post was first held by future emperor Hadrian. Remains from both Roman settlements survive, and Óbuda itself is also interesting for its bourgeois 17th-century Baroque houses overshadowed - but not outshone - by the serried concrete ranks of modern-era solutions to the housing crisis.

Both the civilian and military Roman towns had an amphitheatre. The remains of the military circus - a perfect circle with supporting walls

Ancient meets modern in Óbuda.

ÓBUDA & AQUINCUM
Civilian Amphitheatre
AQUINCUM
HÉV
Ruins of Aquincum
HÉV KASZÁSDŰLŐ
HÉV FILATORIGÁT
HÉV ÁRPÁD HÍD
HÉV TIMÁR U.
Hercules Villa
Flórián tér
Military Amphitheatre
Óbudai-sziget
Margit-sziget
Danube
ÁRPÁD HÍD
SZENTENDREI ÚT
BÉCSI ÚT
VÖRÖSVÁRI ÚT
PACSIRTAMEZŐ U.
Kunigunda útja
Huszti út
Thermae Maiores
Umbrella Women
Kassák
Vasarely
Fő tér
Flórián tér
Tavasz u.
Hídfő
Polgár
Kórház
Vöröskereszt u.
Harrer P.
Miklós u.
100 200 300 400 500 m
1
2
3

and gateways - stand in what amounts to a traffic island, between Nagyszombat utca and Pacsirtamező ('lark meadow'), next to which the traffic streams toward Árpád Bridge. At Flórián tér, the old centre of the garrison town, there is an underpass adorned with fragments of Roman statuary, insouciantly displayed next to hole-on-the-wall boutiques selling cigarettes, children's toys and cheap knitwear. Behind glass panels is an excavation of the *thermae maiores*, the old military bathhouse. Flórián tér itself is ringed around with high-rise housing developments designed for a brave new working-class world. The notorious 'panel apartments', now universally despised, are no more than prefabricated concrete panels hung onto a reinforced concrete skeleton.

Central Óbuda

Óbuda's main sight is its main square, Fő tér, just on the far side of the Árpád Bridge flyover. (To get there by public transport take the HÉV train from Batthyány tér - *map p. 262, B2* - to the Árpád híd stop.) Fő tér's pretty, cobbled expanse is surrounded by Baroque buildings: a clutch of traditional taverns and an imposing town hall with its portal borne by moustachioed caryatids. In the north-east corner (the top right-hand corner as you face the town hall) you will find sculptor Imre Varga's *Umbrella Women*. Flanking the eastern side of the square is the enormous, crumbling Zichy palace, once home to the lords of the manor of Óbuda and now the domicile of the Kassák museum (*Open Tue-Sun 10am-6pm*) dedicated to Constructivist artist, writer and lifelong champion of the working man, Lajos Kassák (*see opposite*). Hungarian-born Op and Kinetic artist Victor Vasarely (1908-1997) is also celebrated with a museum in Óbuda, at Szentlélek tér 6.

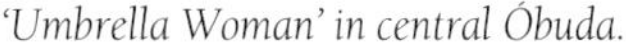

'Umbrella Woman' in central Óbuda.

Lajos Kassák (1887-1967)

Kassák was introduced early to the working man's cause: he dropped out of school as a boy and was set to work as a locksmith's assistant, taking a variety of factory jobs after that. As a member of the Workers' Movement, he organised strikes and demonstrations, after which he was blacklisted. Undaunted, he embarked on a self-tailored, self-educatory Grand Tour of Europe on foot, visiting museums and galleries by day and sleeping in doss-houses by night. On his return to Hungary he began to publish poems and short stories in literary journals. He took a strongly anti-war stance during the build-up to the First World War. When the war ended he joined the Hungarian Communist Party and became editor of the radical arts periodical *Ma* ('Today'). When the Republic of Councils fell in 1919, he fled to Austria with a price on his head. He continued to edit *Ma* from his Vienna apartment, publishing prose, poetry and art by a number of leading avant-garde figures, including Cocteau, Schwitters and Le Corbusier. He also began to experiment with graphic art himself, designing many of the magazine's covers. Kassák's political leanings were anathema to the Horthy government; he was not permitted to return to Hungary until 1926, and even then he was constantly in trouble with the authorities, charged with inciting public unrest and taken into custody more than once. Nevertheless he continued to publish novels and stories addressing social problems such as unemployment and the plight of the rural peasantry. He also married his partner of twenty years, the actress and reciter of Dadaist poetry Jolán Simon, to whom he was everlastingly unfaithful. Simon took her own life in 1938, worn out by the sacrifice involved in being the prop and mainstay of an egotistical creative spirit.

Kassák came into his own after the Second World War as a member of the Hungarian Arts Council. He staged a number of exhibitions and his poetry was intoned at party rallies. But trouble was always waiting in the wings. Though a Socialist by conviction, he was not a zealot, and had more sympathy with the Social Democrats than the Communists. He had been outspoken in his condemnation of the show trials of Stalinist Russia, which had claimed the life of his brother-in-law. When the Hungarian Communists and Social Democrats came to blows in the late 1940s, Kassák was evicted from the Communist Party. Then, in 1956, he came out on the side of the anti-Soviet revolutionaries. After that his movements were closely monitored. Though he was permitted to exhibit privately, he was not allowed to mount public shows. A retrospective exhibition was mooted in 1966, but turned down as politically inappropriate. It was not until the following year, the year of his 80th birthday, that he was finally rehabilitated, and given the official state recognition he had always known he deserved. He died soon afterwards.

Roman Óbuda

The Hercules Villa: In 1958, workmen digging the foundations for a school came across something unexpected: the remains of a twelve-room Roman villa, once home to a high-ranking military officer. The name 'Hercules Villa' comes from its most famous mosaic, which depicts Hercules's wife being abducted by the centaur. That has now been removed to the museum at Aquincum (*see opposite*), but a number of other mosaic fragments remain at the villa site, which you will find huddled under angular blue roofing in the middle of a small housing estate. *Buda III, Meggyfa utca 21. Open mid-April-1st May & all of October Tue-Sun 10-am-5pm; May-end Sept Tue-Sun 10am-6pm.* *Map p. 219, C2.*

Aquincum: West of the main road are the remains of the civilian town's amphitheatre. The beasts that were kept here are said to have been so wild that a specially high fence had to be built to stop them breaking out and attacking the population. Today

Roman tombstones and masonry at Aquincum.

the roar of the lions and the screams of the Christians have been replaced by the hum of crickets in the grass and the roar of the main road. Across that road are the remains of the civilian town. The site contains the ruins of houses and courtyards, and a market place and public baths. The museum at the site contains artefacts unearthed here, including some exquisite glassware, a beautifully designed folding table and stool, and a 'hydra' or water organ. There is also a memorial to the organ-player's wife, Aelia Sabina: '*She was well versed in the arts; she alone could surpass her husband. She had a sweet voice - but suddenly she fell silent...*'. The museum's star exhibit is the mosaic originally from the Hercules Villa (*see opposite*) depicting Hercules's wife Deianera being carried off by the centaur. *Buda III, Szentendrei út 139. Museum open Tue-Sun 10am-6pm (summer); 10am-5pm (spring & autumn). The ruins themselves open an hour before the museum. Map p. 219, A3.*

Where to Eat in Óbuda

Fő tér itself has a handful of taverns offering old-style Hungarian fare. The Új Sípos specialises in river fish, and makes several varieties of *halászlé*, Hungary's traditional carp soup. Slightly further afield, at Kenyeres utca 34 (*map p. 219, D2*), is Kisbuda Gyöngye (*see p. 236*). Gigler, at Föld utca 50/c (*map p. 219, D2*) is an old-fashioned Óbuda inn serving Austrian beer and Austro-Hungarian home cooking (*NB: closed Mon*).

PART V

PRACTICALITIES

PRACTICALITIES

FOOD & WINE

Everyone has heard of goulash. What might surprise you is that in Hungary it is most often encountered as a soup. Traditionally Hungarian meals always start with a soup, and rich meat and bean broths are still popular starters, frequently made even more calorific by the addition of sour cream. In fact, calorie count and high meat intake are the watchwords of the traditional Hungarian bill of fare. This is largely because traditional Magyar cooking is peasant cooking: large portions of bread and meat to fill hungry workers and keep them going in the fields all day. But heavy Hungarian cuisine is fast being replaced by lighter, more Mediterranean-influenced dishes, with emphasis on fresh vegetables and salad. Hungarians haven't completely forsaken their heritage, though. They still eat a lot of pork. Legend says that this culinary habit

'Poppy-seed Cake' (1910) by Adolf Fényes.

began during the Ottoman occupation. The Turkish population didn't want the forbidden meat, so the price dropped and it was left to the poorer locals. True or not, pork is definitely the dominant meat in Magyar dishes, although you'll also find lots of poultry (including good duck), beef and river fish.

Popular Hungarian Dishes

Babgulyás: Goulash soup with dried beans. Usually featured as a starter, but with plenty of bread it makes a whole meal.

Csirke Paprikás: This is the dish that everyone's grandmother makes best in the world. Chicken pieces stewed with onion, mild paprika powder and sour cream.

Gundel palacsinta: Hungary's most famous restaurant (*see p. 235*) invented this dessert crêpe, and it's since become a staple. Rum, raisin and walnut make the filling, and the whole thing is covered with chocolate sauce.

Halászlé: This popular fish soup is a light, spicy broth with chunks of carp, seasoned with onions, garlic and paprika. Every Danube village claims to do it best; one popular way is to include the milt and roe.

Hideg Libamáj: Cold slices of goose liver served in goose grease with toast and raw purple onion rings. French goose liver producers are allegedly up in arms that Hungarian goose liver prices are pushing them out of business. If you're concerned about the treatment of animals or your own cholesterol level, there is nothing to be said in this dish's favour, but from any other point of view it is wonderful.

Lángos: A disc of deep-fried potato batter (yes, that's all it is), spread with garlic, sour cream or grated cheese - or all three. You can find a *lángos* stand at most markets, for example the one behind the Mammut shopping mall on Széna tér (*map p. 262, B1*).

PÖRKÖLT: A rich stew, made of beef, pork, chicken or tripe. It is traditionally eaten with *galuska*, Hungarian flour-and-water gnocchi, though it is equally good with rice.

TÖLTÖTT KÁPOSZTA: Savoy cabbage leaves stuffed with rice and minced pork, flavoured with savory and served on a bed of sauerkraut in paprika sauce, crowned with a spicy sausage and a curl of pork fat, plus liberal dollops of sour cream.

SOMLÓI GALUSKA: Sponge squares soaked in brandy, scattered with raisins and mixed with whipped cream and rich chocolate sauce.

PAPRIKA

Hungary's most famous cooking ingredient was brought to the country by the Ottomans. To begin with it was known as 'heathen pepper'. God-fearing Christians wouldn't dream of eating it; they grew it in their gardens as an ornamental plant. It was not until the 18th century, when trade embargoes during the Napoleonic Wars made pepper unavailable, that paprika, cultivated on the sunny Great Plain, became the prime seasoning. Ground paprika powder can either be hot or mild. When buying a bag of it, *édesnemes* is a good variety to choose: pungent and flavourful without being sharply spicy. Raw paprika, whole or sliced crossways or lengthways, is also a mainstay. Watch out for the long, thin green ones - they're hot - but the fat yellow ones (called *TV paprika* not because they're 'as seen on TV' but to indicate they're good for stuffing) are mild and crunchy. A common summertime paprika is the deep red *pritamin*, rounded in shape and beautifully sweet to taste. Paprika is a good source of Vitamin C, and in fact it was while munching on a piece of raw paprika that Hungarian Nobel Prize-winning chemist Albert Szent-Györgyi first discovered and isolated the vitamin.

Wine

If your palate has been conditioned by the full-fruit flavours of Californian or Australian vintages, you might find that Hungarian wines take some getting used to. Even so, there is no doubt that excellent wine is being produced here, and Hungary can be proud of its viticultural traditions. Admittedly, Hungary is now drifting towards the mainstream, with more and more noble grape varieties being used. But the native varieties are still hanging on, with a number of winemakers taking a definitive stand in their favour. High-acid Hungarian whites and light, spicy reds do not necessarily complement the Mediterranean-style cooking that is all the rage in the wealthier parts of the country, but they are excellent with traditional spicy sausage and paprika-rich stews, and it would be a mistake to sacrifice them on the altar of global trend. Summers here are hot, but relatively short, and winters long and cold - which makes Hungary predominantly a white wine producer.

Major Wine Regions

Villány: In the south of the country, it produces Hungary's heartiest reds. Winemakers to look out for are Attila Gere and József Bock in the premier league, with Mayer, Günzer, Vylyan and Wunderlich coming up behind them. Some of the top producers use a lot of new oak during the ageing process. If you aren't a fan of that, try the region's indigenous Kékoportó, a soft, fruity wine for drinking rather than for cellaring.

Eger: In the north-east of the country, famous for its red Bull's Blood (Bikavér), a light and spicy blend which became popular as a safe alternative to cholera-infested water in the early 19th century. Good winemakers are Vilmos Thummerer and György Lőrincz (who bottles under the Szent Andrea label).

Szekszárd: To the south of Budapest, this is the home of dark red, high-extract wines best drunk with food. There is also a Szekszárd version of Bull's Blood, which locals claim is from an older tradition than Eger's. Look out for the Takler family and Tamás Dúzsi, who makes a good Kékfrankos (a light, peppery red) and a lovely, summery rosé.

Balaton and Somló: Vineyards have been planted on the shores of

Botrytised berries on a Tokaj vine. The grapes shrivel, thus concentrating the sugars.

the great lake Balaton since Roman times. It is primarily a white wine region, producing a lot of unfashionable (though often very good) Italian Riesling (Olaszrizling) and some Chardonnay, along with Traminer (Tramini), Sauvignon Blanc and Pinot Gris (Szürkebarát). The northern shore of the lake is volcanic, with a soil rich in acids, making for some interesting wines. Good winemakers are Huba Szeremley (Szent Orbán Pince), Ottó Légli and János Konyári.

Somló is Hungary's smallest wine region, tiny and compact, clinging to the slopes of an extinct volcano and producing white wine only. The volcanic soil here is even richer in acids and minerals than north Balaton soil, which means that traditionally 'flowery' varieties like Traminer taste much bolder. Somló also produces plenty of the traditional Hungarian white-wine varieties Hárslevelű and Furmint. Allegedly Somló wine was administered to Habsburg brides to ensure the production of a male heir. Winemakers to look out for are Imre Györgykovács and Béla Fekete.

SOPRON: In the north-west of the country, on the Austrian border, Sopron is home to light rosés and some good reds, mainly made from the traditional Kékfrankos grape. Successful Pinot Noirs and Syrahs have also been vinified here. The Weninger winery is the best in the region.

TOKAJ: This is undoubtedly Hungary's most famous wine region. What most people mean when they talk about 'Tokaj wine' is Tokaji Aszú, an aged dessert wine made from adding berries infected by the noble rot *botrytis cinerea* to the base wine. The botrytis shrivels the grapes and gives them their characteristic flavour and sweetness. Traditionally the *aszú* berries were added to the other grapes by the hod, or *puttony*. Technology and instinct have supplanted the *puttony* now, but the word is still used as a measure of sweetness. The higher the *puttony* number the sweeter - and pricier - the wine. The lowest *puttony* number is 3 and the highest is 6, though not every year yields enough botrytised grapes to make a 6-*puttony* wine, and increasingly 3-*puttony* wines are being marketed as 'noble late harvest', or some term which sounds less bottom-of-the-scale. Vast sums of money have been spent by the French, British and Spanish on buying Tokaj wineries, and small individual growers and winemakers are also coming to the fore. Some say the *aszú* wine is better since the so-called post-Communist Tokaj Renaissance; others like it less. This is something you can only judge for yourself. Good years for old-style Tokaji Aszú are 1972, 1975, 1983 and 1988, and, for the new style, 1993, 1995 and 1996. The top private producer of *aszú* is István Szepsy. The best of the large, internationally owned wineries are Disznókő, Oremus and Hétszőlő.

The term 'Tokaj' can otherwise be used either to mean any white wine

Bottles of tawny-coloured Tokaji Aszú, historically the elixir of kings.

made in the region, but typically from the native grape varieties Furmint and Hárslevelű. There is also Tokaji Szamorodni, which is more akin to sherry and takes its name from a Polish word meaning 'as it comes', because the grapes are fermented together unsorted: some bunches will have more *aszú* berries, some fewer. As a result of this, the wine can be either sweet or dry. Because of complicated laws regulating what a

Szamorodni is or isn't, most producers have now ducked the issue and are calling their non-botrytised wines 'late harvest' (*késői szüret*) instead (not 'noble late harvest', which would be a low-*puttony aszú*).

Where to Buy Wine

If you are interested in going into detail on the wine subject, visit the Magyar Borok Háza on Fortuna utca on Castle Hill (*map p. 262, C1, opposite the Hilton Hotel*). A huge cellar space has been given over to displays from all the wine regions, with open bottles of selected vintages for visitors to sample. For advice on what to buy, visit one of the specialist merchants. The best are the Bortársaság at Buda I, Batthyány utca 59 (*map p. 262, B1*) and Pest IX, Ráday utca 7 (*map p. 263, E4*); La Boutique des Vins at Pest V, József Attila utca 12 (*map p. 262, C3*), and Monarchia at Pest IX, Kinizsi utca 30 (*Map p. 263, E4*).

RESTAURANTS

This selection reflects the current dining scene in Budapest. Some places have been chosen for their food, others for the way they look, for their atmosphere, or for what they tell you about contemporary Budapest. Listings are arranged by locality. The coloured numbers refer to the map of city-centre restaurants given on pp. 238-39.

Key to Pricing:

$ = cheap (around 5,000 Ft for two)
$$ = moderate (up to 10,000 Ft for two)
$$$ = moderately expensive (up to 20,000 Ft for two)
$$$$ = expensive (20,000 Ft or over for two)

Wilma wishes you bon appétit, serving up nicely grilled pork sausages and slices of white radish.

Central Pest

1 Baraka Map p. 239, D3 $$$$
Friendly, stylish-looking little place known for its inventive menus and ingenious combinations. The wait staff is friendly and the food is cooked with flair and a loving touch. The chocolate volcano dessert has set a city-wide trend. *Pest V, Magyar utca 12-14. Tel: 483-1355. Open from 6pm to 11pm every day.*

2 Biarritz Map p. 238, A2 $$
This favourite haunt of a generation of literary figures is nestled in a cold, windy corner near Parliament. It serves light, Mediterranean-inspired nouveau grill food in a comfortable environment. Good salads, even in the depths of winter. *Pest V, Kossuth tér 18. Tel: 311-4413. Open Mon-Fri 9am-midnight; Sat-Sun 10am-midnight.*

3 Bouchon Map p. 239, B3 $$
Relaxed bistro-style atmosphere in the heart of Pest. Serves Hungarian dishes with a contemporary flavour. Wide range of daily specials. A good place to linger over lunch on rainy afternoons. *Pest VI, Zichy Jenő utca 33. Tel: 302-2301. Open Mon-Sat 9am-11pm.*

4 Café Kör Map p. 238, C3 $$
Good-looking, lively bistro-style restaurant interpreting Hungarian cuisine for international tastes, plus classic Magyar puddings such as *mákos guba*, a sort of sugary concoction of bread, milk and poppy seeds. Popular with locals and expatriates for its jolly atmosphere. Booking essential. *Pest V, Sas utca 17. Tel: 311-0053. Open Mon-Sat 10am-10pm.*

5 Café Picard Map p. 238, B3 $
A good place to stop for sandwiches and coffee if you're in the official district, near Parliament. The interior is cramped but there's street seating in

Warm style at Baraka.

nice weather. Good bruschetta and decent salads. *Pest V, Falk Miksa utca 10. Tel: 331-4576. Open Mon-Fri 7am-10pm; Sat 9am-10pm.*

❻ **DUPLA** Map p. 239, C4 $
A sister restaurant to the small and smoky pub Szimpla next door, Dupla (it means 'double', essentially in the sense of a double shot of espresso) serves up simple, tasty dishes at almost unbeatable value. Informal atmosphere. *Pest VII, Kertész utca 48. Tel: 342-1034. Open noon-2am every day.*

❼ **FAUSTO'S** Map p. 239, D4 $$$$
Enduringly popular with a predominantly business clientele. Resolutely slick and stylish, it serves Italian haute cuisine and good wine. Booking essential. *Pest VII, Dohány utca 5. Tel: 269-6806. Open Mon-Sat noon-3pm & 7pm-midnight.*

❽ **KÁRPÁTIA** Map p. 239, D3 $$$
Magnificent old restaurant, with not an inch of space left ungilded or undecorated, in a neo-Gothic style reminiscent of the Mátyás Church. The best dishes are the traditional staples such as stuffed cabbage, the soups and stews (*pörkölt*), or goose liver. Most of the other dishes are rather ordinary. Gypsy band in the evenings. Beer bar area with a more informal feel. Candlelit terrace in summer. *Pest V, Ferenciek tere 7-8. Tel: 317-3596. Open 11am-11pm every day.*

❾ **KÉT SZERECSEN** Map p. 239, C4 $$
Attractive, inviting bistro bar, with Mediterranean-inspired salads, grilled meats and good wine. *Pest VI, Nagymező utca 14. Tel: 343-1984. Open Mon-Fri 8am-1am; Sat-Sun 11am-1am.*

❿ **KRIZIA** Map p. 239, B4 $$$
Talented chef from Bergamo combines a warm, relaxed atmosphere with some of the best cooking in Budapest. Everything always fresh and in season. Stunning truffle risotto. Booking recommended. *Pest VI, Mozsár utca 12. Tel: 331-8711. Open Mon-Sat noon-3pm & 6.30pm-midnight.*

⓫ **LOU-LOU** Map p. 238, C3 $$$
French-inspired cuisine in an elegant setting. The restaurant has a number of classic dishes, such as duck à l'orange with chocolate sauce or the - usually excellent - lamb chops with French beans. *Pest V, Vigyázó Ferenc utca 4. Tel: 312-4505. Open Mon-Fri noon-3pm & 7pm-midnight; Sat 6pm-midnight.*

⓬ **M** Map p. 239, C4 $
Decorated in brown paper with pen sketches of furniture, M is a curiosity. Homely and filling rather than gourmet, the menu changes every day.

The place is tiny, but, if you can, try to secure a place by the window. *Pest VII, Kertész utca 48. Tel: 269-2786. Open 6pm-midnight every day.*

13 NEGRO Map p. 238, C3 $$
Long thin bar, made to look more expansive with mirrors, serving competent fusion cuisine and a range of well-mixed cocktails. Popular with thirty-something professionals. On a winter's night it can get crammed to the gills. In summer the whole operation spills outside onto the square. Unbeatable views of the Basilica. *Pest V, Szent István tér 11. Tel: 302-0136. Open noon-midnight every day.*

14 RÉZKAKAS Map p. 239, D3 $$$
Though old-fashioned restaurants with gypsy fiddlers and ceremonious waiters have gone right out of vogue with most younger Hungarians, the best of them are still an event that has to be sampled at least once. Here, Róbert Kuti and his band fill the over-decorated space with haunting strains, the menu tempts you with rich game dishes, and your wine will be decanted before serving. Dress up swell and enjoy yourself. *Pest V, Veres Pálné utca 3. Tel: 318-0038. Open noon-midnight every day.*

15 TG'S Map p. 238, C3 $$
The food is cheerfully mediocre, and the back wall is decorated like a carpet showroom. But Budapesters love this place, and it is always humming and alive. The sushi has a good reputation, too. *Pest V, Október 6. utca 8. Tel: 266-3525. Open noon-midnight every day.*

16 VÖRÖS ÉS FEHÉR Map p. 239, B4 $$$
Budapest's best wine bar, with a selection of vintages to sample by the glass, and tapas to taste with them. Also doubles as a restaurant, with tasty, inventive cuisine. Its location makes it a good choice for dinner after the Liszt Academy or Opera. *Pest VI, Andrássy út 41. Tel: 413-1545. Open noon-midnight every day.*

OUTER PEST

17 MOSAIC CAFÉ Map p. 239, A5 $$$
Situated in a 1930s hotel building, Mosaic offers 'Mediterranean' food, while the walls mimic the swirling style of Ravenna. A pleasant terrace fronting Andrássy út makes it good for a summer evening. *Pest VI, Andrássy út 111. Tel: 462-2100. Open 6.30am-11am & 11.30am-11.30pm every day.*

Bagolyvár Map p. 258, B3 $$$
This restaurant shares a kitchen with the famous Gundel, and advertises itself as 'entirely staffed by women'. The food is old-fashioned Hungarian comfort food - look for hefty stuffed cabbage and crispy roast duck. In summer you can sit out on the terrace overlooking the zoo. *Pest XIV, Állatkerti út 2. Tel: 468-3110. Open noon-11pm every day.*

Gundel Map p. 258, B3 $$$$
Founded in 1894, this is Budapest's premier restaurant, serving time-honoured Hungarian fare in glittering surroundings. The food does not always live up to the promise of the atmosphere, but it's still a place worth dressing up for (jacket required for men). Garden in summer. Weekend buffet brunch. *Pest XIV, Állatkerti út 2. Tel: 321-3550. Open noon-4pm & 6.30pm-midnight every day.*

Castle Hill & Inner Buda

18 **Arany Kaviár** Map p. 238, B1 $$$
Ice-cold vodka, a choice of caviar, and classic Russian specials such as Volga sturgeon and superb Stroganoff cooked up by smiling chef Sasha. *Buda I, Ostrom utca 19. Tel: 201-6737. Open 6pm-midnight every day.*

19 **Café Gusto** Map p. 238, A2 $$
Tiny café bar serving cold food only. Good pasta salads; excellent carpaccio and tiramisu. Freshly squeezed orange juice and homemade lemonade. Street terrace in summer. *Buda II, Frankel Leó út 12. Tel: 316-3970. Open Mon-Sat 10am-10pm.*

If you like your sturgeon, Arany Kaviár is the place.

20 **HORGÁSZTANYA** Map p. 238, B2 $
This place has made no concessions to changing tastes and fashion. It still resides in the 1970s: slightly dingy and grubby, with waiters who turn grumpiness into an art, but serving some of the best fish soup (*halászlé*) in town. Especially good is the *korhely halászlé*. *Buda I, Fő utca 27. Open noon-11pm every day.*

21 **RIVALDA** Map p. 238, C2 $$
Almost the only restaurant on Castle Hill that is patronised by locals. Good varied menu, a sort of Magyar-Mediterranean fusion. Very pretty inner courtyard in summer, part of what was formerly a nunnery. *Buda I, Színház utca 5-9. Tel: 489-0236. Open 11.30am-11.30 pm every day.*

THE BUDA HILLS & ÓBUDA

ARCADE Map p. 261, D3 $$$
Popular haunt located in a primarily residential area. Careful attention has been paid to both décor and menu, which is short but with something for everyone. Slick service. *Buda XII, Kiss János Altábornagy utca 38. Tel: 225-1969. Open Tues-Sun 11am-11pm.*

KISBUDA GYÖNGE Map p. 219, D2 $$$
This cosy little restaurant in Óbuda is panelled with beautiful wood that on closer inspection turns out to be the doors of armoires and the headboards of beds. Seating is tight and the atmosphere is intimate; the food is the game-and-liver high Hungarian style. Piano music. Garden in summer. *Buda III, Kenyeres utca 34. Tel: 368-6402. Open Mon-Sat noon-midnight.*

MATTEO Map p. 260, A1 $$$
Built into the lower floor of a 1930s bus shelter, this restaurant has a café at street level and a full-blown restaurant below, offering international cuisine with a slightly Italian twist. The Bologna-style veal (wrapped in Parma ham and served with mashed potato and spinach) is usually excellent. An ideal solution for lunch after visiting Napraforgó utca (*see p. 84*). *Buda II, Pasaréti tér. Tel: 392-7531. Open 11.30am-midnight every day.*

NÁNCSI NÉNI Map p. 4, B1 $$
Out-of-town taverns were once a Buda speciality. This family-style place aims to prolong the tradition with good old Hungarian recipes, and tables in the garden in the summer. Booking essential. *Buda II, Ördögárok út 80. Tel: 397-2742. Open noon-11pm every day.*

Liszt Ferenc tér

The Liszt Music Academy (*see p. 122*) is not the only reason to visit this square (*map p. 263, B4*), nor is the fine bronze statue of Liszt himself, with hair flying and fingers crooked in a frenzy of organ-playing (he is supposed to have regularly broken pianos with his impassioned touch). This charming square, shaded by trees and blocked to vehicle traffic, is in fact one of the city's most popular spots for an afternoon of idling over coffee or a night of cocktails at a fashionable bar. At dusk the place comes buzzingly alive. If you're sitting outside, it hardly matters which of the more than half a dozen cafés you choose - especially since new places open all the time - but the retro flair of Menza at No. 2 is an entertaining choice for a rainy day. There are also usually a few breakfasters at Café Vian at No. 9, which is also known for its coloured glass bar. Karma at No. 11 is a dark and cosy restaurant serving Asian-inspired dishes, while the red-and-silver Pesti Est Café at No. 5 opens a dance floor downstairs at night and caters to the late crowd. If dancing is too much for you, Buena Vista, at No. 4-5, has couches and the pale shades of a 1970s living room.

CITY-CENTRE
RESTAURANTS
0 100 200 300 400 500 m
Gül Baba
MARGIT
HÍD
SZT. ISTVÁN
KÖRÚT
Millenáris Park
Bem
Király baths
Danube
MARGIT
KÖRÚT
Moszkva tér
MARGIT
MOSZKVA TÉR
Batthyány
BATTHYÁNY TÉR
Parliament
Kossuth Lajos tér
Ethnog.
Alkotmány
KOSSUTH TÉR
VÍZIVÁROS
Military Hist.
Music Hist.
Tel.
Mátyás templom
LIPÓTVÁROS
XII
VÁR
Hunyadi János út
Acad. Sciences
Széchenyi
Roosevelt tér
Deák
JÓZSEF A.
DÉLI PU.
Krisztina krt.
Palota út
CHAIN BRIDGE
(LÁNCHÍD)
Clark Ádám tér
Funicular
KRISZTINAVÁROS
I
Ludwig
Alagút
Krisztina tér
Mészáros u.
Vörösmarty tér
VÖRÖSMARTY TÉR
Vigadó
National Gallery
Bud. History
NAPHEGY
Naphegy tér
Attila út
TABÁN
ERZSÉBET HÍD
RAKPART
Convention Centre
HEGYALJA
Rudas baths
Gellért-hegy
Citadel
Liberation Monument
Jubileumi park
XI
Gellért baths
ALKOTÁS
BUDAÖRSI ÚT
19
2
5
18
20
11
15
21

HOTELS & ACCOMMODATION

This list is not exhaustive, but gives a cross-section of the kind of hotel accommodation Budapest has to offer. Charming, small, privately run hotels are sadly a category that does not exist in the Hungarian capital, and the visitor is left to choose between an admittedly wide selection of luxury hotels or less expensive and less glamorous chains.

Telephone numbers are Budapest, +361 from abroad. Prices are for a double room in high season, excluding taxes unless otherwise stated.

Luxury Hotels

Corinthia Grand Hotel Royal Map p. 263, C4
Recently renovated; only the façade is original now, plus the splendid ballroom on the first floor. The public spaces hark back to the 'gracious living' days of the original hotel that stood here. Central location on the Nagykörút.
414 rooms. € 150 (breakfast extra)
Pest VII, Erzsébet körút 43-49
Tel: 479 4000; Fax: 479 4333
www.corinthiahotels.com

Hilton Budapest Map p. 262, C1
Built in the 1970s on the remains of a mediaeval monastery. Not much character but every comfort.
322 rooms. € 180-220
Buda I, Hess András tér 1-3
Tel: 889-6600; Fax: 889-6925
www.hilton.com

Inter-Continental Map p. 262, C3
Decorated in the Inter-Continental corporate style. Boasts an excellent Danube-bank location, comfortable rooms, and stunning panoramic views of the Danube and Castle Hill.
398 rooms. *€ 170 (breakfast extra)*
Pest V, Apáczai Csere János utca 12-14
Tel: 327-6333; Fax: 327-6357
www.interconti.com

Kempinski Hotel Corvinus Map p. 263, C3
Classic international luxury hotel with a business flavour, in a well designed modern building right in the centre of Pest.
369 rooms. € 139 (breakfast extra)
Pest V, Erzsébet tér 7-8
Tel: 429-3777; Fax: 429 4777
www.kempinski-budapest.com

Lounge of Le Méridien.

Le Meridien Map p. 263, C3
Cool, tasteful French Empire-style decor, very comfortable rooms. Completely renovated early 20th-century building in central Pest. French pastry chef lays out wonderful afternoon teas.
218 rooms. € 139 (breakfast extra)
Pest V, Erzsébet tér 9-10
Tel: 429-5500; Fax: 429-5555
www.lemeridien-budapest.com

Medium-Range Hotels

Art'Otel Map p. 262, C2
Filled with contemporary art by Donald Sultan, this hotel is an intriguing mix of 1990s modern and early 18th-century Buda Baroque. Rooms on the front have good Danube views; rooms in the old, stone-built section on the other side are cooler and quieter.
165 rooms. € 132
Buda I, Bem rakpart 16-19
Tel: 487-9487; Fax: 487-9488
www.parkplazaww.com

Astoria Map p. 263, D3
Elegant, early 20th-century public rooms with lots of gilt and green marble, survivals of Budapest's belle époque. Bedrooms disappointing but adequate.
131 rooms, double or twin - you need to specify what you want. € 140
Pest V, Kossuth Lajos utca 19-21
Tel: 889-6000; Fax: 889-6091
www.danubiusgroup.com/astoria

Carlton Hotel Budapest Map p. 262, C2
A modern, largish place on the Danube-facing slope of Castle Hill. Rooms are basic and functional but small, with bland, 'airport hotel' furniture.
95 rooms. € 75-126
Buda 1, Apor Péter utca 3 (A.P.u)
Tel: 224-0999; Fax: 224-0990
www.carltonhotel.hu

Gellért Map p. 262, E3
One of Budapest's classics, attached to the Art Nouveau Gellért thermal baths. Most of the main rooms have a slightly 1970s flavour, but the hotel is comfortable and well run, and still maintains a character of its own.
234 rooms. € 110-140 (use of thermal baths included)
Buda XI, Szent Gellért tér 1
Tel: 889-5500; Fax: 889-5505
www.danubiusgroup.com/gellert

Hotel Andrássy Map p. 263, A5
Housed in a classic 1930s structure by Olympic swimmer and architect Alfréd Hajós, this newly renovated hotel fronts a side street, though many rooms have views of the lovely Andrássy boulevard after which the hotel is named.
70 rooms. € 100-400 (breakfast extra)
Pest VI, Andrássy út 111
Tel: 462-2100; Fax: 462-2195
www.andrassyhotel.com

Hotel Astra Map p. 262, B2
In a quiet side street on the lower slopes of Castle Hill, this small,

The restaurant at the Art 'Otel.

private hotel is housed in a 300-year-old building. Fully renovated, it retains little that is truly ancient, but rooms are light and airy, and keep to an 'old world' style.
12 rooms. € 90-135
Buda I, Vám utca 6
Tel: 214-1906; Fax: 214-1907
www.hotelastra.hu

K+K Hotel Opera Map p. 263, C3
Light, bright modern decor: clean lines, lots of wicker, and a definite preference for sunflower yellow. Good central Pest location, right by the Opera House.
205 rooms. € 130 (including taxes)
Pest VI, Révay utca 24
Tel: 269-0222; Fax: 269-0230
www.kkhotels.com

Uhu Villa Map p. 260, A1 (just beyond the map)
A small, intimate hotel in a secluded turn-of-the-century villa at the top of a perilously steep, twisting lane in the Buda Hills. Rooms are well decorated and appointed, and the bar and lounge area cosy and inviting. The restaurant offers Italian home cooking.
9 rooms. € 280-480
Buda II, Keselyű utca 1/a
Tel: 275-1002; Fax: 398-0571

Victoria Map p. 262, C2
Small, privately run modern hotel on the Danube bank in Buda. All rooms face front, with views of the river. Dated decor, but the size and location are big points in its favour.
27 rooms. € 102
Buda I, Bem rakpart 11
Tel: 457-8080; Fax: 457-8088
www.victoria.hu

Basic

Burg Hotel Map p. 262, C1
Small modern hotel on Castle Hill, with views of the Mátyás Church. Rooms basic but functional. Key location in historic Buda.
26 rooms. € 109
Buda I, Szentháromság tér
Tel: 212-0269; Fax: 212-3970
e-mail: hotel.burg@mail.datanet.hu

Kulturinnov Map p. 262, C1
Early 20th-century neo-Gothic twinned with basic Communist-era, make-do-and-mend Functionalism. Amenities are basic, but the Castle Hill location is excellent.
16 rooms (all twin). € 78
Buda I, Szentháromság tér 6
Tel: 355-0122; Fax: 375-1886
e-mail: mka3@matavnet.hu

Medosz Map p. 263, B4
An unashamed relic of Communist days. This place shows its age with shades of brown and unsympathetic lighting, but the location just off the main section of Andrássy út is unrivalled. It is a short walk to the bars and restaurants of Liszt Ferenc tér, Budapest's most happening square.
70 rooms. € 45
Pest VI, Jókai tér 9
Tel: 374-3000; Fax: 332-4316

Private Rooms & Pensions

There are some reasonable town centre guesthouses - try, for example, City Panzió Pilvax (Tel: 266 7660, www.taverna.hu) - and some quieter suburban bed and breakfasts, such as the award-winning Beatrix Panzió (Tel: 275-0550, www.beatrixhotel.hu) at Buda II, Széher út 3 (*map p. 260, B1*).

Private rooms can be booked through IBUSZ at Pest V, Ferenciek tere 10, Tel: 485 2767, and at Keleti Railway Station, Tel 345 9572, e-mail accommodation@ibusz.hu - both only open during working hours Monday to Friday.

PRACTICAL TIPS

Public Transport

Buses, Trams and the Metro

Budapest transport is cheap, well run and efficient, and will get you anywhere you want to go with - usually - minimal waiting time. All forms of public transport require a ticket bought in advance, either at a metro station or newsstand. Weekend or weekly passes are also available, or you can just buy a book of 10 or 20 tickets (don't tear the cover off; it invalidates it). Use one ticket for each journey you make. To validate it, you must punch it by sticking it into a ticket machine as soon as you board the tram, bus or trolley bus. The newer machines are automatic. On some of the older buses and trams they are manual: insert your ticket in the top, and pull the black funnel towards you until you hear the punching sound. If nothing happens, it is probably because prankster saboteurs have filled the funnel with 10 forint coins. If you're travelling by metro, you must punch your ticket before you get on the escalator. Random spot checks are carried out by inspectors sporting red and gold armbands, and you will be fined if you can't show a valid ticket.

Many trams stop automatically at every stop, but on some trams and all buses and trolley buses you must press a button by the doors if you want to get off. And try not to scramble off at the last minute: that, as well as failing to give up your seat for an elderly person or someone with young children, will brand you as thoughtless.

The HÉV railway network links Budapest with its outlying suburbs. The HÉV from Batthyány tér takes you to Óbuda and Aquincum. Public transport tickets are valid on the HÉV within city limits. Punch them to validate them when you get on the train.

Taxis

The public transport network stops for the night at 11.30, but there are night buses on most major routes. If you feel it's too late to take a bus, don't jump into the first cab that comes along. Budapest taxis often take their passengers for a ride in more ways than one, so it's better to stick with reputable companies like

City Taxi (*Tel: 211-1111*); Fő Taxi (*Tel: 222-2222*) and Rádió Taxi (*Tel: 377-7777*). You'll get cheaper fares if you call a cab instead of picking one up on the street. If you are calling from a mobile phone, you need to add the prefix 061 before the number.

The Budapest Card

The Budapest Card gives unlimited travel on public transport, free entry to most museums and some sights, and discounts on certain sightseeing tours, restaurants, baths, performances and car rentals. You can pick the card up at the main metro ticket counters, as well as at tourist offices and some hotels. There are two versions: the Ft 4,350 card is good for 48 hours, while the Ft 5,450 lasts for 72 hours.

Opening Hours

Shops generally open at 10am and close at 6pm. Most high-street shops are shut on Saturday afternoons, and there is almost no Sunday opening, except for the shopping malls. Banks tend to close at 4pm, but there are plenty of ATM machines around the city, and money-changing outlets stay open later, so access to cash should never be a problem. It is often worth getting an exchange rate quote from more than one bureau de change before parting with your money, as rates do tend to differ.

Public Holidays

Long gone are the days when schoolchildren paraded in red neckerchiefs to honour the glory of the Soviets. Today's national holidays are strictly Hungarian in origin, the most important being March 15th, August 20th, and October 23rd. **March 15th** celebrates the doomed revolution of 1848-1849, when Hungarians rose up against Austrian rule only to be crushed a few months later, and is celebrated by Hussar parades, impassioned speeches, and recitals of patriotic poetry. **August 20th** is the saint's day of King Stephen, first Christian ruler of a united Hungary, who was crowned in 1000. Folk markets and fairs fill the town, the relics of the saint are paraded in the streets, and the event culminates in a magnificent evening fireworks display on the Danube. **October 23rd** marks the beginning of the Hungarian uprising against Soviet rule in 1956, when workers, students and even members of the Hungarian army joined forces against Soviet tanks for a brief but glorious twenty-two days.

Christmas is a family affair in Hungary, but New Year's Eve (*Szilveszter* in Hungarian) sees people thronging the streets with cardboard trumpets, whistles and firecrackers for a grand and raucous street party.

Festivals

Spring Festival (*Tavaszi fesztivál*): Budapest's largest cultural festival features many fine guests and local artists. The emphasis is classical, with ballet, opera and chamber music leavened with some folk dance and jazz. Usually held the second half of March. *www.festivalcity.hu*

Dance House Festival (*Táncház-találkozó*): Dance troupes and folk bands from all over present-day and historic Hungary congregate in the Budapest Körcsarnok in late March. The whole event lasts several days, with a variety of programmes: concerts, dance classes, childrens' events, crafts and cookery. *www.tanchaz.hu*

Autumn Festival (*Őszi fesztivál*): Born as a counterweight to the cultural classicism of the Spring Festival, the Autumn Festival showcases cutting edge theatre, dance and various media arts, as well as music and film. Usually held in the second half of October. *www.festivalcity.hu*

WoMuFe: WoMuFe is an annual world music festival featuring acts from the Central and Eastern European region and beyond. It's always held in July, at the Budai Parkszínpad. Dates and programmes are released in April.

Sziget Festival: Held every year in early August, this is primarily a pop festival, but world music also has a significant presence. An enormous throng of mostly young people completely take over an entire island in the Danube (Hajógyári-sziget), turning it into a tent megalopolis. During the day it's lectures and more subdued events; at night it's party time. *www.sziget.hu*

Wine Festival (*Borfesztivál*): Held on Castle Hill in late September, this event allows visitors to sample wines from around the country. There's also always a 'guest nation', and concerts to watch while you sip.

Climate

In winter (Dec-March) it often hovers around freezing, usually with snow. Temperatures get hot and humid at around 30°C in summer (July and August). Spring tends to be extremely short, just a week or two in April. Autumn is the best (although it can rain), often with Indian-summer temperatures of around 20°C in October.

Personal Safety

Watch out for pickpocket gangs who get on buses and trams in a huddle, cause a diversion, and then jump off at the next stop, laden with tourists' handbags. Other known scams include thieves flashing bus passes and pretending to be undercover policemen - they'll then attempt to 'check' your passport. Another common nuisance is overcharging in restaurants. Just take a look at the bill and be prepared to hold your ground if you think a waiter is trying to slip in an extra charge.

Place Names

Though most Budapest sights and landmarks are referred to in English throughout this book, when consulting maps or asking for directions, you will need to understand Hungarian names too. Below is a brief list of the toponyms used in this book, with their English equivalents.

utca - street
út - road
templom - church
tér - square
híd - bridge
kert - garden
körút: ring road or boulevard. The Nagykörút is the wide ring road that traverses Pest.
sétány - promenade
korzó - corso, esplanade
palota - palace

The Budapest Metro

The red, blue and yellow lines are metro lines. Deák tér is the only place where thee lines intersect and where you can change from one to another. The yellow line is the *földalatti* (underground railway), which runs all the way up Andrássy út. (The green lines are the HÉV suburban railway.)

INDEX

Numbers in italics refer to illustrations. Numbers in bold are major references.

PEST
XIII
XIV
VI
Danube
Margitsziget
Citypark
Széchenyi baths
Fine Arts
Parliament
Hősök tere
Nyugati PU
MARGIT HÍD
SZT. ISTVÁN KRT.
RÓBERT KÁROLY KÖRÚT
HUNGÁRIA KÖRÚT
VÁCI ÚT
DÓZSA GYÖRGY ÚT
KÓS KÁROLY SÉTÁNY
STEFÁNIA ÚT
THÖKÖLY ÚT
NAGY LAJOS KIRÁLY ÚTJA
ANDRÁSSY
TERÉZ
ALSÓ RAKPART
KOSSUTH TÉR
Lehel tér
Béke tér
0 200 400 600 800 1000 m

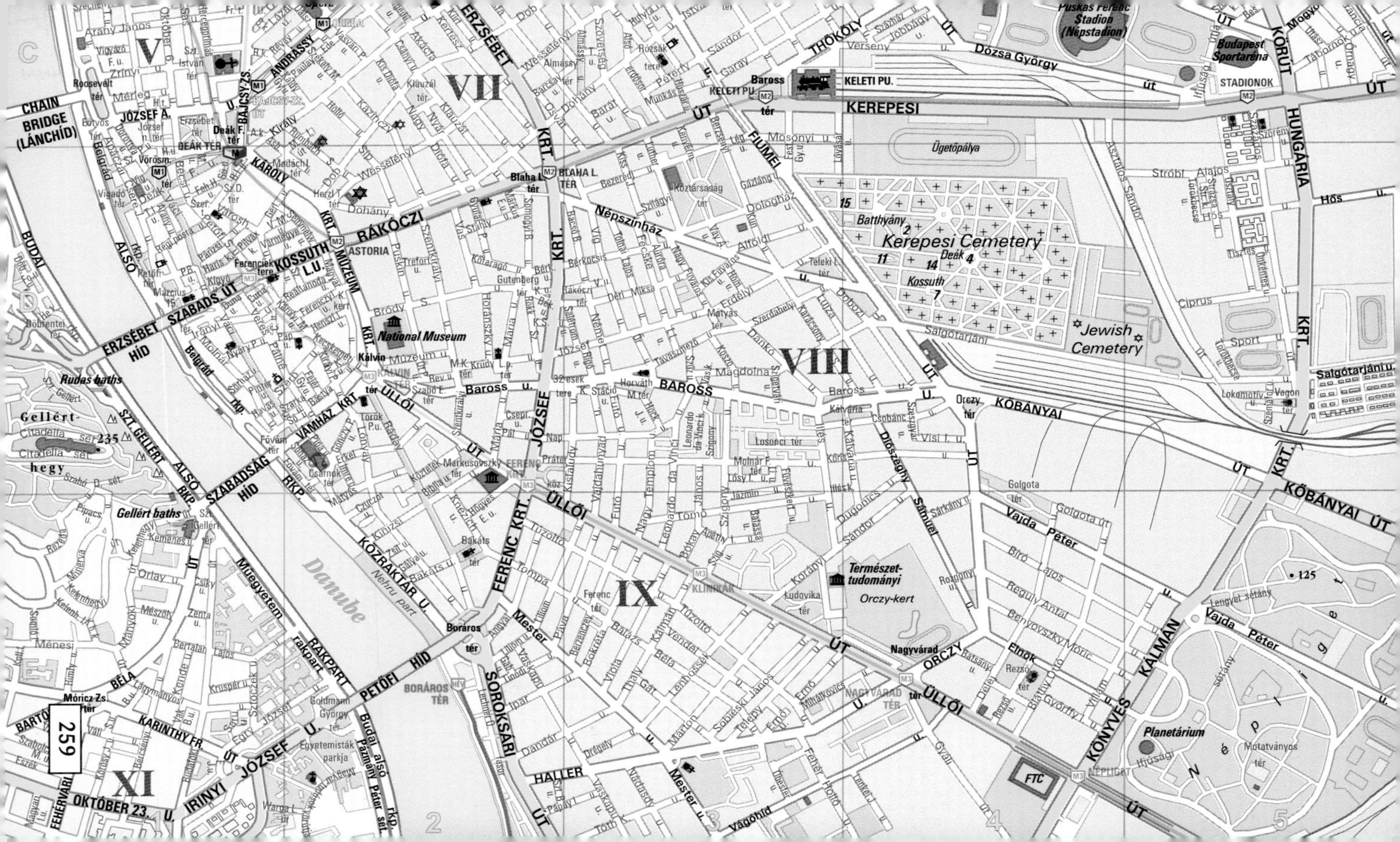
V
VII
VIII
IX
XI
CHAIN BRIDGE (LÁNCHÍD)
Roosevelt tér
JÓZSEF A.
Deák F. tér
DEÁK TÉR
BAJCSY-ZS. ÚT
ANDRÁSSY
KÁROLY
ERZSÉBET KRT.
THÖKÖLY
Dózsa György út
Puskás Ferenc Stadion (Népstadion)
Budapest Sportaréna
STADIONOK
KÖRÚT
Baross tér
KELETI PU.
KEREPESI ÚT
HUNGÁRIA KRT.
Ügetőpálya
FIUMEI ÚT
Blaha L. tér
BLAHA L. TÉR
Népszínház
Kerepesi Cemetery
Jewish Cemetery
Salgótarjáni u.
RÁKÓCZI
ASTORIA
KOSSUTH L.U.
MÚZEUM KRT.
Ferenciek tere
SZABADS. ÚT
National Museum
Kálvin tér
BAROSS
Baross u.
JÓZSEF KRT.
KŐBÁNYAI ÚT
Orczy tér
Diószeghy Sámuel
ERZSÉBET HÍD
Rudas baths
Gellért-hegy
Citadella
SZT. GELLÉRT ALSÓ RKP.
BUDAI ALSÓ rkp.
VÁMHÁZ KRT.
ÜLLŐI ÚT
SZABADSÁG HÍD
Gellért baths
Danube
Nehru part
KÖZRAKTÁR U.
FERENC KRT.
Természet-tudományi
Orczy-kert
Vajda Péter
KÖNYVES KÁLMÁN KRT.
Planetárium
Boráros tér
PETŐFI HÍD
SOROKSÁRI ÚT
Műegyetem rakpart
RAKPART
Móricz Zs. tér
KARINTHY FR. ÚT
IRINYI JÓZSEF U.
OKTÓBER 23. U.
FEHÉRVÁRI
HALLER
Mester u.
Nagyvárad tér
FTC

BUDA
Danube
Margit-sziget
MARGIT HÍD
SZT. ISTVÁN KRT.
Parliament
KOSSUTH TÉR
BUDAI ALSÓ RKP
Batthyány tér
ÁRPÁD FEJEDELEM ÚTJA
Újlaki rakpart
BÉCSI ÚT
LAJOS
Lukács baths
Király baths
Apostol
Rómer Flóris
MARGIT KRT.
MOSZKVA TÉR
Városmajor
FASOR
SZILÁGYI E.
SZILÁGYI ERZSÉBET
Pasaréti út
Szépvölgyi út
Mátyás-hegy caves
Pál-völgy caves
Ferenc-hegy
Szemlőhegyi barlang
Törökvész út
Bimbó út
Fillér u.
Vasas
Bartók
HŰVÖSVÖLGYI
Zugligeti
Napraforgó u.
Kútvölgyi
Cogwheel railway
II
0 200 400 600 800 1000 m

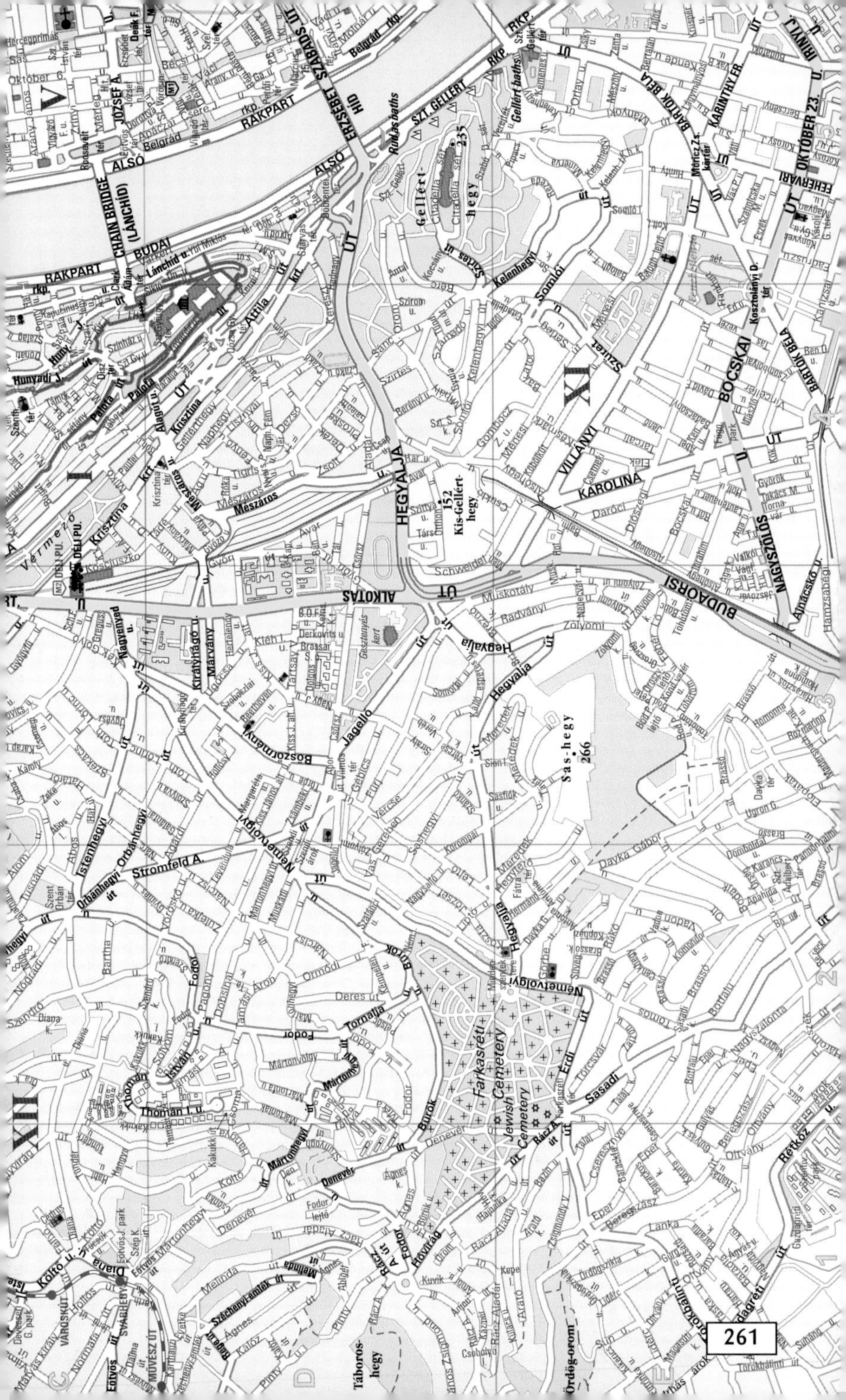
V
I
XI
XII
CHAIN BRIDGE (LÁNCHÍD)
ERZSÉBET HÍD
SZABADSÁG HÍD
BUDAI ALSÓ RAKPART
SZT. GELLÉRT RKP.
Rudas baths
Gellért baths
Gellért-hegy
Citadella
235
Kis-Gellért-hegy
152
Sas-hegy
266
DÉLI PU.
Vérmező
Krisztina krt.
Attila krt.
ALKOTÁS
HEGYALJA
BUDAÖRSI
BOCSKAI
VILLÁNYI
KAROLINA
NAGYSZŐLŐS
BARTÓK BÉLA
FEHÉRVÁRI
OKTÓBER 23. U.
Böszörményi
Jagelló
Németvölgyi
Stromfeld A.
Istenhegyi
Orbánhegyi
Mártonhegyi
Sasadi
Érdi
Farkasréti Cemetery
Jewish Cemetery
Táboros-hegy
Ördög-orom
VÁROSKÚT
SVÁBHEGY
MŰVÉSZ ÚT

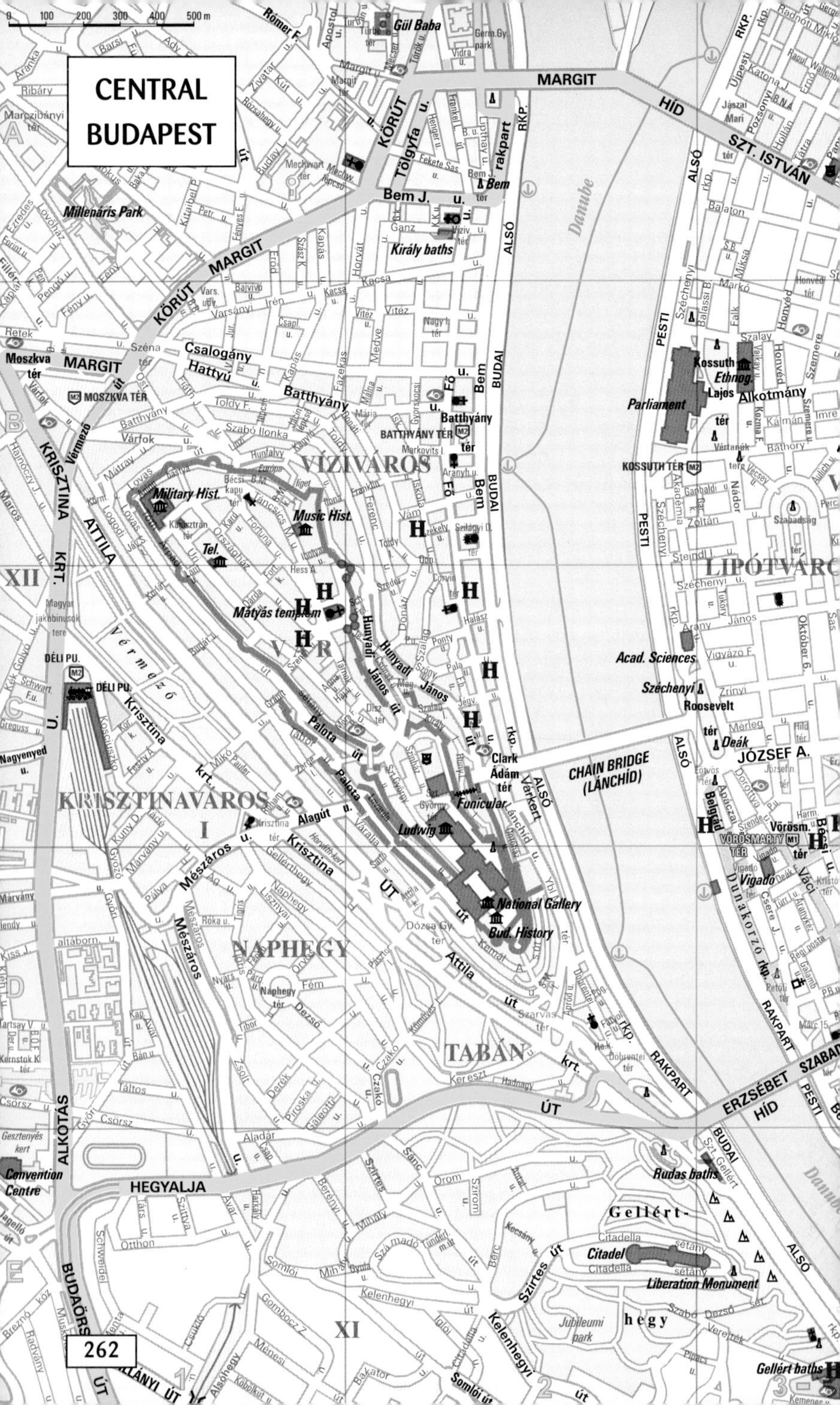
CENTRAL BUDAPEST
0 100 200 300 400 500 m
Gül Baba
MARGIT HÍD
SZT. ISTVÁN
MARGIT KÖRÚT
Millenáris Park
Király baths
Danube
Moszkva tér
MOSZKVA TÉR
Batthyány tér
BATTHYÁNY TÉR
VÍZIVÁROS
Military Hist.
Music Hist.
Tel.
Mátyás templom
VÁR
Parliament
Kossuth Lajos tér
Ethnog.
KOSSUTH TÉR
LIPÓTVÁROS
Acad. Sciences
Széchenyi
Roosevelt tér
Deák
JÓZSEF A.
CHAIN BRIDGE (LÁNCHÍD)
Clark Ádám tér
Funicular
Ludwig
National Gallery
Bud. History
DÉLI PU.
KRISZTINAVÁROS
XII
I
NAPHEGY
TABÁN
VÖRÖSMARTY TÉR
Vigadó
Dunakorzó
ERZSÉBET HÍD
Rudas baths
Gellért-hegy
Citadel
Liberation Monument
Jubileumi park
Gellért baths
Convention Centre
HEGYALJA
ALKOTÁS
BUDAÖRSI ÚT
XI

TERÉZVÁROS
VI
ERZSÉBETVÁROS
VII
JÓZSEFVÁROS
VIII
XIII
IX
Citypark
Fine Arts
Hősök tere
Műcsarnok
Vajdahunyad Castle
Agric.
Nyugati tér
NYUGATI PU.
Westend City Center
Terror House
Liszt
Kodály körönd
Oktogon
Operett
Music Academy
Opera
Ernst
Madách
Új
Post
DEÁK TÉR
BLAHA L. TÉR
Blaha L. tér
Baross tér
KELETI PU.
KEREPESI ÚT
Erkel
Köztársaság tér
ASTORIA
National Museum
Kálvin tér
Petőfi
Fővám tér
Applied Arts
ANDRÁSSY
RÁKÓCZI
BAROSS
ÜLLŐI ÚT
JÓZSEF KRT.
FERENC KRT.
MÚZEUM KRT.
VÁMHÁZ KRT.
KOSSUTH L. U.
TERÉZ KRT.
ERZSÉBET KRT.
VÁCI ÚT
DÓZSA GYÖRGY ÚT
FIUMEI ÚT
Városligeti fasor
Népszínház

SOMERSET LIMITED
Lövőház utca 39, 1024 Budapest, Hungary
Felelős kiadó: *Ruszin Zsolt, a Somerset Kft. igazgatója*
Repro studio: *Timp Kft.*
Set in Berkeley Book 9.8pt and Barmeno
Print production: *Print-X Rt.*
Printed by: *Dürer Nyomda Kft, felelős vezető Megyik András*
ISBN 963 212 986 5